THE SECRET BILLIONAIRE

ERIN SWANN

BECAUSE YOU DON'T ALWAYS HAVE TO BE A LADY.

Copyright © 2018 by Swann Publications

Cover image licensed from Shutterstock.com

Cover design by Swann Publications

Edited by: Jessica Royer Ocken, Donna Hokanson

Typo Hunters Extraordinaire: Lynette Hamilton, Renee Williams

ISBN-13 9781980668022

The following story is intended for mature readers. It contains mature themes, strong language, and sexual situations. All characters are 18+ years of age, and all sexual acts are consensual.

Find out more at: WWW.ERINSWANN.COM

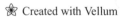 Created with Vellum

ALSO BY ERIN SWANN

The Billionaire's Trust - Available on Amazon, also in AUDIOBOOK

(Bill and Lauren's story) He needed to save the company. He needed her. He couldn't have both. The wedding proposal in front of hundreds was like a fairy tale come true—Until she uncovered his darkest secret.

The Youngest Billionaire - Available on Amazon

(Steven and Emma's story) The youngest of the Covington clan, he avoided the family business to become a rarity, an honest lawyer. He didn't suspect that pursuing her could destroy his career. She didn't know what trusting him could cost her.

The Billionaire's Hope - Available on Amazon

(Nick and Katie's story) They came from different worlds. She hadn't seen him since the day he broke her brother's nose. Her family retaliated by destroying his life. She never suspected where accepting a ride from him today would take her. They said they could do casual. They lied.

Previously titled: Protecting the Billionaire

Picked by the Billionaire – Available on Amazon

(Liam and Amy's story) A night she wouldn't forget. An offer she couldn't refuse. He alone could save her, and she held the key to his survival. If only they could pass the test together.

Saved by the Billionaire – Available on Amazon

(Ryan and Natalie's story) The FBI and the cartel were both after her for the same thing: information she didn't have. First, the FBI took everything, and then the cartel came for her. She trusted Ryan with her safety, but could she trust him with her heart?

Caught by the Billionaire – Available on Amazon

(Vincent and Ashley's story) Her undercover assignment was simple enough: nail the crooked billionaire. The surprise came when she opened the folder, and the target was her one-time high school sweetheart. What will happen when an unknown foe makes a move to checkmate?

The Driven Billionaire – Available on Amazon

(Zachary and Brittney's story) Rule number one: hands off your best friend's sister. With nowhere to turn when she returns from upstate, she accepts his offer of a room. Mutual attraction quickly blurs the rules. When she comes under attack, pulling her closer is the only way to keep her safe. But, the truth of why she left town in the first place will threaten to destroy them both.

CHAPTER 1

*P*AT

"MISTER PATRICK, WHAT KIND OF WOMAN WEAR A THING LIKE this?" my housekeeper, Juanita, asked.

She held up the pink thong Lisa had left last night at the end of her pick-up grabber, the kind of tool they used to pick up trash on the freeway. She'd bought the tool specifically for this weekly undies game. She was scared shitless to touch the panties.

"A pretty one," I answered.

Each week, I made a point of placing the panties out in the open, where Juanita would find them on cleaning day, my little game. She normally came on Monday, but this week, Juanita had family in town, so we'd moved the cleaning forward to Sunday.

She shook her head. "This *chica* no good."

Juanita said the same thing every week without fail.

"You need to find you a nice *señorita*."

I smiled. I knew what women were for, and what they weren't. Obsessing over one woman wasn't for me. My work didn't allow time for that. *Variety is the spice of life*, a wise man once said.

1

Variety in women was the right thing for me, and I certainly didn't need someone telling me to pick up after myself.

Juanita was half right this morning, though. Lisa was no good for me, just not for the reasons Juanita thought. Most girls lasted at least a week or two with me. It took that long to sample the pleasures they had to offer, but not Lisa. One helping of Lisa had been enough. She had all the right equipment but was cold as a fish.

Juanita wagged her finger at me. "You need to settle down with a real woman, Mister Patrick. One that make babies for you. These *chicas*, they no good. I can tell. You going to catch something, make it fall off. Then you have no *niños* and you wish you listen to Juanita."

I loved these weekly lectures. It was our little game.

"Where you want me put it?" she asked as if she didn't know, holding the thong away from her with the grabber.

"In the laundry," I said.

I had a dresser drawer reserved for forgotten ladies' panties, and a bra or two, which was getting full. A few were ripped, most not. Most weren't forgotten either. They'd gotten tangled up in the sheets at some point or lost under the couch. But if I told my guests the cleaning lady was due soon, they usually gave up looking pretty quickly on their way out the door.

There was nothing quite as hot as a girl leaving in the morning going commando. And if one got a little too clingy, leaving the drawer open one morning usually solved the problem.

As she left the room, Juanita repeated her warning about it falling off. Not what I wanted to hear before breakfast.

I finished buttoning up my work shirt and headed downstairs to meet Phil at Starbucks, leaving Juanita to mumble to herself as she cleaned the kitchen.

Settle down with a nice señorita. *Fat chance.*

∽

PHIL WAS WAITING FOR ME INSIDE WHEN I ARRIVED. PHIL
Patterson was my Sunday workout partner, and we often hit this
place after an hour on the machines, but today we were headed
over the hill.

I got in line behind the Gladys twins. "Morning Gladyses."

"Good morning to ya, Patrick," the taller Gladys replied. They
weren't actually twins, just two older ladies both named Gladys.
They rolled in with their walkers and sat at the table by the
window almost every morning. The shorter of the two smiled and
echoed the taller one's greeting.

In a conversation with them a few months back, I'd learned
that they both lost their husbands last year. Since then, I'd made a
point of saying hello every time I saw them. They'd told me
Gladys was a Welsh name that meant princess, and they were both
proud of that.

I pulled out my tattered brown wallet, and a picture dropped to
the floor. I really needed a new wallet, but I couldn't bring myself
to get rid of this one, a gift from Dad. It was my link back to him.

It was so like Dad to give me a simple gift, something practical
that I would use every day. The wallet was embossed with the
Covington Industries logo——his subtle, daily reminder that he
expected me to join my brothers in the family business. The other
side was embossed with FCF, our first rule: *Family Comes First*.

"Pardon me." I stooped down to retrieve the picture my worn
wallet had released.

It was the last picture taken of my dad before his accident.
Living overseas, I hadn't seen much of him in the two years before
he died. This image showed him at his birthday party, the last one
I'd been able to attend. He was smiling brightly, opening a present
from my sister Katie.

He had been my role model. He'd taught me how to be a man.
Always give, never take; always compliment, never brag; always
protect, never hurt; and always be strong, never cry.

And I hadn't cried, until the day I got the call telling me he was gone.

"I'm sorry, ma'am, but there's not enough on this card," the barista behind the cash register said to Gladys, waking me from my reverie.

Short Gladys shrank a few inches and started fumbling with her wallet. "Oh, dear."

I moved up to the counter. "Let me take care of this, ladies. You just go sit down."

"But Mr. Patrick," short Gladys protested.

"No arguments, ladies. My treat this morning."

They begrudgingly turned and wheeled over to their usual table.

I picked up the Starbucks card short Gladys had left on the counter and handed it to the pretty coed behind the register along with a Benjamin. "Put the change on her card, and I'll have a grande mocha, extra shot, please, with a bacon, cheese, and egg sandwich."

Poor short Gladys had looked so ashamed when she'd come up short for their hot chocolates. I pulled a second Benjamin out of my wallet.

"And put this on the card as well." Her name tag said *Jamie*. She was at least an eight on my scale. "You're new here, aren't you, Jamie?"

She blushed, marking my cup with a smile. "No, just a different shift." She returned a warm, inviting smile, tucking a stray curl behind her ear.

I would add her name to my list later. Phil and I were running late and would have to scarf down our sandwiches while driving over the hill to the project in the valley. I walked the card over to the Gladys twins with my warmest smile and added an admonition to keep it safe because I had put a few dollars on it. I grabbed some napkins and waited for my order at the end of the counter while Phil ordered.

"Don't look now, bud, but your soul mate is right outside," Phil said after giving the barista his order and a wink.

I turned to see Tiffany, of all people, opening the door. Her figure was striking, backlit by the bright Los Angeles sunshine.

"Maybe she's here to see you," I offered.

"No fuckin' way, Romeo. My bank account is a half-dozen zeros short of interesting to her."

Tiffany Lawrence was one woman I had hoped to never meet up with again, but today was not my lucky day. She'd already spotted us and was sashaying in our direction with a hip swivel that was exaggerated even for her. For a moment, I was reminded of what those hips did when I put her on top.

She made an alluring picture in black yoga pants with a wide diagonal pink stripe and a black spandex crop top with a Nike logo on it, which hugged all of her surgically enhanced curves. The crop top accentuated her tanned, bare midriff, and the outfit was likely meant to look like she'd just come from yoga or a spin class, which was such a joke.

The only exercise she ever did outside the bedroom was the two-finger lift of taking her credit card out of her wallet. She was only five foot two, so she wore high heels everywhere. She seemed to have no idea how incongruous this morning's outfit was with five-inch stilettos.

She bounced her ample assets our way and placed a hand suggestively on my arm when she arrived. "Patrick, fancy running into you here," she said with a smile as fake as her surprise.

She knew my routine and had obviously planned this meeting. She was back like a bad rash. Her problem was not how she looked or her bedroom skills. And she wasn't stupid, or at all mean. Instead, she was incredibly self-absorbed. Tiffany was on the hunt for a sugar daddy and not at all bashful about it. I had been her target a few months ago until I cut it off.

There was no spark. The spell had been broken.

"You remember Phil," I said.

She offered Phil her hand, palm down and bent at the wrist like he was supposed to kiss it or something.

"Sure, I do."

Phil had been right. Her tone indicated she knew he didn't have enough cash to interest her.

Phil had always disliked her, but he shook her hand with a smile like the gentleman he was. "Miss Lawrence."

She glanced at Phil only momentarily before returning her focus to me. "Patrick, I was thinking we could…" She traced a finger up my arm.

Her thinking had always resulted in me taking out my credit card somewhere. I had to concentrate to keep it civil and avoid swearing at her.

"Tiff, there is no '*we*'. There is no '*us*'."

"Can't we just talk privately for a minute?" she pleaded as she stroked her fingers up my arm.

The grin on Phil's face told me he wasn't going to come to my rescue. He was enjoying this way too much. He'd had Tiffany figured out from the first night I met her and had reminded me of that more than once.

Tiffany brushed her ample breasts against me as she leaned in close. "It will just be a minute, darling," she added with syrupy sweetness.

"I'll leave you two lovebirds alone for a moment," Phil said wryly as he turned away.

I was raised to be polite, so I gritted my teeth as he ambled a few steps away, and I tried to keep a semblance of a smile on my face, which was not easy.

Tiffany leaned in closer. "I think we should give ourselves another chance, Patrick. We are so good together."

There was no denying she was enjoyable in bed, but there wasn't enough below the surface. Shopping and high-brow social functions were the only things Tiffany found interesting. She was exceptionally pretty arm candy, but that was all.

I thought back to the day I broke it off with her. We'd been at a barbecue a few months ago when I noticed an attractive blonde walking by.

"Patrick, don't be so obvious. I don't care who you play with in your spare time after we're married, but it's just uncouth to look around when you're here with me," she'd said. *"It's embarrassing to have such bad manners, don't you think, darling?"*

Where she'd ever gotten the notion that she would someday be Mrs. Patrick Covington was beyond me. We'd been dating for less than a month. I'd told her we wouldn't be seeing each other any more when I dropped her back at her place that evening.

She moved in close. "You've had your break, and now I think we should be together again." She used her practiced sultry voice.

I met her eye. "Tiff, I thought I made it plain. It's over." I spoke as calmly as I could.

Her plastic smile was replaced by her equally plastic pouty face. "But darling, we are so good together."

She was persistent, like the mosquito you swat at and miss that comes back again and again.

The barista called our orders, and Phil picked up the coffees and sandwiches at the end of the counter.

"No, we weren't good together. I want someone who loves more than just my money or my name, and we both know that isn't you," I told her quietly.

Her eyes narrowed. "How silly, Patrick. Every woman you meet is going to be with you for the money."

I made a move to join Phil. "No means no, Tiff. You will make a fine wife for the right guy." I wanted to say *trophy wife* but held my tongue. "But I'm not that guy."

Anger flashed across her face. "Patrick, you're going to regret this someday. You'll marry a girl thinking she's in love with you and be crushed when you find out all she loves is your wallet."

"Like it's any different with you?"

She huffed. "Well, at least I'm honest about it." She scowled and left as quickly as her expensive red-soled Louboutin heels would allow.

Phil handed me my coffee. "You know, I think she friggin' nailed it."

I followed him toward the door. "So you caught that?" I waved goodbye to the Gladys twins, who waved back.

He took a sip from his cup. "The whole fucking place heard her."

"Nailed what?" I asked quietly as we exited into the bright sunshine and turned toward our cars.

"Being a Covington, you'll never know if the girl falls in love with you, or your name and your money, until it's too fucking late."

"I'll know."

"Bullshit, you will."

"Well, I know it's not her."

"Just sayin', once you whip out the black Amex card and she finds out you're one of THOSE Covingtons, you can't fuckin' know for sure. No way."

I walked along with Phil as I pulled my keys out of my pocket. "Thanks for the pep talk."

Phil had been one of my best friends since high school. He had a thriving construction business and a sideline string of rental houses he'd accumulated by buying rundown single-family homes and renovating them. Today he was joining me at the Habitat for Humanity project where my family volunteered. Today's house was in Reseda, a bedroom community in the valley. The previous house on the lot had burned down, and the land had been donated to Habitat. We were putting up a duplex, and two deserving families would shortly have brand-new homes to live in.

Phil stepped up into his pickup as I settled into my Corvette, parked right behind him. I noticed the extra writing on my coffee cup as I went to put it in the holder.

Jamie had written her number on it.

Things are looking up.

I pushed the *Start* button, and the supercharged engine rumbled to life. Phil's words rattled around in my skull.

"Bullshit, you will. You can't fucking know for sure. No way. Not until it's too fucking late."

CHAPTER 2

*P*AT

THE HABITAT PROJECT SITE WAS CRAWLING WITH VOLUNTEERS
when Phil and I pulled up. My brother Bill waved from the sign-up
tables. My sister Katie was handing out hard hats. Our family had
been volunteering once a month or so for going on two years now.
It was a down-to-earth way for us to give back to the community
that had treated us so well over the years.

The neighborhood was nice——not well-to-do, but most of the
yards and houses on the street showed pride of ownership. Phil and
I unloaded the cutoff saw, compressor, power nailers, and drills
from the back of his truck. Phil had been a great addition to the
team, providing us with his tools and another set of experienced
eyes to keep the weekend rookies from doing anything stupid and
hurting themselves.

I was surprised to see old man Benson on site again. He'd hurt
his back last month, and I'd expected he might take today off, but
there he was at the plan table, going over the blueprints and writing

down measurements for one of the carpentry leads who was a regular.

The whole project was a bit like an old-fashioned, midwestern barn raising. Old man Benson barked directions left and right all morning, rattling off measurements, stud counts, and electrical and plumbing locations from the plans. At one point, Steven had to run out to the local Home Depot when it looked like we might run short of Simpson Strong-Ties.

This was a bigger project than the last one because we were doing a duplex. Still, by the lunch break we had all the walls framed, and with some luck, we would finish placing the rafters this afternoon.

Bill's wife, Lauren, made a run to Subway for sandwiches for our family group, including Phil. Katie had brought a potato salad and two big bags of chips. Bill kept busy razzing her, now that she was going to be a big movie star. That earned him some potato salad flung his way, which landed in his hair. And also in mine because I was sitting next to him.

"It serves you right for picking on her," Lauren told him.

Katie got ready to fling a second spoonful at him, but Bill put up his hands in surrender.

"It's just three lines," she said.

"But you get to walk the red carpet just like the rest of them," Lauren noted.

She was right. Katie had landed a bit part in a rom-com that was premiering soon, courtesy of Steven's movie-star ex, Victoria Palmer. Katie had lines, so she'd gotten her name in the credits, and she was looking forward to walking the red carpet for her first, and she insisted only, time.

Katie rolled her eyes. "And I still have to find a date."

"I'll go with you," I offered.

Katie smiled and nodded, but she didn't say anything. As her brother, I was clearly not her first choice.

I felt around in my hair to remove the potato salad, but ended up mashing it farther in.

Phil leaned over. "See? If you'd brought Tiffany with you today, she could help out with that."

"Tiffany wouldn't be caught dead out here. It would ruin her manicure," I replied.

"Did I hear you're seeing Tiffany again?" Steven asked.

I tried a napkin on my hair. "No way."

"I didn't like her very much," Lauren said.

"You should have seen her try to undress him right there in Starbucks," Phil added.

Katie put down her Mountain Dew. "Well, he can't help it that he's gorgeous and rich."

Phil laughed. "It's the rich part that has them swarming all over him. He ought to try walking a mile in my shoes. They wouldn't give him a chance if he didn't drive around in that chick magnet car of his with his flashy clothes and big wallet."

Phil was right. The 'Vette was a chick magnet.

Katie defended me. "I think he'd be a great catch for any of them, even without the money."

I continued working the mess out of my hair.

"I agree," Lauren chimed in. "You guys are the shallow ones. You drool over a girl with big boobs and a short skirt before you've learned anything about her."

I cast a sideway glance at Bill. He and Steven were both smart enough to not get dragged into this conversation.

"And women are any different?" Phil asked.

Lauren laughed. "Of course. We look below the surface to see the character of the man."

Bill smiled at his wife.

The horn announcing the end of the lunch break saved us from continuing the debate.

"I still say it's the 'Vette that makes him so fuckin' irresistible," Phil added as we cleaned up the plates.

We worked on the duplex into the afternoon, finishing early. I credited this to Lloyd Benson's organizational skills, and I told him so as we packed up.

Benson patted me on the back with his signature, "Thanks, son," reply. To him, every man under the age of fifty was *son* or *sonny*, except his own sons, of course, who warranted their actual names.

Phil and I lifted the last of his equipment into the bed of his dented, twenty-year-old Ford dually, which was even bigger than the average contractor's pickup. It was a sturdy F350 crew cab with his company name on the back and a huge V-8 engine under the hood. He still had his old high school girlfriend's name stenciled on the door: *Maggie*. It was a real working man's truck, but not the kind of thing you'd drive around town. It was a bitch to park.

Phil held out his keys. "I say we trade for a week. I bet you can't pick up a girl without the fuckin' chick magnet."

Phil had his share of success with the ladies, but not lately, I knew. He'd complained about it during our morning workout. It had been three months, and he was getting desperate. I kept telling him to take it slow and clean up his language, but that had gone in one ear and out the other. He was a nice guy after you got past the four-letter words and sexual innuendos, but Phil was convinced that when he showed up in his truck, the girls wrote him off.

He was such a tightwad, plowing every dime he earned back into his business. He refused to buy a car to go along with his work truck. He said if it was going to cost him that much to get laid, it would be cheaper to spend his money on Hollywood Boulevard.

"Why not?" I told him, offering my keys in exchange. "Just don't haul any lumber in it."

Phil was a great friend, and he needed this.

"Thanks, bud. You know the 'Vette gets 'em wet," he said with a huge smile. "And hand over the card too. No fair waving your black Amex card around."

I grabbed my wallet and gave him the card. "You'll only pull it out for show, right?"

"Got it. No big fuckin' charges." He smiled. "Meet up at the usual place?"

"See you there," I responded as I searched his huge key ring for the truck key.

He climbed into my 'Vette and started it up as he rolled down the window. "At least nothing *YOU* would call big." He laughed and roared off.

I gave him the finger. The car trade was no big deal. I also had a BMW back at the condo, and as my brother had taught me long ago, the value of a car was only the deductible it would cost me if someone wrecked it.

I climbed up and grabbed Phil's company logo baseball cap from the dash.

"The 'Vette gets 'em wet." He has that part right.

~

LIZ

THE LETTER MADE ME INSTANTLY NAUSEOUS.

A bright yellow envelope with *Allied National Collections* on it in impossible-to-miss giant red letters, addressed to *Elizabeth Turner*. I could see it on the front table.

It should have been addressed to Trent Stover, Assholus Maximus.

I tore open the envelope and pulled out the letter, putting it in my purse to read later when I had some time. I left the gaudy envelope upside down on the table. The last thing I needed was its hideous color attracting attention at work.

I had stupidly co-signed a car loan for my asshole ex-boyfriend, Trent, and this was my lesson for being such a dumbshit. It didn't matter to them that the loan was for his truck and in his name. I had co-signed, so it was my problem now that he'd skipped out and left the state. I was the easy target.

I closed my purse and put off the bad news for now. I didn't feel like starting my day pissed off and having my tips suffer for it.

I told my sister, Stacey, I was leaving for work and tousled Timmy's hair on my way to the door.

"Bye," he said, straightening his hair without glancing up. He hated my tousling, but he let me get away with it.

"Amy, I should be back by nine," I yelled to our babysitter in the kitchen.

"See ya," she replied from around the corner.

Amy was a godsend on days like today. She was always available when my sister, Stacey, and I had to be out at the same time. Today I had the dinner shift at The Ironhorse, and Stacey wouldn't be back from the hospital until late. Timmy was well mannered and mature for his age, but a seven year old couldn't be left alone in the house.

Missy, our Australian Shepherd, waited by the door. She was smart enough to figure out when I was getting ready to leave. Roxy, our King Charles, remained oblivious, passed out on the dog bed. I patted Missy on the head as I left.

Outside, the air was surprisingly clean for a change. Yesterday's wind had blown all the smog out, and the mountains both north and south were clear in the bright California sun. My trusty little blue Corolla needed to be hosed off, but it would have to wait till tomorrow. The door squeaked as I closed it. I crossed my fingers. Turning the key brought the normal slow wheezing sound as the engine barely turned over and finally sputtered to life. My luck was holding.

The service station guy had said it probably needed a new battery or a starter or something, and it would be at least a hundred bucks. This week's budget didn't allow for that, and neither did next week's, for that matter. I'd have to beg for some more shifts at the restaurant to cover it, and that meant dealing with my manager, Ben. That thought brought the taste of bile to my throat. He was such a creep.

I'm not braving that today.

Since moving up to The Ironhorse from a nearby Olive Garden, my tips had improved significantly, but we still barely covered the bills. I cracked the windows a bit because the air conditioning in my shitmobile barely worked. Just another thing I'd have to spend money on.

Tonight was bingo night at the senior center, which meant a bigger than usual after-dinner crowd. The problem was, they weren't great tippers, and they didn't order much beyond appetizers and pie. I was mentally calculating what a decent tip should be on a table with an order of prawns, one calamari, and four pieces of pie when it happened.

The red Camaro in front of me swerved abruptly to the left, but not far enough.

I heard the yelp, and my heart jumped to my throat.

HE HIT THE DOG.

CHAPTER 3

LIZ

THE YELLOW LABRADOR LIMPED OFF TO THE SIDEWALK AS THE
jerk in the Camaro that hit him kept right on going. I flipped him
the bird, for all the good it did. Hitting a poor defenseless dog and
leaving the scene? I couldn't believe it.

"How would you like it if someone ran down your dog or your
kid, you asshole?" I yelled through the windshield.

Dr. Phil was probably right that Mr. Camaro with the big
engine was compensating for something else that wasn't so big.
Fuckhead.

I stopped in a clear space and parked. I got out and ran toward
the dog, which promptly ran away, scared of me. I stopped, and he
stopped as well, eyeing me like I was the local dog catcher. I
moved toward him, and he moved off with a limp. He didn't seem
to be bleeding, but you never could tell about internal injuries. I'd
learned as much from my sister, the nurse in training.

I talked softly and moved slowly. At first the dog stayed still, allowing me to get closer, then it ran around a parked van and across the street.

I followed.

Tires screeched.

My heart stopped. A big-ass truck was barreling down on me. I covered my eyes.

The truck stopped just feet from me.

"Asshole," I yelled as I got my breath back.

The fucker shouldn't have been going so fast on a street like this.

The dog trotted down the other side of the street, and on wobbly legs, I gave chase again.

The big, white pickup pulled over and parked as the dog laid down and I slowed to a walk.

"Need some help?" A man's voice shouted from behind me where the pickup had stopped.

I turned and put my finger to my lips to get him to shut up. I was getting close now, and I inched forward in small steps. I didn't need some cowboy yelling and scaring the lab away again.

The dog raced around me.

Mr. Pickup moved into place to block the space between a homeowner's fence and a parked car.

The dog tried to get by him, but he dove and grabbed his collar.

I trotted up to him.

"I got him. Miss?"

"Liz," I answered.

Pickup man got to his knees, holding the retriever by the collar. His forearm was scraped and bloody from lunging onto the sidewalk.

"You shouldn't run out in the street like that," he told me. "I almost hit you."

As if it was my fault.

"You shouldn't be going so fast," I shot back.

"Next time keep your dog on a leash," he hissed.

"He's not my dog! He got hit by some jerk that just drove off, and I was trying to catch him to get him back home where he belongs. I was afraid he might be hurt."

I knelt down to check the tags on the dog's collar. "So don't go run me over and then yell at me."

"Of course it's not your dog. This isn't a he, and you would know that if she was yours."

I read the tag on her collar. "Her name is Tosca, and there's a phone number here. Do you have a phone? Mine is in my car." I glanced up at him and caught his eyes, the amber eyes of a cat, dangerous eyes.

"Sure." He pulled out a phone and handed it to me.

I dialed the number on the tag.

He ran his hands over the dog's back and legs, checking for injuries. Tosca didn't react or pull back, probably a good sign that nothing serious was wrong with her.

"Disconnected," I said after I got the annoying warble sound the phone company reserved for calls that didn't go through. "Now what am I going to do? I have to get to work."

I hadn't considered what I'd do with her if I couldn't reach the owner. Tears welled in my eyes. I would be late if I took her back to my place.

"Just put your number in the phone, Liz. I'll take her to a vet and let you know what they say. Maybe I'll be able to track down the owner through the rabies tag number, or maybe she has a chip."

I punched my number into his phone.

I finally got a good look at him when he stood up. He towered over me, well over six feet with broad shoulders, a chiseled square jaw with a bit of a stubble, and warm amber eyes over prominent cheekbones. Heat rose in my cheeks as I noticed the bulging muscles beneath his work shirt. I began putting together how handsome he was now that he wasn't on the ground holding the dog. I licked my lips. Quite the find. I tucked some stray hair behind my ear.

Control yourself, girl, and stop preening.

He escorted Tosca to his truck. *Patterson Construction* it said on the back of the dented old pickup, which matched the writing on his baseball cap. *Maggie* was stenciled on the door in script. It was one of those long trucks with four doors and big dual wheels in the back——the kind I move over to avoid on the road, half because they're so big, and half because they have a few dents that tell you they don't mind pushing little cars like mine out of the way.

Eyeing my ass, he asked if I had pets, and I admitted I did.

Mr. Pickup opened the back door and effortlessly lifted Tosca inside.

The dog seemed to be quite at ease with him. A good sign. I'd always found animals a better judge of character than people. Mine had never cared for Trent——a warning I should have heeded at the time.

I offered my hand with my best smile. "I didn't get your name?" His touch emitted sparks of promise that ran up my arm.

"Pat."

He had big, strong hands, and not as rough as I expected from a construction guy. The smile he returned was warm and generous, with dimples to die for.

"I'll take care of Tosca for you today. Go get yourself to work, Liz. I don't want to make you late."

I waved goodbye and smiled as I walked back to my little blue car. Too bad he was in construction. Trent had worked construction, and so had Mike, my boyfriend before him. They'd both been complete losers. Why did all the hot guys have to be losers or gay? As my little car wheezed and finally rumbled to life, it dawned on me: Pat had my number, but I didn't have his.

He doesn't seem gay.

~

PAT

I DON'T KNOW WHY I TOLD HER MY NAME WAS PAT.

I've always gone by Patrick, but when she had said her name was Liz, Pat just seemed a better fit.

Liz waved as she drove past. The bumper sticker on her car read *My Aussie is Smarter than your Honor Student*. She liked her dogs, all right. I had her number in my phone, and the dog in my backseat was my ticket for another meeting.

She was on her way to work, she'd said. She had her hair up. It probably was even prettier down. This woman had it all, if she'd just dress up a little.

I readjusted myself in my pants. The sight of that ass when she bent over had started to get me hard——and that chest. I could already feel those soft tits in my hands.

Tosca licked at my neck as I reached for Phil's first aid kit under the backseat. Labs were the best dogs. I gave her a quick pet.

As a 4-H project, I had raised a black lab puppy for Guide Dogs for the Blind when I was little. Her name was Jessie. I was so proud the day I got the postcard saying she'd graduated from the program and gone to be a guide dog for a man in St. Louis.

I finished tending to my arm and climbed into the pickup. I was looking forward to meeting up with Liz again tomorrow to give her the dog. I needed to get out of these work clothes and into a proper suit and my BMW for this woman. Something about her clicked for me.

What restaurant would I take her to? And what should I get her? Maybe a nice ruby necklace to match those kissable lips. No, a sapphire one to match those gorgeous blue eyes of hers would be better.

She had all the right curves, but the best one had been that smile. I just couldn't get it out of my mind as I drove off.

What a smile.

CHAPTER 4

LIZ

LOUISE AND I BOTH ARRIVED AT THE IRONHORSE JUST IN TIME FOR our shift. We walked in together. Tina was already handling tables, so we were greeted by Ben, our creepy new manager. Sticking close to Louise was my plan; she was like creep repellent. Ben gave her a wide berth. She had been among the first three people hired by the restaurant's owners, the Vandersmoots. That gave her clout in our little ecosystem. The Vandersmoots had three other restaurant locations, so if the situation with Ben got too bad, I could ask to transfer to one of the others. But I kept this only as a last resort, because the tips would be lower at the other more casual spots.

While I was putting my purse in my locker, Louise patted her butt and gave me a meaningful look.

"Thanks," I said.

I still had cat hair on the seat of my pants. Having a Ragdoll and an Exotic Persian at home meant a constant battle, since I had to wear black for work. I used the lint roller I kept in my locker and turned back toward Louise.

"Any news?" I asked.

"Not yet. Selling an upscale place like this takes a while. It's not like selling a franchise."

The Vandersmoots had confided in Louise a few weeks ago that they'd put The Ironhorse up for sale.

Shortly after I reached the dining room, three guys in jeans with a sprinkling of sawdust on their clothing grabbed table seven. Carpenters, from the looks of them. Plumbers almost always came in with dirty fingers from putting pipe together. The bearded one of the group had driven up in a bright red Corvette. Good thing for him it wasn't a Camaro, or I might've needed to spill a carafe of coffee in his lap in case he was the one who'd hit the dog. The other two had driven up together in a BMW. One had a buzz cut, and the other curly hair.

I walked up with a smile. Waitressing rule number one: always smile, even if they have BO.

"What can I start you gentlemen off with today?"

Beard guy and curly ordered beers, with iced tea for buzz cut, and a fourth that hadn't arrived yet would also take an iced tea.

Before I left, beard guy asked if it was safe to park his Corvette near the entrance where he had it, his way of making sure I knew what he drove.

Like I care?

A half hour later, my heart raced as I glanced outside to see the big, white Patterson Construction pickup parking in the shade on the far end of the lot. Pat, my gallant dog catcher, disembarked from the truck and walked Tosca for a minute on the grass before joining the three guys at table seven.

After a minute, I went back to the table to get their dinner order, my smile in place. "You guys decided yet?"

Beard guy eyed me up and down, pretending to try to read my name tag, which meant he was checking out my boobs. Creep.

I need to move my tag up higher.

I hoped they weren't all going to be like that. At least Pat had seemed more refined when I'd met him earlier, but sometimes guys got rowdier and raunchier when they were in a group. It became a testosterone competition or something.

"How'd we get so lucky to have a pretty girl like you to wait on us, Elizabeth?" the beard asked, laying it on thick. "My name's Phil, by the way."

Pat hadn't glanced up from his menu yet.

"That's so nice of you," I answered with a smile. Rule number three: never respond angrily. "Now, what will you gents have?"

"Hank, you go first," Pat said to curly.

Hank ordered, and I learned buzz cut was called Winston.

Pat was the last to order. He eyed me so hungrily, a shiver rolled over me as his amber eyes held mine. "I'll have the T-bone." His dimples grew as his smile slowly expanded, ratcheting up my temperature.

I tucked a stray curl behind my ear and wrote slowly, trying to keep my gaze on my pad for fear I would be hypnotized by those eyes if I looked up.

"And how would you like that cooked, Pat?"

The beard shot a sideways glance at Pat, apparently baffled that I knew Pat's name.

"However you take it," he said before adding, "Liz."

The way he said my name dripped with sex appeal, and his gaze sent a rush of heat through me. He told me he'd already taken Tosca to a vet, and she would be all right.

I looked up to find him still staring at me with those enticing amber eyes, which pulled me in like a tractor beam. I broke eye contact and retreated quickly to get the orders started.

Louise had been at the next table over and came back to the kitchen with me. "I like the one in the baseball cap," she said. "I think he's cute, and he likes you."

"I don't need a guy unless he's a nice, stable professional type ——a doctor or a lawyer or something."

Louise filled a water glass. "In the meantime, you could date around a little and least get a free dinner or two out of it."

"Been there, done that. Not interested." I was tempted to drink some of the water to cool down.

This was typical Louise. She was always handicapping the field for me, trying to get me to go out with someone like a mother hen trying to get the chick out of the nest. But this chick had already been out there and gotten burned.

I didn't dare tell her Pat and I had already met, and he seemed like a very nice guy. She'd be relentless then. Trying to get the single waitresses married off seemed to be Louise's sole pastime.

She ran her check through the left-hand register, and I ran table seven through the one on the right. Having two new touchscreen registers meant we didn't ever have to wait, and it also now printed out several tip suggestions on the receipt, making it easier for the math challenged. These were the only improvements Ben had made that I could tell.

Tina came over. "Which one?" she asked.

"Baseball cap, table seven," Louise reported. She took the bill and the card and left.

Tina pivoted to eye my table. "Cute times ten," she whispered. "If you don't want him, that's your loss. I hear carpenters have big tools." She giggled.

Tina had a saying like that for every kind of guy.

Those eyes. I just can't get them out of my head.

PAT

SIRI HAD HELPED ME FIND A VET THAT WAS OPEN ON SUNDAY, AND

a quick visit had confirmed that Tosca was bruised, but not badly injured from her run-in with the car.

The Ironhorse was my regular spot to meet the guys after a Habitat day, if the project was in the valley. It was close to the freeway and let us relax while the traffic was dying down before we headed over the hill to west LA. It wasn't quite as upscale as my brother's restaurant, but it beat stopping at Denny's. Winston and Hank lived in Santa Monica, Phil in Palms, and I was on Wilshire.

Today the guys had all beat me here because of my doggy detour, but at least Phil had parked my 'Vette where it wouldn't get a door ding.

I'd parked in the shade, rolled the windows down a bit, and taken the dog out before going in.

When I found their table, Phil, Winston, and Hank had already gotten me my usual iced tea to start.

"What's with the arm?" Hank had asked, pointing to my bandage. "Your girlfriend bite you again?"

I'd put my arm under the table. "Little accident catching a dog."

I'd almost choked on my iced tea when Liz walked up to take our order. Her black apron only partially hid the enticing figure I knew was behind it.

Phil was ogling her tits like a high school kid, and he'd laid one of his pickup lines on her, which she politely ignored.

I'd kept my face in my menu to avoid staring at her like Phil.
She deserves better.

I was the last to order, and when I did, I was mesmerized by her light blue eyes again, and the symmetry of her features.

I found myself wondering again what her hair would look like down. Liz carried off beautiful with only mascara and that terrific smile, which grew as she looked at me. Her sultry voice had my cock straining against my jeans under the table.

"She's fuckin' into me. I can tell," Phil mumbled as she left the table with our orders.

"In your dreams, kid. She's just too polite to tell you to shove it," Hank said.

Winston rolled his eyes. He agreed with Hank.

"Patrick, what are you smirking about?" Winston asked, kicking me under the table.

"I met her on the way over here is all, and I kinda like her," I told him.

Phil gave me the evil eye. "Bet you don't get anywhere with her if you don't wave your wallet around. No wallet, no car, no girl. No fuckin' way."

"I say you're wrong," Hank said. "She has eyes for Patrick here, not you."

I put my hands up in mock surrender. "I didn't say it."

Phil scowled. "I still bet you strike out."

Hank saved us by asking Winston to fill us in on his latest escapades.

Liz brought out our food, and for nearly an hour, Winston regaled us with stories of guarding Hollywood celebrities, and their antics.

Then Hank and Winston decided it was time to head over the hill, but Phil and I stayed for dessert.

"Go ahead. Give it a try. I'm gonna laugh all the fucking way home. No car, no wallet, crash and burn, baby," Phil said.

After she'd brought us both a slice of cheesecake, I made my move. "Liz, I think you and I should go out some night this week."

She stopped, and a soft smile tugged at her lips. "Pat, that's so nice of you to offer."

Phil smirked.

"What do you two do for a living?" she asked.

"Cousin, why don't you fill her in?" I said, elbowing Phil.

Phil gave me a sideways glance and smiled. "I run a construction company, darling, and Pat here works for me."

She put her pen up to her lip before continuing in a soft voice. "Well, Pat, I'd love to, but I have a rule that I only date professional men. Lawyers and doctors and such. So, the answer is no." She turned and walked off.

Phil grinned. "I told you. Crash and burn."

"Your radar needs a serious adjustment, bud. She is going to be mine. I can feel it."

I tried two more times to get a *yes* out of Liz when she came by, but I was politely shot down each time.

I tried one more time when she brought our check. No luck. Phil gloated.

She started to leave, then turned around. "Phil? It is Phil, isn't it?"

He nodded eagerly.

"Is Pat always this persistent?"

"Pretty much," he answered.

I put on my best puppy dog face.

Liz smiled at me. "And does he always get what he wants?" she asked.

"Yup."

Her smile grew. "So this is a new experience for him?"

Phil laughed. "Yeah, a first. He's seeing how it is for the rest of us."

Liz smirked in my direction. She turned and left without another word.

I followed Phil out and gave a little wave to Liz behind his back.

She waved in return. There was a lot more to this beautiful girl than she was letting on.

Tosca greeted me with a few licks on my neck as I climbed up into the truck. She'd decided the front seat was more to her liking than the back. I pulled out my phone and sent Liz a text.

ME: Have a nice evening - Pat

On the drive back, I kept thinking about Liz and contrasting her with Lisa, Tiffany, and the others like them I'd been with recently. Liz was a beauty with compassion and down-to-earth honesty. And I'd always found you could tell a lot about a person by the way they treated animals.

But what Tiffany had said this morning still bugged me. I'd insisted I would be able to tell if a woman was truly into me, not my money, but what if Tiffany was right and I couldn't tell until it was too late? What if Tiffany was the only honest one of the bunch, as she claimed?

When I got home, I still couldn't answer my Tiffany question. Would I really be able to tell?

Oliver, the doorman, was at his usual post. "Good evening, Mister Patrick. Fine-looking dog you have there, sir."

I brought Tosca over, and the old man pulled a doggy treat out of his pocket. He always took special care of the residents' dogs. I took Tosca up in the elevator with me, and once inside my condo, I gave her some water and found sliced turkey breast for her to eat. I'd forgotten to stop for dog food.

I dialed up Phil. "Hey, Phil. I'd like to keep the truck a while, if it's okay with you?"

"Sure, if I can keep the 'Vette. But I'll need some of the tools out of the back. I'll send a guy over in the morning to pick 'em up," he said.

I hesitated before asking him the next thing. "One more thing, Phil. Is the house on Myrtle still empty?"

"Yeah. The fucking paint crew pushed me out a week. Why?"

"I'd like to rent it for a while."

He was quiet, waiting for me to explain.

"I'm going to take you up on your suggestion and walk a mile in your shoes, buddy. For a while I want to be Pat Patterson, construction grunt, instead of Patrick Covington, and I'd like to live in the house on Myrtle and drive your truck."

He laughed. "About fucking time you saw how the other half lives. I like it. Do I get to use your penthouse condo?"

"Let's not get carried away. You can drive the 'Vette," I answered.

"The key to the house on Myrtle is the blue one on the key ring," he said.

My phone dinged, announcing an incoming text message.

"I knew you'd strike out without the 'Vette." He laughed. "And take proper care of my Maggie."

He stayed on the phone and insisted on busting my balls some more before he signed off. I pulled up the text when he finally hung up.

LIZ: U 2 how is Tosca

I composed a reply, but before I could send it, another came in.

LIZ: Can I see her tomorrow

ME: You must miss me already

The reply took a while; she was obviously still working.

LIZ: In yur dreams

ME: You already know what I dream about

ME: Bet you dream about me tonight too

I didn't get a reply to that.

Now I needed to get some things organized for tomorrow.

Sleep didn't come easily. Her smile kept coming to mind, followed by that body and all the things I could do with her. I imagined how good the smile would look with her under me.

After that I couldn't get to sleep at all.

I grabbed a washcloth and took matters into hand with a vigorous jerk-off session.

I was going to have this girl. She just didn't know it yet.

CHAPTER 5

LIZ

IT WAS A BEAUTIFUL MORNING, SO OUR NEXT DOOR NEIGHBOR,
Teresa, and her son, Jack, had just collected Timmy to walk to
school instead of taking the bus.

Stacey closed the door behind them and raised an eyebrow as
she headed for the kitchen.

"So who is this guy Pat, anyway?" She poured us some orange
juice to go with the scrambled eggs she'd made.

She'd been asleep when I got home last night, so I hadn't told
her a thing about Pat or the dog. I checked the counter where I kept
my charger. My phone was missing.

"You reading my messages again?" I asked. "Give me that
back." I held out my hand.

Stacey was the nosiest sister ever.

She produced the phone from her pocket and started scrolling
through my messages again. "Come on, Liz, you know it's the only
way I get any excitement these days."

That was true. With school full time and working as a nurse's aide thirty-plus hours a week, she didn't have a lot of time for dating——not that my dance card had been very full lately either. Having a child around was like having a skunk in the house to most guys our age.

"And who is Tosca?" she asked, still holding the phone.

I picked up my glass of juice. "Pat is the guy that helped me catch the dog."

"What dog?" Stacey asked.

"The dog that got hit by a car while I was driving to work yesterday." I sipped some juice.

Stacey waited expectantly.

"Pat was nice enough to stop and help me catch the dog," I repeated.

Stacey finished off a forkful of eggs. "Is he hot?"

"Anyway, I tried the phone number on the dog's tag, and it was disconnected. I couldn't take the dog to work, so he volunteered to take her for a day."

"For a day?" Stacey exclaimed. "What are we going to do after that? You can't take in every stray. For God's sake, we barely convinced the agent to rent us this place with the critters we have."

It had taken forever to find this house. Once they heard we had four animals, most of the agents showed us the door.

"Your soft spot for animals is going to get us all in trouble."

"He thinks he can find the owner through the rabies tag."

"And if he doesn't?" she asked.

I didn't have an answer. I would have to find a way to place the dog with a good home. I couldn't just put her back on the street.

I put out some food for the cats, and Candy came running from her perch on the window sill. Tasha was nowhere to be seen, probably under my bed.

Stacey finished another forkful of eggs. "And don't think I didn't notice that you avoided my question about this guy's hotness. That means you like him."

"I do not," I lied. "I just think he was very considerate. That's all." I filled my mouth with toast to keep from having to say anything else.

"Liar," she replied. "I can read you like a book. So tell me more, or I'm going to send him a text saying you're horny."

I grabbed across the table for the phone. "Give me that."

She jerked it out of reach. "Not till you share."

I relented. "He's tall, and yes, he's cute, with these gorgeous amber eyes. He and his buddies stopped in the restaurant for dinner, and I found out he works for Patterson Construction. That's all there is. That's all I know."

"And did you?" she asked.

"Did I what?"

"Did you dream of him last night?"

I lunged for the phone, but she was too fast for me. "None of your business!"

She ran into her room with the phone. The door closed before I reached it.

"Give me that back," I yelled as I banged on the door.

Stacey opened it and eyed me for a moment. "Did you?"

"I don't remember my dreams," I protested as I held out my hand.

Evidently she'd decided she'd gotten enough information out of me. She handed me the phone. I saw the screen.

ME: I did and I miss u already

ME: Wish u were here

"You can't do that," I yelled, glaring at her. She was always messing with my private life.

She giggled. "Just be nice to him when he comes to see you." She cocked an eyebrow. "He is coming by to see you again, right?"

"I guess." I tried to hide how much I wanted that to be true, because at the same time, I dreaded it. He was another stupid construction guy, and Stacey and I both knew what that meant.

"From over the hill?" she asked.

I hadn't thought about it like that. "I guess."

"Hmmm…" she said. She didn't seem to think Pat was making the drive for a loose dog.

His response came a half hour later.

PAT: See you tonight

I scratched my neck. *Now what do I do?*

AT THE BEGINNING OF MY SHIFT, BEN CORNERED ME AND suggested coffee after work, which I declined, explaining that my sister was picking me up. His suggestions were becoming more frequent. He didn't understand the concept of *no*.

I checked again for a message from Pat. So far nothing. I'd hoped he would call and tell me how Tosca was doing.

Well, that's what I told myself. He seemed like a nice guy, and those eyes were something else, but he was still just a dumb, broke construction guy, and I couldn't get my hopes up for someone like that.

I opened my purse during my ten in the break room and pulled out the letter from the collection agency. I hadn't read it yesterday. As I did now, horror congealed in my stomach. Twenty-one thousand and some odd dollars it said I owed in big red letters. And below that was worse news in even bigger print: GARNISHMENT TO START IN 30 DAYS OR LESS.

"Oh dear, Liz, what happened?"

It was Louise. I hadn't heard her come in. The printing on the page was so big anybody could read it from across the room.

I quickly folded the paper. "My ex…" I didn't quite know how to explain it. "I signed on a car loan for my ex. He didn't have insurance, and he wrecked the car, so he still owes the money, but he skipped out and so…"

"And so they're coming after you for it?" she asked, sitting down and putting her arm around me.

I felt so shitty that I'd gotten myself into this mess. It would make it impossible to afford Stacey's schooling.

"I was stupid. I should never have signed it."

"Was this that Trent guy?"

"Yeah, he's the one."

Trent was only the latest in my string of failures. I could never seem to get it right with guys. I always fell for the sweet talk and promises, but they were all losers from the beginning. It was always the same story, just a different character. He lied to me, then he left. The guys I dated never had steady jobs and real futures. Construction was fine when things were good, but the cycle changed and they always ended up out of work sooner or later, and off to greener pastures and other gullible girls.

Louise placed a kind hand on my arm. "So what are you going to do, hon?"

"I don't know. Just have to get some extra shifts to make up the difference, I guess."

What I didn't say was that if they took a few hundred a month, this could go on for years. With paying for Stacey's schooling and everything else, we might have to move again, farther out of town to find a lower rent.

"What about finding the jerk, so he can pay?" she asked.

I wrung my hands. "I would, if I had any idea where he went, but I don't." My stomach felt progressively more sour.

I got up from the table and put my purse in my locker. "My ten is up. Back to the real world." I grabbed my notepad and headed out front. My heart sank a little as I surveyed the room and came up empty checking for Pat.

Get Trent to pay. That'll be the day.

P*AT*

I GOT UP EARLY, DECIDED TO SKIP MY WORKOUT, AND PUT ON MY running clothes. I drove Tosca to the house on Myrtle, stopping to get some dog food on the way.

I quickly toured the house, making mental notes of what I would need to make it livable. I walked the backyard fence. It was good enough to keep the dog in, and I left Tosca there with some food and water. The house was an older one from before this area had been developed. It was tiny, but sat on eight-tenths of an acre with a large backyard that included some fruit trees left over from when this area had featured more orchards than houses. It also had a pool, which was surprising.

Phil had explained that the previous owners had put the pool in for the grandkids and had planned to expand the house, but they didn't get to it for some reason. Phil had bought the property as an investment. When he got the money together, he planned to split the lot and put up two bigger houses. In the meantime, he'd been fixing up this house as a rental.

I locked the door to my new home and smiled as I started the three-mile run back to my condo, leaving the truck in the driveway. My phone dinged twice with new messages.

LIZ: Yes I miss u already

LIZ: Wish u were here

Liz filled my thoughts the whole way back. I kept running toward her smile. I felt like I was getting closer to her with each step. I needed to shower and change before my ten o'clock meeting on the Fellsman acquisition, but I returned Liz's text when I got to the condo.

ME: See you tonight

The Fellsman family had built a nice chain of hardware stores in the western states that were heavy into garden, landscaping, and backyard accessories and were different enough from the big box stores to survive on their own. The family wanted to retire and was looking for an owner that would follow their basic business model and keep the stores intact. They were worried about the impact the sale could have on their current employees.

I had assured them last week that as a family-run business, Covington was a better fit as a buyer for them than selling out to one of the national chains who would take over the real estate and downsize their company.

I was proud of the work my family did, but I didn't want to work for either of my brothers at Covington. So ever since I'd come back from Europe, we'd settled on having me work loosely for Bill, looking at acquisitions for our company. So far it had been comfortable for both of us. I was contributing to the family business, but I felt like I was running my own not-so-little show. Bill didn't try to manage me, and I didn't get in his way. My step-brother Liam was still out in Boston and running a section of the company from there——sort of Covington East, for the time being.

When I got upstairs in the Covington building, I corralled Judy, the assistant I shared with Bill, and gave her the address of the Myrtle Street house and a list of things I needed. Judy was sweet, and efficient to a fault. She could handle any assignment I gave her without a fuss.

The Fellsman meeting ate up my morning, and I spent most of the afternoon going over the numbers on the Popovich transaction with our CFO, Uncle Garth. It was not a day with a lot of down time for reflection.

As I walked to the car at the end of the day, I finally thought back to the Fellsman meeting. It had gone well, with one exception. I hadn't been one-hundred-percent engaged. I'd had trouble staying focused. I'd been distracted by memories of Liz all day. This was a new problem, and it bothered me. Usually I was laser focused on the objective of a meeting, checking my notes before starting and analyzing my progress at the breaks.

Women were for evenings and weekends. After work, I'd relax, get some exercise, some release with her, then park any lingering thoughts about her at the door when I got back to work. This had always worked for me before, through both school and work, until today.

Somehow Liz was different. I couldn't compartmentalize her. She monopolized my thoughts.

Today I'd been tempted to text her during the breaks, and I resisted, but only barely. I kept picturing her smile and drifting away. If my job had involved driving a truck, I would have been a menace to everyone else on the road. I was way too distracted.

She's in my head.

CHAPTER 6

LIZ

My breath hitched as I saw Pat walk in.

He wore clean jeans and a faded blue button-up shirt with the same cap as yesterday. He waved as he took a seat at the far end of the room.

I waved back and carried the three plates of food in my arms to table 8. On my way back, I motioned for Louise to join me by the kitchen. "Could I switch and take table eighteen and you take ten?"

Louise checked around the corner toward table eighteen. A smile came across her face. "I see that cute guy from last night is back."

Heat rose in my cheeks as I waited for an answer.

"Sure thing, Liz, and keep table ten. I'm not much good carrying six plates anymore."

That was a lie. She was looking out for me.

"Thanks. I owe you." I straightened my skirt and freshened up my lip gloss before heading to Pat's table.

His eyes met mine as I approached, and the same feeling of

being lost took over before I reached him. Anticipation fizzed in my stomach. Just like last night, a slow, deliberate smile grew by the second until it covered his entire face and spawned those tremendous dimples. Just the sight of him excited me.

I took a deep breath to calm myself.

He held my gaze. "You look lovely tonight, Liz." My name slid off his tongue with the same liquid sex appeal as yesterday, heating me between my thighs.

I broke eye contact to get my tongue working. "Thanks, Pat." The cotton of his shirt stretched to accommodate the breadth of his shoulders. His sleeves were rolled up, and he still had a bandage on the arm from catching the dog yesterday.

He motioned for me to sit down with him. "Take a load off."

I took out my pad. "I can't. I'm on duty, and we're pretty busy."

He handed me a tiny paper umbrella, the kind you put in a tropical drink. "This is for you."

"And this is for?" I asked.

He grinned. "Tell you later." He winked.

"Thank you." I put the little umbrella in my apron pocket. "What can I get you tonight?"

He perused the menu slowly.

Ben came out from the back office.

"I'll be back when you've made up your mind."

He nodded. "Sure."

I came back five minutes later after taking care of my other tables.

The menu was still open in front of him, and he watched me walk up with a look that devoured me. I'd been watched by guys before, but not like this. It wasn't lecherous, but admiring. I concentrated on my words so I didn't sound like an imbecile.

"Have you decided?"

Coffee, tea, or me would have been a better line, if I'd been willing to ditch my rule.

He grinned. "I know what I want; I'm just not sure how to ask for it."

I smiled. "Pointing works if the words are too big for you."

He pointed a finger at me. "Tosca and I would like to take you out for coffee."

My heart fluttered, but I just couldn't. "You told me last night that you work construction, right?"

"Yeah, that's one of the things I do."

"Did you also just graduate from medical school or something?"

His amber eyes threatened to break my resolve. "No."

"Like I told you, I have a rule that I only date professional men."

I did have a rule, after all.

"I'll have the filet tonight, please, while you reconsider."

I wrote it down, careful to avoid eye contact with him again. "How do you want that cooked?"

"Same as always, just the way you would order it."

I needed to change the conversation. "How is Tosca, by the way?"

"She's fine, and she's waiting to see you outside when you get off."

My stomach churned. *Did he mean he was dropping the dog off with me?* I wasn't ready for that.

"I'm not off till ten tonight."

"It's a date," he said with a smile.

Those eyes and the way the words flowed over his lips had me frozen for a moment. I gave myself a mental slap. "Not a date."

He winked. "Anything you say, Buttercup. Not a date...yet."

I wrote down M for medium and turned tail to get away from him and his effect on me.

Tina caught me in the back. "You're blushing. So? Did he ask you out yet?"

"I told you, not interested."

Tina crossed her arms. "You're so full of it. The way you look at him has horny written all over it."

I turned toward the kitchen.

"I hear carpenters do really good work with their hands," Tina added as I walked away.

She can be so annoying sometimes.

As the evening wore on, I kept glancing in Pat's direction.

My manager, Ben, managed to be where I would have to step around him more often than normal. He was so obvious when he was trying to brush up against me. It was disgusting. And the stares ——somebody had to teach the man how to keep his eyes *up.*

Creep.

For the rest of my shift, Pat ate slowly. Actually, *very* slowly, and I occasionally caught him glancing in my direction. But not in a creepy way, quite the opposite.

Pat added cheesecake and coffee to his order when he'd finished his meal, followed by ice cream. He kept complimenting me when I came back to check on him. He liked my smile and my eyes. It was all quite gentlemanly. Which was a complete turn-around from the normal comments I got, like "*nice rack"* or "*nice ass.*"

He asked me to compliment the chef as well, which I did.

Joey stuck his head out of the kitchen for a moment. "Which one?"

I pointed Pat out. "Baseball cap, table eighteen."

Joey smiled and waved to Pat, who waved back. Joey ducked back into the kitchen for a moment and reappeared with a piece of apple pie. "Give him this from me. Anybody who likes my cooking is my kind of customer."

I walked the dessert over to Pat. "Compliments of the chef. If you have room, that is."

The mind-melting dimples appeared again. "Why, thank you very much, Liz. This is my favorite, after my sister's of course. Katie's apple pie is just to die for."

I went back to working my other tables.

Tina had noticed what was going on and pulled me aside. "So?" she asked, nodding in Pat's direction.

"So what?" I didn't want to go there.

She smirked. "Did he ask you out? He obviously likes you, and I can tell you like him."

I huffed. "Yes and no. Yes, he asked, and no, I'm not going."

"You and your stupid rules. I hear carpenters really know how to handle their wood." She giggled.

Louise had left, and I still had another half hour in my shift.

Ben was at the registers, printing out a summary. I went the long way around back to my tables.

My phone vibrated in my pocket.

STACEY: I have to stay late sorry - be there by 11

She had my car because hers was in the shop. Now I had a problem. The restaurant was emptying out as it neared ten o'clock. Pat walked outside and stood by his truck as I retrieved my purse.

As creepy as Ben was being, I absolutely didn't want to wait in the back till Stacey showed up. When my shift was up, I hurried out to the parking lot while Ben was busy in his office for a minute. I was safer waiting with Pat than staying inside.

Pat held Tosca on a leash. The dog wagged her tail furiously as I approached. "She's almost as happy to see you as I am," he said.

She sniffed my leg then my crotch.

I leaned down to pet and hug her. "So I see."

After a moment Ben followed me out of the restaurant and came our way.

"Elizabeth," he said loudly as he approached. "Since your sister isn't here yet, how 'bout if I give you a lift home."

"No thanks, Mr. Perham."

He kept walking in our direction, and I made a snap judgment.

I put my arm around Pat. "My boyfriend is taking me home."

Ben stopped in his tracks. "Just making sure you're safe." My statement surprised him.

I knew he'd asked Louise a few days ago if I had a boyfriend.

Pat played along, putting his arm around me.

I gasped. His touch sent shocks through my body that I wasn't prepared for. His hand on my waist scorched the skin beneath my shirt. I instinctively molded myself to the warmth of his side.

He waved at Mr. Perham as he pulled me close.

Being in his arms was wrong, but it felt so right. His body was hard and warm, his arm around me strong and protective, melting my resolve.

Ben stood there watching, not entirely convinced.

Pat kissed my ear and whispered. "It'll cost you dinner for me to play along."

What choice did I have? I nodded and turned to face him. A fire raged inside me as my breasts pressed up against his chest.

His lips came down to claim mine, and his tongue sought entrance. I opened to him. Our tongues began the dance of acquaintance as they sought each other. One hand snaked around my waist to grab my ass and pull me to him as his cock surged noticeably against my stomach, sending sparks through me.

He tasted like sex and power. The faint scent of pine and spice in his hair drew me closer. His other hand came up, and his thumb lightly traced the underside of my breast, leaving a trail of heat that instantly hardened my nipples as I pulled more tightly into him, needing the pressure, the heat, the closeness.

I couldn't keep the kiss simple, short, or friendly. It was impossible to stop, and I no longer wanted to. I only heard the pounding of my heart as I speared my fingers through his hair, pulling myself up to him.

He broke the kiss and loosened his grip on me, but I kept my breasts pressed against his muscular chest, feeling our synchronized breathing.

"He's gone now," Pat said, kissing my forehead.

I let go and stepped away. "Thanks," I said, trying to keep the words simple as I slowly reengaged my brain. "He really gives me the creeps."

"I could tell," Pat said with a smile. "And no problem. I enjoyed it just as much as you did."

"I did not." I looked down, hoping to hide my lie. I petted the dog some more.

"Hop in." He opened the door to his truck for me, and when I was in, he loaded the dog into the back.

I scanned the inside of the truck nervously. No ax, no knives, no chainsaw, no blood stains. It appeared safe. It was actually clean and orderly for a work truck.

"What time for dinner tomorrow?" he asked as he started the engine.

"I thought you were kidding."

He stopped the engine. "I can take you back in to Mr. Creepy, if that's what you want, because I don't drive liars in this truck." His eyes showed his determination.

"Okay, okay, already. Tomorrow." Facing Ben right now was the one thing I could not do.

He started the engine and looked at me expectantly.

His gaze melted me. I sighed. "Six work for you?"

"Six is good."

I gave him my address, which he told Siri to navigate to. I texted Stacey that I had a ride home.

Had I dug myself into a hole here trying to avoid Ben? I had hugged Pat, I had kissed Pat——or rather he had kissed me. Or actually we'd kissed each other. I was so mixed up right now.

I'd pledged to not date him, and now we'd kissed and he was driving me home with a dinner date scheduled. This was so messed up. I'd gotten into Pat's truck even though my rule said to stay clear of him.

But I wasn't really breaking a rule because he was just giving me a ride. We weren't going out or anything... It was just a fake kiss to fend off Ben, and just a ride home, if I didn't count the dinner I'd agreed to. I tried not to glance over at him.

Just a fake kiss.

"So, I don't have a lead on Tosca's owner yet," he told me after we drove off.

"Oh."

He glanced over. "The bureaucracy doesn't move very fast down at County Animal Services. They said they would be able to look it up tomorrow, if I called back."

"Didn't you tell them the dog was lost?"

"Sure, but they were even less helpful than the Department of Motor Vehicles. They said I'd have to wait until Janice somebody is in on Tuesday."

I nodded. Pat had been so nice. "I appreciate you following up with that, and thank you for giving me a ride. I really didn't want to go with Mr. Perham."

He reached over and touched my shoulder. "It was my pleasure, Buttercup. I want you to be safe. I'll talk to Mr. Creepy tomorrow and warn him to stay away from you," Pat announced as he turned on to my street.

"No. I fight my own battles."

"Suit yourself, Buttercup."

It gave me a warm, tingly sensation to be protected by such a tall, strong man. He obviously kept himself in great shape. His offer to warn Ben sounded a lot like an offer to beat the crap out of him, which tempted me. Then there was the off-the-charts kiss.

I was in dangerous territory.

Being near Pat was easy and hard at the same time. He drew me like a magnet. But I knew getting involved was the wrong thing to do. Like eating a whole pint of Ben & Jerry's in a sitting, I would regret it later and wonder how I could have been so stupid.

When we parked, he insisted on walking me to the house. Tosca came with us, and he held my hand. It was such a simple gesture, but so hard to resist. My brain told me to refuse, but I couldn't. The warmth of his touch ignited my skin and torched all my functioning brain cells on the way to my lady parts. It was as if his hand was coated with some aphrodisiac, melting my inhibitions.

I squeezed his fingers as we walked. "This doesn't mean I agree to date you." I meant it. Sort of.

His eyes pierced me straight to my soul, and I feared he saw right through me.

"Right. Not a date, just a ride home from a friend. And a kiss. We can't forget the kiss."

I barely managed enough coherent thought to answer. "You know what I mean."

He smirked. "So, do you kiss every man you plan to not date?"

I hit him in the shoulder. "You're incorrigible."

"I'll take that as a no."

He has that part right.

We stopped in front of my house.

He brushed something off my shoulder. His touch once again sent a lightning bolt through me.

"Man glitter," he said.

"Huh?"

"Sawdust. Man glitter," he answered.

I smiled. "Thanks. We wouldn't want my sister getting the wrong idea."

"Yeah, you need a doctor. I get it."

He clearly didn't agree.

What will I do if he dumps the dog off with me?

He surprised me by offering to keep Tosca for now.

I let out an audible breath. *What a relief.*

I explained that we already had two dogs and two cats, and how hard it was to find a place to live with that many animals.

He mentioned that he had a big backyard for the dog.

I couldn't stay out here and talk with him forever. Amy had to get home. I told him I had to go in to relieve the babysitter.

He cocked his head. "You have kids?" he asked.

It was time to end this once and for all, before I got myself in too deep. I hesitated, then I pulled out my anti-boyfriend Kryptonite.

"A seven-year-old boy." That always sent them running for the hills.

Confusion crossed his face. "Married?"

I held up my left hand. No ring. "No."

He let out a breath, looking relieved. "It must be hard."

I backed up toward the house. "You have no idea." That was the truth. Juggling jobs, school, and Timmy had been hard for the two of us.

Why is he still here? He should be a mile away by now.

A smile grew from the corners of his mouth, and those eyes held me. "I'd love to come in and meet him."

Now what do I do?

"He's already in bed." I gave him a smile and and took a step toward the house. "Goodnight, Pat. Thanks for the ride."

"I'm great with kids," he called as he walked back to his pickup with Tosca.

My Kryptonite had failed. It never failed.

CHAPTER 7

*P*AT

Her house was a small, light-colored bungalow with a lawn in front and a driveway off to the right leading to a small garage in the back. The yard was sparse, just the lawn and a few shrubs——the kind of low-maintenance yard you put in for a rental house. The paint wasn't fresh, but it wasn't dilapidated either.

I bid her good night and walked back to Phil's truck as her little blue Toyota drove by and into her driveway——undoubtedly her sister arriving home.

I turned back, and the sister waved.

I returned the wave and climbed up into the truck with Tosca.

No wonder she needs financial security in a boyfriend. She has to worry about more than just herself.

She has a son.

She had meant the kiss to be fake, but that was a lie. Her response told me what I needed to know. Her passion wasn't faked. She just needed to give herself permission to let it loose.

She is going to be mine.

LIZ

I WAITED AT THE STEPS AS STACEY DROVE IN AND PARKED.

"Is that him?" she asked quietly as she closed the door to my trusty bucket of bolts.

I nodded.

She waved to him, and he waved back before getting into his truck.

"He's tall," she said as we walked into the house together.

The dogs were all over us the minute we entered.

Amy was already in the front room, ready to leave. "Timmy's asleep," she told us as she picked up her purse. "Tomorrow night?" she asked from the door.

"Same as always," Stacey replied with a wave.

"So he was your ride, huh?" Stacey asked as the door closed.

"Yeah, and he sort of offered to beat up my boss for me."

"No shit?"

"Well, not exactly. He said he could warn him, but the way he said it was...well, scary."

"So, you like him?"

"He's okay."

"Liar," she said. I'd never had much luck getting anything over on Stacey.

My Kryptonite failed.

I blurted it out. "He kissed me."

Stacey's jaw dropped halfway to the floor. "I knew it." She pointed her finger at me. "You little liar. I know you. You don't kiss guys that are just okay." She advanced toward me.

Stacey was still waving her finger at me. "You're into this guy.

Admit it."

I folded my arms in front of me for protection. "It wasn't like that. Ben, Mr. Perham, was trying to offer me a ride home, and I had to avoid that, so I told him…"

"Yeah?"

"I told him Pat was my boyfriend, and he was giving me a ride."

"And that's when Pat kissed you?"

"Well, I sort of started it by putting my arm around him… Yeah, that's how it started." I threw up my hands and walked toward the kitchen.

Stacey followed.

"It was just a fake kiss," I insisted.

"So… It was just a peck then?" she asked.

I couldn't lie to her. "Well…not really." I was busted.

"So?" she asked.

I had no way out of it at this point. "It was a real kiss, and it lasted a while."

"Tongue?" she asked.

"Yeah, but I'm not doing a play by play. He's a good kisser, I can say that. And I kept all my clothes on, so what's the big deal?"

She opened the fridge and pulled out a pitcher of decaf iced tea. "I don't have time for a boyfriend of my own, so I have to live vicariously."

I found the little paper umbrella in my purse and put it on the counter.

"What's that?" Stacey asked.

I grabbed two glasses from the cupboard. "He gave it to me."

She picked up the umbrella and opened it. "Moving right along, I see. A good kisser and already giving you little presents. Nice boyfriend."

I poured the iced tea. "He's not my boyfriend."

"Why fight it, Liz? You like the guy. You deserve to have a good time. Screw your rules for once."

CHAPTER 8

Liz

THE NEXT DAY STACEY HAD MY CAR AGAIN——SOMETHING ABOUT her brakes needing more work. It would work out because I was committed to dinner with Pat tonight anyway.

Tina found me shortly after she arrived at The Ironhorse. "You're such a liar, Liz. I saw you making out with that carpenter hunk of yours in the parking lot."

I tried to ignore her.

It didn't work.

"Is it true that carpenters have a tighter fit?" she asked.

"We kissed. He drove me home, and that's all that happened, Tina."

She walked off, letting it go for the moment.

A little before the end of my shift, my phone vibrated in my pocket.

PAT: I will be there at six to take you to dinner and then home - not a date

Louise walked by as I read the message. "Your prince charming coming to pick you up?" she asked.

I feigned ignorance. "What are you talking about?"

"That Pat guy you've been fawning over the past two nights. I just figured that might be him. You could use a night out, and Tina told me you two were hot and heavy in the parking lot last night."

"That little snitch. Does everybody here know?"

She shrugged and grabbed three plates to deliver to a table.

It was infuriating the way everybody else was trying to run my life and tell me what to do.

Tina passed me a little later. "I hear carpenters really know how to screw it in." She giggled and moved along.

Sooner or later she had to run out of those.

Pat arrived slightly before my shift's end, as he had promised.

I got the shivers as he parked, and not because I was afraid. I took off my apron and left to meet him.

Ben was entering the building as I reached the door. He blocked my way.

I got a chill as he leered at me.

He pointed toward the back. "Elizabeth, I need to talk to you in my office." His tone was slightly more menacing than usual.

Whenever he wanted to talk to one of us, it was never good news.

"Sorry, Mr. Perham, but I've already clocked out. How about tomorrow?" I said as cheerfully as I could.

I felt like a gazelle trying to be cheery answering a question from a lion.

"Ready, Liz?" Pat came up behind Ben.

His voice sent relief flooding through me.

Ben moved out of my way. "Tomorrow then."

Pat walked me to his truck and opened the door. "What did Mister Creepy want?"

"He needs to talk to me is all he said."

Anger flashed in Pat's eyes. "Perhaps I should have a talk with him first."

"Like I said, I fight my own battles, and that would probably make it worse. It might be nothing, anyway. I'm due for a raise. Maybe that's what it is."

That last part was not a lie, but Ben's tone had not indicated he wanted to share good news with me.

"So where are we off to?" I asked.

"Hawaii," Pat said with a grin as he started the truck.

"Isn't that a little far for dinner?"

"Ten minutes tops."

I asked about his day as we drove, and he answered without offering any particulars. I took out my phone to text Stacey.

ME: Going to dinner with Pat be home later

Hawaii turned out to be a place called Tropics Burgers. The walls were covered with pictures of beaches and surfing and Hawaiian Airlines posters. There were little thatched umbrellas over the tables inside and out. All the tables were covered with retro gingham tablecloths.

The menu was Hawaiian themed, with pineapple, mango, and papaya on the burgers, and tropical drinks as well.

Pat tapped me on the shoulder. "I forgot to ask. You aren't vegetarian, are you?"

Just a simple touch on the shoulder ignited warmth in my chest. I assured him I ate normal food, and we ordered two Surf Burgers with fries and a couple's Mai Tai. The drink was a monster, with two straws and two little paper umbrellas in it.

He pulled out a ratty old brown wallet that was falling apart.

I noticed FCF stamped on it. "What's FCF?"

"My family's rule number one: Family Comes First. My dad gave me this as a birthday present," he said with obvious fondness.

My phone dinged.

STACEY: Have fun don't do anything I wouldn't do

Not very limiting.

"Just my sister, Stacey, checking on me," I told him.

We took a table near the back.

"This is a cute place," I said.

His amber eyes probed mine as his smile grew and the dimples appeared.

"It's as close as I can get to Hawaii tonight, but I plan to take you there someday, or maybe Bora Bora."

It sounded romantic, but I couldn't do romantic with him.

"You're obviously a dreamer if you think two working stiffs like us can get the time and the money to go on a vacation like that."

"What kind of attitude is that? Of course we can. I know I can do anything I set my mind to. You should have faith."

His sentiment was nice, but not very practical. After Trent, I didn't need another trip down that road.

Pat fetched our tray when our number was called. When he returned, he hoisted the big drink.

"To Hawaii," he said as he leaned forward.

We both sipped from the straws on opposite sides. The drink was cold and soothing.

He asked about my day, and I filled him in as we munched on the burgers.

He grinned as I took another bite.

I wiped my lips with my napkin. "What?" I must have gotten something on my face.

"I just enjoy a girl that can eat without being self conscious about it."

Heat rose in my cheeks as I smiled. He obviously meant it as a compliment rather than a joke. He was always complimenting me, and I was really beginning to like it.

"So many girls in this town think they can't eat anything but rabbit food."

"Those are just the girls that aren't as fat as me." I had real curves, and I was not going to be mistaken for a Victoria Secret model by anybody.

He threw a fry at me, which hit me in the forehead. I squealed.

He grabbed his straw out of the drink and pointed it at me. "You are the most gorgeous girl in the valley. Don't you ever put yourself down like that again." His tone was commanding, almost scary.

His words were a complete surprise. I wasn't homely, but nobody had ever called me gorgeous before, and certainly not a hunk like Pat. Pretty, when they were being nice, but not gorgeous. The compliment warmed me all over.

He put the straw back in the drink and offered it to me. "We need to drink this together for good luck," he said. "We both get to make a wish."

I leaned forward, and we sipped on the drink.

He reached out and placed his hand on mine, sending sparks up my arm. "What did you wish for?" he asked.

His touch, his smile, and his dimples were inhibiting my brain function.

"That you were a doctor or a lawyer instead of a carpenter." The words escaped my mouth before I had a chance to consider them. I'd admitted I was falling for him.

"I turn wood into things. So what's your super power?" he shot back.

I felt terrible; I had insulted him. "I'm sorry…"

"No worries, Buttercup." A wicked smile lifted the corners of his mouth. "So you're wishing you could date me, then?"

His words sent liquid heat to melt my panties. He had seen through me.

This is getting far too intense.

I looked down and took another bite of my burger. "This is delicious."

"They taste even better by the beach."

"Pat, that's not happening. I can't take the time off, and even if I could, I can't afford it. No way."

Dreams like that can only disappoint me.

"What was your wish?" I asked as I sipped more of the Mai Tai.

He smirked. "Seeing you in a bikini on Waikiki."

I coughed and almost spit my drink all over my plate. "In your dreams, cowboy."

He licked his lips and slowly inserted a French fry. His grin grew as he chewed. He chuckled. "You know me so well; you know exactly what I dream about."

It was my turn to throw a fry at him. I got him in the chest.

He threw one back.

It hit me in the neck and dropped down my shirt. I fished it out of my cleavage. I held it in front of my mouth, teasing him as I licked my lips. I licked the fry and sucked on it as seductively as I could manage.

The fire in his eyes was unmistakable. "I'll settle for dinner Saturday."

I popped the fry in my mouth and started to chew. "Pat." I pointed to my mouth. "Watch my lips: WE ARE NOT DATING."

He laughed. "I got it. This is not a date. Just two friends sharing a burger and talking about the future." Playfulness came to his eyes. "We really have to talk about this hang-up of yours."

He was right. Just saying no was not working with him.

"I told you, I have a rule that I only date professional men."

My statement didn't faze him one bit.

"And why is that?" he asked.

My rules weren't up for debate. "Just because." I picked up the pineapple slice my little umbrella had impaled and took a bite.

His eyes conveyed his feelings. He wasn't about to give up

on this. "Just between friends talking over a burger…" He
paused to eat another fry. "You could explain it to me." He took
another fry. "Just between friends." His eyes were as kind as his
tone.

"As a friend, I would ask you to understand that I have had bad
experiences with men…" I searched for the right way to put it.
"That didn't have stable jobs."

He reached over the table and took my hand. His touch was
warm and soothing.

"I'm sorry you were treated poorly. So now you need to find
yourself a proper professional man, is that it?" His smile grew,
those dimples returned, and his thumb traced a circle on my hand,
breaking my concentration.

"Something like that."

His thumb continued to trace tiny circles. "And how many of
these professional types have you dated since then?"

I changed the subject. "Have you been to Hawaii before?"

His hand tightened on mine. "I'll take that as a solid zero. You
have no idea what these professional types are like, do you?"

I pulled my hand back.

"I can see that you haven't met enough of these guys to know
that they're no better than you or me."

They have to be. I looked up. "And I suppose you know a lot of
them?"

He took off his hat and laid it on the table. "Sure. I grew up
with a gazillion of them. And not one of them is good enough to
deserve you."

I took a sip of the drink to cool myself down. "You can flatter
me all you want, but we're still not dating."

He smirked. "And when you do go on a date with me, you're
going to have the best time ever." He took a sip from the monster
drink. "What do you have planned this weekend?"

I finished chewing the bite of Surf Burger I had started,
ignoring his date comment. "I pick up some work with a catering

company on the weekends, so that shoots Saturday, and I have the dinner shift at The Ironhorse Sunday."

He finished the fry he was chewing. "Which catering company?"

"Lusso's Catering."

He dipped a fry in ketchup and offered it to me.

I took it.

"Lusso's is a good company," he said.

How could he know a high-end catering company like Lusso's? It had taken a recommendation from The Ironhorse's owners to get me on their crew.

"You know them?"

"Buttercup, like I told you, I know lots of people." He winked.

A dollop of mustard fell from the burger he was waving around and landed on the bill of his cap on the table. He wiped it off, but it was going to be another stain on his well-worn hat. As we continued the meal, he told me about Hawaii and how much I was going to enjoy it there.

I quit arguing the subject with him.

His dimples danced as he talked and laughed. He was such a pleasure to share a meal with. It had been a long time since I'd felt so at ease across the table from a man, and he was all man. His shoulders were broader than Trent's by a mile.

I caught myself making more comparisons, and he came out ahead of Trent in every way except his hair. Pat's hair was too short.

In no time at all, we'd reached the bottom of the giant Mai Tai glass.

He pulled a coin out of his pocket. He flipped it in the air, caught it, and placed it on the back of his hand, covered. "Heads says we both get our wish.

I peered over as he uncovered it. Heads it was. That couldn't be right. We couldn't afford Hawaii.

"No way," I said. "We're not on a date, and we're not *going* to date, remember?"

"I have faith."

Those eyes froze me for a second. He was serious, and seriously hot with that look in his eye.

He turned in our tray. "Ready to go? I'm sure I need to get you home to your son."

I started to correct him, but I couldn't. I followed him out to his truck, caught in my own deception.

My own tangled lie.

PAT

I DROVE HER HOME, CONTEMPLATING HOW TO MEET UP WITH HER this weekend. I needed to figure out where her catering job was on Saturday.

We parked in front of her house, and I walked her toward the door.

She turned before we reached the house, seeming reticent.

Before she could say anything, the door opened and a woman emerged.

"You must be Pat," the woman said, waving us in. "Come on in."

Concern flashed in Liz's eyes. She wasn't sold on inviting me into her home, but she didn't fight it.

Inside, a furry black, brown, and white dog with no tail and one blue eye and one brown eye pounced on me immediately. I took a knee to nuzzle and pet the dog, whose name I learned was Missy.

"She's just a little over-friendly is all," Liz said.

"No problem. I love dogs. She's an Aussie, right?" I asked.

Liz confirmed that Missy was an Australian Shepherd, and she introduced me to her sister, Stacey, and her boy, Timmy. The other dog, a King Charles, watched from the dog bed. A fluffy gray and white cat sprawled out on the back of the sofa, and another perched on the windowsill, watching birds in the trees outside.

Timmy had brown hair, more like Liz's sister's than Liz, but the same kind eyes that seemed to run in the family.

The house was homey and inviting, with comfortable, clean overstuffed furniture and a shelf of kids' board games. Prints of outdoor scenes adorned the walls.

"Where'd you go to dinner?" Stacey asked.

Liz glanced to me furtively.

"Hawaii," I answered. I pulled another paper drink umbrella out of my pocket. "Even brought back souvenirs."

Liz laughed. "Taste of Hawaii was more like it."

I offered Timmy the paper umbrella.

He took it and began opening and closing it. "Did you swim in the ocean? I want to swim in the ocean."

Liz quickly explained. "No, we didn't go to the ocean. It was just a restaurant that was like Hawaii."

"If you want to go swimming, you can come over to my place. I've got a pool," I offered.

Timmy turned to Stacey. "Can we, Mommy? I want to go swimming."

The blood drained from Liz's face, and understanding dawned on mine.

I'm calling bullshit. Timmy isn't her son.

CHAPTER 9

LIZ

I WAS BUSTED. THE GLINT IN PAT'S EYE AND HIS BROAD SMILE told me he hadn't missed Timmy calling Stacey *Mommy*.

"How about Sunday, Stacey? Would that be good for you guys?" Pat asked.

Not only had my Kryptonite failed, it had pulled me in deeper.

Stacey grinned and answered before I had a chance to object. "Sure, I have a shift at Memorial, but you two can take Timmy. Just make sure he wears his life jacket." She patted her son on the head.

Timmy jumped up and down for joy.

"I have a shift too. I'm afraid we can't on Sunday," I said, trying to get out of this date Stacey was setting up for me.

"But that's not till late in the afternoon. You'll have lots of time," she said with a wicked smile. "You can take Timmy, right?"

The trap had been sprung, and I was caught. I couldn't disappoint Timmy now.

"I guess that would work," I said weakly.

Timmy's smile was all the reward I needed.

So my weekend was totally booked now: catering on Saturday and swimming at Pat's with Timmy on Sunday, all on top of evening work at the restaurant both days.

And another not-date with Pat.

~

PAT

THURSDAY MORNING I VISITED UNCLE GARTH. I KNEW HE USED Lusso's Catering regularly. It only took him two calls to find out for me that Liz was scheduled to be part of the catering crew for the Children's Hospital fundraiser on Saturday. My brother Bill and his wife headed the organizing committee, and all of us locals except Katie, who was out of town, were planning to attend.

Bill had greased the skids for me with Bob Hanson, whose company was providing security for the grounds. Bill had used them extensively in the past. I now had a cover to be there as Pat Patterson, security guy.

That evening I joined Bill, his wife, Lauren, and my sister-in-law Emma for dinner at Bill's restaurant, Cardinelli's. Emma was in town for a few days from San Francisco to help Lauren with the fundraiser this weekend. Then she needed to get back to her *tripod* husband. Steven had broken his leg on a skateboard trying to keep up with his younger employees. Only an idiot with a death wish skateboarded down a San Francisco hill.

I'd just looped them in on my plan to be at the fundraiser as Pat Patterson instead of Patrick Covington.

"You come up with the craziest ideas," Bill said, leaning back in his chair and sipping the last of his cabernet.

I put my fork down. "It's just for a while. I'm sick of being paranoid every time I meet a girl that she's more interested in my name and my money than me."

Bill nodded. He knew as well as any of us the power of the family name to distort our personal relationships. Lucky for him, he and Lauren had been forced together by fate when our father died. He'd told me once about how Lauren couldn't stand him at first, and he had given up everything to chase her. It had all happened while I was in London.

Bill put his glass down. "Just be careful about the lies. I've always found honesty to be the best policy, as the saying goes."

Lauren gave him an evil grin. "And the omissions," she added.

Bill smiled back at his beautiful wife. They obviously shared a secret I wasn't privy to.

Emma's face revealed her concern. "Are we supposed to ignore you, then?"

"Not quite," I answered. "You just know me as Pat Patterson, the security guy."

Emma nodded. "I want to hear about the woman that brought this about."

Lauren's eyes lit up. "I'd like that too."

I put my fork down. "Her name is Elizabeth Turner, and she'll be on the catering crew Saturday."

"And?" Lauren asked.

"She's extremely compassionate. And she has the most captivating smile." I stopped myself from going any further.

The women gave up after a few more questions that I avoided answering in any detail. All they learned was that I'd met her on the road after last Sunday's Habitat project, I'd helped her catch a stray yellow lab that had been hit by a car, and I had the dog for now.

"So how long do you plan to keep up this charade?" Emma asked.

"As long as it takes."

"Just be careful that you don't get caught in your own web of lies," Lauren said.

I nodded. That was the plan.

CHAPTER 10

Liz

"You'll have a great time, Liz. Rich guys, sunshine, free food, and horses," my sister assured me.

"I'll be back this afternoon." I grabbed my purse and left to cater this stupid polo match. I'd sought out the job with Lusso's Catering precisely because they routinely handled events like this one, occasions that should be teeming with rich, professional types. So far I had come up empty at four of these weekend shindigs, but this could be the one.

"If the guys are donkeys, just go hang out with the horses." Stacey laughed at her own joke.

The lady in my phone led me to the address I had been given, which was located in a not-very-nice part of town. This probably had been an area full of large ranches before all the people arrived. I could tell right away that the event was high class compared to the neighborhood. Four sheriff's cars were parked out front, probably to protect the rich folk from the riffraff inhabiting the surrounding territory. I was in the valet line behind a Porsche, a

BMW, and a Bentley. No shortage of automotive bling at this event.

Driving my little shitmobile Toyota, I hoped they wouldn't send me away. Tony Lusso, our boss, had told us to arrive at the front entrance, as the back gate was chained off for some reason. At the valet stand, I grabbed my duffel with my change of clothes and resisted the urge to make sure the guy who gave me my ticket stub had an up-to-date tetanus vaccination before he got into my car.

The banner over the gate was quite a mouthful: *Covington Annual Children's Hospital Charity Polo Match.*

I felt like an interloper among all these rich people. I'd noticed the price on the tickets at the gate: five hundred dollars a head, a thousand for a couple. Anyone who could blow that much money in an afternoon, didn't live in my neighborhood.

Tony had me assigned to hors d'oeuvres service, and I would be off the clock after the meal had been served. That would give me time to wander a bit and mingle. For now, the guests were gobbling up the appetizers. I was on my ninth tray.

"Hey there, gorgeous. I was hoping I'd see you here."

I turned.

The sight of him took my breath away. There was Pat in a security uniform. My heart started to pound. The shirt was a little tight on him and showed off his broad shoulders and that muscular chest that tapered down to a slim waist. The aviator sunglasses and too-short hair gave him a military look. I braced myself as he approached, as the reaction he caused in me was worrisome. I was here to meet professional men, not swoon over him all over again.

"What are you doing here?" I asked.

"Working, can't you tell? When you told me you worked for Lusso's, I hoped we'd run into each other today." Pat waved over Jimmy, one of my coworkers. "Jimmy, could you get me a Diet Coke, please?"

"Sure thing, Mr…"

"Pat," he corrected.

Jimmy nodded as he walked away.

"He knows you?"

Pat smiled back at me, his dimples making another appearance. "Yeah, I've been at a lot of these things. I guess I make an impression."

Odd. Perhaps I'd never paid proper attention, but I had never remembered the names of any of the security guys.

"I have work to do," I told him, getting a grin in return. "And I want you to leave me alone."

This flustered him, but only for a moment. He followed me.

"Don't you have to be somewhere guarding jewelry, or the liquor or something?"

He took one of the pastries off my tray. "No. Privileges of rank. I'm the floater, so I just take care of any special problems that come up." His radio crackled to life. "I'll find you again when you're in a better mood," he said as he wandered off.

I assessed the crowd: ladies with gobs of jewelry and men exuding the confidence that came with wealth and power. The place reeked of upper-class money. I smiled as I served the little delights. Stacey had been right. This crowd must contain the kind of man I needed to find. He was here somewhere.

I continued to make circles through the crowd, offering my tasty morsels. Over time, I gave out another eight trays' worth, but the guests became less interested in the tiny pastries I had to offer and more interested in the roast beef, pork chops, and barbecued chicken at the lunch buffet.

Pat had fetched a plate full of lunch and sat at one of the tables with some of the guests.

Floater, my ass. More like freeloader.

Tony called me over and told me to stop the hors d'oeuvres service, wrap the remaining pieces in individual napkins, and place them in some paper shopping bags he had brought. He said the

Covingtons would take the excess food from the meal down to the local soup kitchen when the party was over.

That was the nicest thing I'd heard in a long time. At every other party we catered, the excess food was thrown away, and it had been the same at my previous catering company. When I finished a half hour later, I closed myself in the back of the catering truck with my duffel and changed into the sundress and sandals I had brought. Climbing out of the truck, I felt the weight of a stare on me, and I turned to find those wonderful dimples on Pat's face as his gaze met mine.

"You have the most beautiful smile," he said. "You should wear it more often."

Heat immediately rose in my cheeks. "I thought you'd agreed to stop doing that."

"Doing what?"

"Complimenting me, like we're on a date or something."

The twinkle in his eyes told me to expect a wiseass answer. "This is not a date, yet. But I would never agree to stop complimenting such a gorgeous woman, and I like the dress, by the way."

"Stop that. You're doing it again." I punched his shoulder, which was rock hard under the shirt. I needed to get away from his distraction. "Are we done here?"

He brought a plate of potato salad out from behind his back. "I noticed you didn't get a chance to eat, so I brought you this."

How thoughtful of him. "Occupational hazard, I guess. We serve, they eat."

We took seats at an empty table.

"Diet Coke or high test?" he asked me.

"Diet works for me."

He hustled off and returned with two sodas.

"You never told me you worked as a security guard."

"There's a lot you don't know about me yet." He winked. "I have my fingers in a lot of pies. Dig in, this isn't as good as my sister Katie's potato salad, but it's still good."

I took a bite as Jimmy brought us our drinks.

Pat thanked him and shoveled some salad onto his fork. "So, you see any targets yet?"

"What?"

"I saw you checking out the guys. You think this is a target-rich environment for finding one of those stupid rich, professional types you've been talking about, right?"

The heat of a three-alarm blush instantly hit my chest and rose to my cheeks. "Can't blame a girl for looking."

"I can save you some time. I know most of these guys, and I can tell you that not one of them is as right for you as I am."

"I'll be the judge of that." I had located a nice-looking candidate and pointed to him. "How about that guy in the blue polo over there?"

Pat rolled his eyes and laughed. "You set your sights high, I can see. That's William Covington. He and his family are putting on this shindig. He's a very nice guy, and rich as sin, but he's married."

The words sent a chill straight through me. "I don't do married." I scanned a little farther. "What about the guy just to his left?" I asked.

"That's Gordie Mossbacker, a nice enough guy, but he's in insurance and boring as hell. I think he's been on fifty SuperSingles dates in the last year and not had a second date yet. On top of that, he'll be drunk before the afternoon is out."

I asked Pat about another two men nearby, and he recognized each of them.

I narrowed my eyes. "How do you know all these people?"

Pat the security guy didn't seem like the kind of man who would have all these corporate types on his speed dial.

"Because I grew up with some of them and went to school with the rest. We lived in a rich part of town when I was little."

I checked farther down the field, contemplating his answer. "And where do you live now?"

"A tiny little house on Myrtle Street. You'll see it tomorrow when you and Timmy come over to swim."

That reminded me that this weekend was now wall-to-wall Pat.

"Phil, the guy with the beard you met at The Ironhorse, owns it," he added. "I just stay in them while he's fixing them up so nobody messes with them, sort of on-site security."

The polo players had mounted their horses, and the crowd gathered around the edge of the field to watch. We did the same.

I stood next to Pat near the midpoint of the field and watched the game with no idea what was going on. The good part was the horses were beautiful——shorter than race horses and a lot more muscled. The ease with which they galloped and turned was a sight to behold.

The players were something else, riding at full speed, swinging long mallets, and hitting the ball most of the time at a gallop, while half hanging off the horse. This was real teamwork between man and animal, but definitely not a sport I wanted to participate in. I considered skateboarding dangerous.

Pat brought me champagne during the break.

We moved down toward the far-end goal where most of the action had been happening.

Near the end of the match, his radio crackled to life as someone called him to a disturbance at the back gate.

I hustled after him, curious to see what he did as a security guy. I rounded the corner, and there they were.

Three biker dudes were climbing down from the fence on the inside of the back gate, and there were a few more outside the chain link, straddling their Harleys and having a good ol' time. The security guy at the gate, a skinny young kid, was backing away from the three *hombres*.

"You guys can stop right there," Pat yelled as he came to a stop.

"Fuck off, pretty boy," the closest one yelled back.

He had long hair and was almost as wide as he was tall. All

three of them looked like they probably downed beer by the twelve pack every afternoon.

"He called me fat, and I'm gonna get an apology," the one with a scar on his face yelled, pointing at the young security guard.

I stopped.

Pat put his hand behind him and grabbed his belt. "If you guys make me draw my gun, I'm gonna use it, and then I'm gonna cut off your pathetic little dicks and feed them to you," he yelled.

He didn't have a gun behind his back, but they couldn't see that.

Pat pointed to the turnstile with his other hand. "Out."

They looked at each other for a moment and decided to leave.

Two had gone out when Long Hair changed his mind. "Mall cops don't carry guns," he yelled, running toward Pat.

My heart crawled to my throat and puffed up like a blowfish. I backed away and cringed. He had called Pat's bluff.

Pat braced himself, and the biker swung but missed as Pat jerked to the side. In a blur, Pat took hold of Long Hair's arm, shifted his stance, heaved him over his shoulder, and threw the monster to the ground so hard it probably registered on the seismograph at Cal Tech.

Long Hair scrambled back to his feet. He hiked his pants up. "You're going to pay for that," he snarled as he lunged at Pat.

I gasped.

Pat sidestepped the huge biker, grabbed his arm and his leather vest, and hurled him like a sack of potatoes. He landed with another loud grunt.

The biker wasn't giving up, though. He got up, a lot more slowly this time, hiked his pants up again, brushed the hair out of his eyes, and danced around Pat. His look was pure rage. He moved forward and kicked at Pat.

Bad move.

Pat grabbed the leg, twisted, and raised it up. Long Hair ended up face first in the dirt, with Pat on top of him, bending his leg in a leg lock.

The biker screamed so loud it hurt my ears.

Pat released a little pressure. "Are we done yet?" he asked the guy.

The gorilla on the ground nodded vigorously and mumbled something I didn't hear.

Pat released him and jumped away.

Long Hair's butt crack was showing as he stumbled out. When he reached his buddies, they quickly mounted their motorcycles and roared off, just before two sheriff's cars pulled up. The deputies talked to the other guard for a minute before getting back in their cars. One drove away, but the second car stayed by the gate.

I felt myself shaking. I couldn't believe what I'd seen. Pat had thrown that monster to the ground like it was nothing. He hadn't hit him; he'd just leveraged him and thrown him down so hard that it must have hurt like hell. There wasn't any grass here to cushion the fall.

I was trying to start breathing again when Pat took my hand, and we walked back toward the people watching the polo match. The crowd was completely unaware of what had just happened at the back gate.

If they were anything like my friends, they would've rather seen Pat lay some whoop-ass on that biker than watch a bunch of wussies hit a little ball around on horseback.

Pat put his arm around me. "You're shaking." He pulled me tightly into him.

"They were scary." I didn't want to admit how worried I'd been for him. "What was that all about?" I asked.

"The last two years in a row, those A-holes have tried to crash the party. They just seem to think it's a fun thing to do on a Saturday afternoon."

"Is that why the sheriffs are out front?"

Pat looked straight ahead. "Yup, that's where they came in before."

"That guy was huge. How'd you do that?"

"I know a little judo is all."

A little was a clear understatement. He'd flattened that monster without throwing a punch. I had seen plenty of guys fight before, but this was my first fight where no one had landed a punch. My carpenter was some kind of black belt or something.

The horn blew to announce the end of the polo match just before we reached the sideline.

"Time to get back to people watching, so you can figure it out," Pat said.

"Figure what out?"

"That I'm the one for you, Buttercup."

I didn't respond.

The crowd dispersed from the sidelines of the field and moved toward the food tables for dessert.

We left the food line with apple pie and cheesecake and found a table along the edge of the seating area. Pat sat next to me, facing the crowd.

I surveyed the scene again. That was supposed to be why I was here, after all.

"The guy in the blue shirt over there, he's a doctor." Pat pointed two tables over.

I checked him out for a few seconds. The guy was not as fat as the bikers, but he looked like a few flights of stairs would turn him into a heart attack victim.

"A little on the heavy side, don't you think?"

"He's a gynecologist, if that helps."

I elbowed him in the ribs. An overweight slob who spent all day looking at other women's vaginas? Not what I needed.

"Got it; no fat guys." He grinned at me. "I'm not fat, or a gynecologist."

I rolled my eyes. He just wouldn't give up.

Pat scanned the crowd. "Wilbert over there." He pointed farther left. "In the button-down shirt with the tie? He's an asshole doctor. You said you liked doctors, right?"

I huffed. "Professional is what I said, and you don't need to be nasty just because you don't like doctors."

"I wasn't being nasty. He's a real asshole doctor, a proctologist."

Pat was funny in a high school kind of way. I tried to stifle the laugh, but failed.

"We call him Doctor Fish," Pat continued. "He thinks the solution to what ails is you always a nice, warm fish oil enema. After two days of the runs and the awful smell, you're cured of whatever you started with."

I couldn't control my laughter. "You really don't like doctors, do you?"

The man he'd pointed out was wearing a bow tie, of all things ——the first tie I'd seen this afternoon. He was on the far side of fifty or sixty and completely bald on top.

"Anyway, he's a little old. No thanks."

"Picky, aren't we? So no May-December match for Elizabeth. Got it. I'm not old, so that's three points for me, right? Not fat, not old, and not a gynecologist."

I chuckled and located another prospect. "What about the guy on the far side over there? Brown hair with the yellow shirt? He doesn't look too old."

Pat followed my gaze to locate the man. "Yeah, Ross. He's perfect for you. Owns a couple of car dealerships. A lot of money in cars. Want me to introduce you?"

I considered for a second. He didn't look too old, he was fit enough, and he wasn't a gynecologist, thank God.

Before I had a chance to say anything Pat got up. "He's always looking for the next ex-Mrs. Rohrbacher. He just divorced number five, so I think he's available now."

I cringed and grabbed Pat's arm.

He sat back down. "I thought not."

Behind the serial divorcer, I spotted another one. "What's the story with blondie in the green?"

Pat chuckled. "Well, he might be okay. A dentist, I think. But you'd have to convince him to stop batting for the other team."

I shook my head. "No thanks. I tried that once. It didn't work." *Why are the good-looking ones always gay?*

When I glanced back at Pat, I realized that wasn't *always* true.

The man in the blue polo who Pat had called Mr. Covington wandered in our direction with two women. They were laughing up a storm about something.

"Pat, they seem to be having a bit of a problem with Gordon Mossbacker at the front gate," Mr. Covington said. "He's been drinking a bit and doesn't want to take a taxi. Since he's your friend, I thought you could get him to see the light."

The women smiled at Pat as he stood.

Pat placed a hand on my shoulder. "Sure thing, Mr. Covington. Just don't go telling Liz here any nasty stories about me while I'm gone. Liz, this old man is William Covington. This is his lovely wife, Lauren. She's the brains in the family, and the pretty redhead is his sister-in-law Emma."

Lauren and Emma smiled politely while William scowled and rolled his eyes.

Pat walked off as the trio sat down with me.

CHAPTER 11

PAT

I glanced back at the table where I'd left Liz after Bill sent me to the front gate to deal with Gordie. It wasn't so bad, except Lauren and Emma had come over with him, and I had to leave Liz alone with all three. They'd better not blow my cover.

Gordie was sauced as usual when I arrived. "Patrick, maybees you can help. Theeese guys won't gives me my keys."

I took him aside, like I was going to tell him a secret. "Hey, Gordie, the problem is the foundation isn't insured for this. You understand?"

The frustration on his face turned to bewilderment.

"Let us call you a cab, and I'll personally see that your car gets home safe and sound. If you were to have an accident, the foundation would be liable, and the children would suffer. You don't want that, do you?"

Gordie shook his head. "Okay, I guess you're right. But next year, I... I's could writes yuz a policy to covers it."

I patted him on the back. "Sure, Gordie, next year."

I waved the two valets over. "Guys, give me his keys, and

please call Mr. Mossbacker a cab." I handed them a hundred-dollar bill. "This should cover it."

All three of them thanked me, and I set out to get back to my date before my family blew it for me.

The table we'd been sitting at was empty when I returned, and I finally located Bill talking to one of the guests.

I waited until he was done. "Where's Liz?"

He smiled. "They went over to see the horses." He pointed to the far end of the field where the barns were located.

I didn't like the sound of that. "Why did you let them do that?" *The three women together was not a good idea.*

Bill chuckled as he placed an arm around my shoulder, like the older brother he was. "Someday, Patrick, you will learn that the words *boss* and *husband* are not synonymous."

He was right, of course. Lauren was a strong-willed woman. She probably had to be to put up with Bill. And I hadn't known Emma long, but she had to be a tough cookie as well to put up with my brother Steven.

"Thanks for nothing," I told him as I started jogging toward the barns.

The girls were all clustered around the door to one of the stalls and giggling when I found them. They quickly retreated a few stalls farther down as I approached.

When I got to the stall they'd been gathered outside, I found a big black horse taking a piss, with his huge dick hanging down. No wonder they'd been giggling.

It was easy to see why girls liked to hang around horses. I'd have to give Liz a hard time about this later, when the others weren't around.

My radio came to life, calling me to the front gate again. I waved to the three of them as I left.

Bill intercepted me with a frown as he put away his phone. "Patrick." He put his arm round my shoulder and spoke softly as we walked. "I just got a call. Monica Paisley is at the front gate, trying to get in to talk to Emma."

I stopped mid-stride. The name caught me completely off-guard.

Bills eyes were cold and his voice firm. "Would you make it clear to the fellows at the gate how unwelcome she is?"

"Got it." I trotted off.

Monica Paisley blamed my brother Steven and his wife, Emma, for her troubles. It was clear to everyone except her that she was the architect of her own demise, but some people just couldn't accept personal responsibility.

When I got to the front gate, Monica had already given up and left. But I gave the guards and valets Bill's message: she was the ultimate persona non grata.

∾

LIZ

THE COVINGTON WOMEN WORE POLO SHIRTS WITH THE CHILDREN'S Hospital Logo on them and jeans with tennis shoes. They were a lot of fun to be around, and not at all what I'd imagined for ladies with the Covington name. They had it all——money, prestige, good looks——and yet they were so normal. Somehow I'd pictured snobby women who took afternoon tea or spent the day shopping for dresses or diamonds or something——not girls in jeans who hung out, drank beer, and made jokes about the size of a horse's penis.

After Pat's brief appearance, we'd stayed in the barn and continued petting the beautiful horses.

"You seem to like Pat," Lauren said, more as a question than a statement.

I couldn't prevent the blush rising in my cheeks. "Yeah, he's okay."

Lucky for me, they dropped it at that.

Lauren knew one of the grooms, Rodrigo, and he got us a bag of Mrs. Pasture's brand cookies to give to the horses.

Who knew they made cookies for horses?

The cookies were hard as rocks, but the horses loved them. They were magnificent animals, athletic and muscular, yet gentle. They craved the attention we gave them, nuzzling us and checking our hands for more cookies before returning to munching on the hay in their stalls.

Lauren's cell rang. It was her husband, and she and Emma left to join him while I stayed in the barn.

I told them I would be along in a bit, after I fed cookies to the rest of the horses. I was down to the last three when a slender, dark-haired man wandered in. I'd noticed him hanging around us earlier when I'd been sitting at the table with Pat and the Covingtons.

"Hi, I see I'm not the only horse lover around here," he said as he approached.

I shot him a smile. "Hi."

"I hope I'm not disturbing you."

I gave a cookie to the horse named Shorty. "No, just passing out a few treats."

He looked in the stall at Shorty. "What kind of treats?"

I held one out for him. "Rodrigo told us they're Mrs. Pasture's cookies. Whoever she is, the horses love her recipe."

He took the cookie from me and offered it to Shorty, who snatched it with his lips and began chewing noisily.

"Oh, these are the best," he said. "I think it's the molasses they bake into them."

"You have horses?" I asked.

He smiled. No dimples, but pleasant enough.

"Not anymore. I had one when I was young, though." He offered his hand. "I'm Blaine, by the way. Blaine Willey."

I shook his hand briefly. "Liz, Liz Turner."

"Who's next?" he asked.

I pointed to the last remaining stalls on this end. "I've gotten to all of them but these two here."

We moved down the aisle. He gave cookies to one, and I did the same with the other.

I glanced at him while his back was turned. He seemed nice enough.

"I have to get going," I told him. "It's been nice meeting you, Blaine."

He smiled and followed me. "I'll walk you back."

I thanked Rodrigo and returned the leftover cookies. He was a working type like me, and he clearly cared about the horses. I liked that.

Blaine ignored him.

We walked back in the direction of the tables.

"Would you like to get some coffee after this?" he asked.

"No thanks, I have to get home," I answered before I thought about it. I should have accepted.

"So, you know Emma Covington well?" he asked.

I didn't care to admit that I didn't know anybody here except people in catering and security. "Not really."

"Oh, I just thought because you were with her earlier..."

"Just an acquaintance," I replied.

We continued toward the remaining crowd hanging out by the tables.

I gathered up my courage. "What do you do for a living, Blaine?"

"I'm a lawyer with Dershowitz and Pine downtown."

We walked in silence a few steps.

"That sounds interesting," I said.

"Not really, but I do get to meet all kinds of people, I guess."

He stopped and placed his hand on my arm. "The invitation to coffee still stands, for another time, if you want to give me your number, Liz," he said.

I told him my number. I was here to meet professional types, after all, and lawyers met the criteria.

"I'll call you later," he said as he sauntered off toward the front gate.

I continued back to the tables with a grin. *My first professional type.*

"Who's your scrawny-ass friend?" Pat asked, walking up behind me a few moments later.

I was surprised, and embarrassed. "Just a guy I met in the barn. He said his name is Blaine. Do you know him?"

Pat thought for a moment. "Blaine, huh? Stupid name. Did he give a last name?"

"Willey, I think."

"Willey... Doesn't ring a bell." He chuckled.

"He's a lawyer. And what's so bad about a skinny ass, anyway?" I asked with a giggle.

Pat puffed up his chest. "Nothing, if what's above it is like this." He pointed to himself. "But with a little jerk like him, it's not skinny. It's scrawny. And he's a lawyer. So which kind is he?"

"You mean scrawny or skinny?"

"No, which kind of lawyer?"

"I don't know," I said. "He seemed nice."

He took my arm and guided me toward the refreshments. "He looks shifty to me, and I can see you haven't met many lawyers. There are only two kinds: the boring ones and the shifty ones. The boring ones go into corporate law and write contracts nobody can understand, and the shifty ones, they don't have any morals, so they go into the courtroom and try to keep criminals out of jail."

It was cute that Pat was jealous.

"I think a lawyer sounds pretty good," I told him. "A nice, professional man."

Pat's nostrils flared. I was getting to him. Jealous for sure.

"Why don't we look around some more? Maybe we can find me another prospect even better than him."

Disappointment clouded Pat's face momentarily. "Sure," he said. "Let's see… Can't be dumpy, can't be old." He scanned the group that remained. "Can't be boring, can't be bald, can't be short, can't be poor. What am I missing?"

"Professional, remember? And not gay."

"Yeah, that too." He studied the crowd. "You sure are limiting the field by being that picky."

I didn't think it was too picky to want a nice man, near my age, who took care of himself and wasn't mean or a bore.

"What about the tall guy over there in the brown?" I asked.

The guy was as tall as Pat, which was saying something. He appeared nice-looking from this angle.

Pat scrutinized him for a moment. "Just a sec… What's his name? Oh yeah, that's Justin. He's a nice-enough guy, but he gets around a lot. A real math genius." He laughed.

"What does that mean?" I asked.

"Give it a minute, and I think you'll understand."

A pair of tall, skinny, size-two model types with big boobs walked up to Justin. One of them handed him a glass of champagne, and the three of them broke out laughing. One of the skinny girls draped her arm on him, and the other kissed him and whispered into his ear.

"He prefers the math of two plus one," Pat whispered.

Yuck.

"I think I've had enough for today," I said. This was a good start. Blaine seemed like a nice-enough guy.

My phone dinged, and I read the text. It was bad news.

"Shit."

"What's the problem?" Pat asked.

I kicked the dirt. "My boss just canceled my shift tonight. He knows I need the hours. This is probably because I wouldn't go out with him, the weasel."

"Let's look on the bright side, Buttercup. Now you have time to go to dinner with me."

I couldn't help but smile. "Remember?" I tapped my forehead. "We are not dating."

Pat took my hand. "I'll walk you out."

The heat of his touch confused me. "Don't you have to stay and work?"

"Flex schedule. We're winding down here."

As we exited the gate, Pat stopped me. "Seriously, now that you're done looking for professional losers, how about you join me for dinner? I promise you won't be bored."

He wasn't getting the message.

"No," I told him. "No means no, Pat. You're a really nice guy, but I need a professional man."

Discouragement crossed his face. "See you for swimming tomorrow then, Liz." He turned and walked back through the gate.

Like that he was gone.

I'm doing the right thing, aren't I?

CHAPTER 12

*P*AT

As Liz and I walked out the gate toward the valet stand, I'd asked her again to join me for dinner.

"No means no, Pat. You're a really nice guy, but I need a professional man," she'd said.

I felt like dirt because I wasn't enough for her. But I couldn't tell her I was a Covington.

Phil had been at least half right. This gave me a taste of what most guys had to endure all the time, and it sucked. I thought I had her when her boss canceled her shift, thought she'd be looking for a distraction. But dammit, she'd stuck to her stupid rule.

My stomach had soured, and I found myself unable to stand there and watch her drive off. I had to walk away.

I decided once again to have a talk with her boss, the weasel ——a serious talk. He was going to leave my girl alone.

Fortunately I found Bill and Lauren again, but five minutes later, I got a radio call to come out front. I returned to find Liz waiting with the valets just outside the gate. Anticipation buzzed in my head.

Maybe she changed her mind.

"Her car won't start," the head valet told me as I walked up. He offered the key back to Liz.

I grabbed it before she had a chance. "Let's give it one more try," I told her.

Her brow creased, but she didn't object. I led her into the field of cars. Hers was near the back.

I got in and turned the key. A rapid clicking was the only noise the engine made, a typical dead-battery response.

"He was right. You're going to need a battery."

Her eyes misted over.

I quickly got out of the car. "It'll be okay, Buttercup. This can be fixed."

She shook her head and began to cry. "But I need my car."

I pulled her into a hug. "Don't worry, this is easy." She was warm and soft against my chest.

She shook. "But I need it for work."

I stroked her hair. "Just call Triple A."

"It costs too much. I don't have it."

I should have realized not everyone had all the things I took for granted.

I lifted her chin to gaze into her eyes. "It must be your lucky night. We can grant each other's wishes. I'll call Triple A and get your car fixed, and you can go to dinner with me. We both win."

She broke the hug and protested, but I insisted.

She continued to argue, but this was non-negotiable.

"Coffee, not dinner," she said.

"You're out of options," I told her. "Go ahead, call your sister to pick you up and leave the car. In this neighborhood it'll be stripped by morning." I started backing toward the front gate. "Forget I offered to help you. You're a big girl. You take care of it." I turned away.

She fussed and fumed. "Okay already," she called after a moment. "Dinner, but nothing after."

"Because you're being so hardheaded, now it's going to cost you two dinners."

She crossed her arms. "That's not fair."

"Not fair? Okay, you fix the car." I turned again to leave.

I hadn't gotten three paces before she called after me. "Okay already, you blackmailer."

I returned. "Now it's going to cost you three dinners for insulting me."

She stomped her foot. "You can't do that."

"To show you how fair I am, I'll flip you for it." I pulled my lucky coin out of my pocket. "Heads two dinners, tails three dinners."

She huffed and shuffled her feet but didn't bitch any more.

I flipped the coin and showed it to her. "Heads. You win. Only two dinners."

She stood there stoically for a moment before nodding.

That was good enough for me. "Trust me, Buttercup. It's fate. Just give yourself permission to have a good time. Soon you won't be able to resist me."

The smirk that graced her face was what I'd been waiting for. She didn't argue.

I pulled out my phone and stepped away to call Triple A. A few minutes later, after hanging up, I assured Liz they were on the way.

We leaned against her car, watching as the valets slowly pulled most of the remaining vehicles out for their owners one by one.

"I'm going to pay you back," she mumbled. "I pay my own bills."

I smiled, thinking of several ways I would like her to pay me back, that were definitely not what she meant.

"And this isn't a date," she continued. "Just dinner, nothing after."

"Right," I assured her.

She looked out at the road in silence, scuffing her sandals in the dirt.

"There he is." She pointed toward the Triple A truck rounding the corner in our direction.

I had given them the year, make and model and asked for a battery replacement. It took the guy all of fifteen minutes to put in a new battery, and the car started right up. I settled up with the driver and told him where I needed him to tow the car.

Liz had already settled herself behind the wheel, thrilled to have a working vehicle again, but I called to her as I pulled poor, drunk Gordie's keys out of my pocket.

"Come on, I'm drivin'."

The yellow prancing horse on the fob gave it away. Gordie might be boring, but he had automotive style. He drove a Ferrari. There were still two left in the parking lot. I pushed the unlock button, and the red one's lights came on.

Liz's mouth dropped open as I opened the passenger door for her. "You have got to be kidding. This is your car?"

I smiled. "Only the best for you, Liz." I gave it a few seconds before telling her the truth. "This is Gordie's car. Remember the guy who was too drunk to drive himself? We called him a cab, and I agreed to get his car home. I just didn't say when."

I closed the door after she took her seat.

"Are you sure it's all right?"

"No worries. He'll be sleeping it off until morning, and when he wakes up, his car will be there."

She didn't seem convinced, but she gave up on arguing for a change.

I started up the musical V-12 and drove Liz toward the beach.

She tried to wheedle our destination out of me, but I didn't give it up until we'd arrived.

I parked at Santa Monica Pier.

CHAPTER 13

LIZ

DRIVING IN A SLEEK, LOW-RIDING FERRARI HAD BEEN A WEIRD experience. Everyone watched us. On the city streets, and even on the freeway, we were an attraction. Heads swiveled to watch the bright red car and its lucky occupants whiz by. The high-pitched roar of the engine as Pat stepped on the gas was like ferocious mechanical music. This must be how those rich Hollywood folks felt. Step on the gas and everyone within earshot turns to see the red shooting star take off. Nice car. Too bad it wasn't Pat's.

But life isn't a fairytale.

None of them had any idea we were just fakers. Neither of us with much more than a few nickels to rub together, especially since Ben, the jerk, had canceled my shift tonight.

When Pat pulled into the Santa Monica Pier parking lot, the palm trees swayed in the gentle breeze, and the salty smell of the ocean greeted me as he opened my door, like a gentleman.

He walked up to the ticket counter for the amusement park.

"Hey, we agreed just dinner, nothing else," I objected.

"You said *nothing after dinner*. This is before dinner."

Apprehensively, I acquiesced. He was annoying, but right. I hadn't ever been here before. I'd wanted to come but never found the time, so this wasn't so bad.

We went on the Shark Frenzy first, which was like the spinning teacups at Disneyland, except for big kids like us. The ride was a blast and brought out the laughing, silly side of both of us. It was a good thing we hadn't eaten yet, or I would have been wearing my dinner. The contraption seemed designed to make us silly, dizzy, and sick all at the same time.

I could barely walk straight when we got off. I was so unstable that Pat had to grab me, and when he did, the heat of his touch lit my skin on fire. I embarrassed myself by recoiling from him and falling down in the process.

"Careful there, Buttercup." He helped me stand.

"I'm sorry." I sensed I'd injured his masculine pride.

In his macho mind, I should have accepted a man's help and avoided the ground in the first place. He was right. My rules and my feelings were in complete conflict as my hormones battled my gray matter.

"No worries. It's a woman's prerogative to fall on her ass if she wants to. I know first aid, if it comes to that."

I brushed my humiliated ass off and smiled, pretending it didn't hurt as much as it did.

We did a trip on the roller coaster, another ride that was better on an empty stomach. As we buckled into our seats, he put his arm protectively around my shoulder. It was warm and comforting and felt so natural that I didn't pull away, even if it was boyfriend-like. The heat of his touch warmed me deep inside. I was drifting in a dangerous direction with him.

He picked the Pacific Plunge for the next ride. It took us up and up. I trembled, scared shitless, as the ride noisily climbed higher. Instinctively I took his hand, sending tingles up my arm.

The ride reached the top with a clunk, and a second later it dropped us four stories to the ground. I screamed and gripped his hand so hard I was afraid I might leave a mark.

"I'm not doing that again," I said as we unbuckled from the seats.

"Scared?"

"More like terrified. And I don't want to see my lunch again."

He grabbed my hand and dragged me back into line. "The only way to conquer your fears, Buttercup, is to face them head-on."

I pulled away, but it was hopeless.

He lifted me off my feet and carried me back to the line. "Behave yourself or else," he threatened.

The feel of his arms holding me made my heart race. I stopped struggling. "Or else what?"

He put me down, but kept a firm grip on my wrist. He whispered in my ear. "Or I'll have to take you over my knee, pull down your pants, and spank you." He grinned.

I giggled. "What if I like it?" I meant to shock him.

He lightly spanked my butt. "You little minx, you. We're going to get along just fine, and when you're ready, I'm going to teach you how to be really naughty."

That shot heat straight to my core. The wetness between my thighs worried me. How was I going to handle it if he called my bluff? I wasn't sure what he meant by naughty, but I wasn't about to ask.

We went on the Plunge three more times. I still dreaded the drop the first time, but by the third, I didn't scream on the way down. Pat held my hand reassuringly each time. And the concern he showed at the bottom before we got back in line was priceless.

He'd been right. Dealing with the fear made me feel stronger. It had been the right thing to do.

"I want to do it again," I told him.

I needed to prove to both of us I had conquered this.

"I'll flip you for it." He pulled a coin out of his pocket and flipped it, holding it hidden under his hand. "Heads you get to go

again; tails you don't." He lifted his hand, revealing heads. I
had won.

I proved I could defeat the fear and screamed for joy as the seat
fell out from underneath us again.

He intertwined his strong fingers with mine as he pulled me
along to the next attraction.

I couldn't deny the fun we were having together. I was getting
used to the gentle warmth of his touch and the feelings he ignited
in me every time I took in that smile of his and those dimples
appeared.

We tried our hands at the target-shooting booth. I missed
almost everything. American Sniper I was not.

He hit what seemed like every shot and won a cute stuffed
porpoise. He named it Flipper and handed it to me.

I stopped trying to pull away when he put his arm around my
waist as we walked, joined at the hip.

After tossing rings at another booth and shooting baskets at a
third, we linked hands, and he led me toward the food. "What do
you feel like for dinner? We have choices of seafood, Italian,
Mexican, or burgers."

My tastes in food ran to the ordinary, and I didn't want him to
spend much. "Burgers sounds good to me."

"Burgers it is, then."

I ordered a single, and he got a double, with fries and shakes
for both of us. It was more food than I normally had for dinner
because I was always on the other side of the ordering pad.

I sipped on my shake. "Pat, you know so much about me, and I
hardly know anything about you."

"Ask away, Buttercup."

"Let's start by dispensing with the Buttercup shit."

"If you want, I could call you Cupcake instead. Kind of appropriate, given what I want to do with you."

My blush went instantly to three alarms. "No, Buttercup is
better."

The tingling between my thighs wouldn't go away as I pictured his face in my crotch. I wondered what it would feel like. I re-crossed my legs.

He smirked, enjoying my embarrassment.

I tried to calm myself. "Tell me about your family, Pat. Any brothers or sisters?"

He punched the straw through the cap of his shake. "Let's see, long story short, there's five of us. I have one younger brother, two older brothers, and an older sister. None of us are in prison, so I guess we turned out all right. I told you about Katie. She makes the best apple pie, the absolute best. You have to try it someday. My youngest brother, Steven, he moved up to San Francisco with his wife." He sucked on his shake. "And Liam, the second oldest, he's out in Boston, so it's just Katie and me and my oldest brother still here in LA."

"Get to see them often?"

"Yeah, I saw both of them last weekend at the Habitat for Humanity project we worked on Sunday. That was the day we met."

I schooled my features to avoid appearing surprised. Volunteering like that didn't fit the image of Pat I'd built in my mind.

"Habitat for Humanity? I thought you guys were just pulling down weekend overtime."

"No, we were all volunteering. Made good progress too. It's a duplex we're putting up in Reseda, so two families will have brand-new homes pretty soon. I like to go to move-in day. The smiles on their faces when we give them the keys to their new house, well, that's all the payment I need. It's the least I can do to help is the way I look at it."

Trent, Mike, and the other guys I'd dated had always saved their Sundays for beer and sports. Football, baseball, basketball, hockey, the sports rotated with the seasons. But the beer and chips stayed the same.

There was a lot more to this black-belt carpenter than met the eye.

"Back at the polo field, you handled that big guy like it was nothing. What did you say that was?"

"Judo. My dad had us all learn self-defense when I was younger. Our instructor taught us a mixture of martial arts, but recently I wanted to learn a technique that didn't involve hitting, so I took up judo. In judo, you don't hit; you throw the guy to the ground with his own momentum and pin him. With the right technique, you can handle somebody a lot bigger than you, and I'm not bad."

Our food arrived. I couldn't resist the aroma and took a bite of my hamburger.

"You sure looked a lot better than just *not bad.*"

"I practice a lot. That helps. What about you, any other siblings besides Stacey?"

I finished chewing the burger, which was surprisingly good. "No, just the one sister." I sipped my shake. "So, being a carpenter during the week and doing security on the weekends, that must keep you pretty busy."

"Not so busy that I don't have time for you, Buttercup."

I couldn't keep back my smile, but I rolled my eyes intentionally. "Seriously, how do you manage it?"

He took my hand.

The touch sent a rush of sparks up my arm and straight to my heart. If I didn't want this to be a date, why was I reacting like this?

"Liz, I told you I have my fingers in lots of pies. I do a lot of different things, and I'm pretty sure I can do anything I set my mind to. I am much more versatile and accomplished than you give me credit for."

I should have, but I didn't pull my hand back. "Is there anything you can't do?"

"I can't take you on a real date. At least not yet." His thumb traced circles on my hand, melting my willpower. "That's enough about me, though. Tell me about you and your sister."

I wrestled enough brain cells together to compose an answer. "Stacey's getting her nursing degree. I promised my mom I would put her through school." Tears welled behind my eyes. "My mom, she passed away last year, and my dad died when I was very little, so it's up to me now to take care of her and Timmy." I didn't tell him the whole story about my father.

He placed his other hand atop mine. "I'm so sorry, Liz. My parents are both gone as well. It's a cruel fate, when you know your kids will grow up without ever having met their grandparents."

"I hadn't thought about it that way." I contemplated the touching way he'd put it——focused on the issues it created for others, rather than the problems it created for him. Trent, the A-hole, had only asked about the size of my nonexistent inheritance.

Pat squeezed my hand. "How far along is Stacey in her program?"

"This is her last year. Then when she gets a job, she'll help support me while I save up for vet school to get my DVM. At least that's the grand plan. I've also applied for a scholarship, but I haven't heard about that yet. I left UC Davis around Christmas of my senior year when Mom got sick. I was in the pre-vet program, and I'd been accepted to the vet school. I just have to finish up my BS. They've been really good about keeping it open for me."

"I have no doubt that you'll do well, Dr. Turner."

"I hope so. I'm sort of out of practice when it comes to school work."

We ate and talked more about my plans to leave waitressing behind and become a veterinarian someday. Talking to Pat was so easy. He listened and asked questions and kept me relaxed. So many of the guys I'd dated had been more interested in talking than listening. But every time I asked some more about Pat, he would turn the question around to learn more about me.

We finished the dinner, and he suggested a final ride on the Ferris wheel. I agreed, and once seated, he placed his arm around me. I rested my head for a moment on his shoulder and dreamed he was a doctor who owned the red Ferrari and this was a wonderful first date. The ride stopped with us at the top.

I snuggled in close to him. The view from the full height of the slow-moving ride was magical in the failing light. I turned to face him, and his gaze paralyzed me. I was helpless to resist the warm amber eyes of the cat as they drew me in. I moved toward him, and he pulled me closer.

It began slowly, his stubble scratching my cheek as he nibbled at my earlobe. The pine scent in his hair mixed with the salty smell of the nearby ocean. I snaked my arms around him and pulled him close, finding his lips with mine and opening to his tongue. He tasted of ketchup and mustard and desire. His tongue teased me, gliding across mine, stroking, competing in a hungry duel, lighting my blood on fire.

His grip on me was firm as he pulled me closer, pressing my breasts to his warmth, caressing my back with slow, steady hands that released all my tension. He was strong, powerful, insistent, and gentle at the same time. His embrace was a warm cocoon of safety from the world.

He fisted my hair and tore my mouth away from his, gazing into my soul with those piercing eyes. He could see my vulnerabilities, my desires, and my needs. He rubbed his nose against mine, his lips just out of reach, before claiming my mouth again.

We traded breath, our tongues speaking the language of desire. My blood sang, and I melted in his arms. I couldn't resist, and I couldn't stop. He was a magnet that could not be denied. The scent of his hair, the warmth of his embrace, and the taste of sex carried by his tongue were too much for me. Time slowed, and the ride fell away. There was only the ocean, the stars, and us. All I could hear was the hammering of my heart. This was unlike any kiss I had ever experienced. I was with him, and nothing else mattered so long as I was in his arms.

The ride started again, and I broke the kiss, embarrassed that I had broken my own rule. I was falling for Pat, unable to resist the pull he had on my soul. When we stepped off the ride, I faced the reality that I was here with a carpenter or mall cop or whatever he was, in a borrowed car. I was on a non-date that had turned into a date because of a dead battery, with a guy that fished quarters out of his pockets to scrape together enough money for the rides.

I am so lost.

P*AT*

THE EVENING HAD BEEN MAGICAL. LIZ HAD BEEN A REAL TROOPER, trying the rides that clearly made her uncomfortable. She was not a roller coaster or weightless drop kind of girl.

When I'd forced her to take the Plunge again, she'd resisted.

I told her I'd have to spank her if she didn't behave.

"What if I like it?" she shot back before blushing with a glow bright enough to give me a sunburn.

That shot a jolt straight to my cock. I had a real firecracker here under the demure exterior. I'd had to readjust my pants, and I couldn't wait to get Liz behind closed doors and light the fuse.

At dinner she kept asking questions to learn more about me, but I wanted to learn about her——and avoid going into too much detail about myself yet.

Earlier I had instructed the tow truck driver to tow her car back to her house after we left. I wanted to avoid an argument with her. Better to ask forgiveness later than permission ahead. When I told her on the way back that I'd had it towed, she accepted without a fight, which was significant progress.

CHAPTER 14

LIZ

I HAD EXPECTED TO RETURN TO THE POLO GROUNDS TO RETRIEVE my car, but Pat told me he'd had it towed to my house, so he drove me over the hill all the way back home.

I didn't complain.

I had Flipper in my lap and a hot guy driving me home in a hot sports car. It was fine with me to have more time riding in this red rocket ship, imagining Pat as a rich doctor as the people we passed looked at us, the perfect couple, and wondered how we'd gotten so lucky.

He kissed me at the door, and I didn't resist. He was in charge, and I was putty in his arms as his mouth covered mine with insistence and desire, rekindling the fire I'd tried unsuccessfully to quench.

I needed his touch, his embrace. I melded my body to his. My breasts pillowed firmly against his chest as I reached up to pull him down to me.

His hand cradled my ass and pulled me into the growing hardness of his arousal. I rubbed myself against his cock. The heat pooling between my thighs threatened to ignite me.

The hitch in his breath as I rubbed against him was the response I craved. His other hand found my breast, lighting a fire in my chest with the strokes of his thumb as he found my pebbled nipple through the fabric of my dress.

I broke the kiss. I had to stop while I could. He was a temptation I had to resist.

He was a gentleman about it and left with another simple kiss to my forehead.

Any more and I would have been doomed.

I had to stop. It was the right thing to do.

Breathless after that kiss, I closed the door behind me. With Flipper under my arm, I leaned against the door, fighting to get my composure back.

Stacey was parked on the couch, pretending she hadn't peeked out the window. "Was that a Ferrari? You must have landed a big one if he drives a car like that."

I nodded.

Missy demanded to be petted, and Roxy followed.

"You're back after curfew. So who was he that kept you out all evening?" Stacey was not going to be denied her gossip.

"Just Pat."

Her brow shot up. "Hot carpenter Pat? So he's not broke after all?"

I walked over to the couch. "My car wouldn't start." I plopped down. "He got it fixed, and I agreed to go to dinner with him."

"Go on."

"He drove me in a Ferrari down to Santa Monica Pier."

"Did you break the sound barrier or anything?"

"No, but it's really cool. We're in this expensive, loud car, and everybody was turning to look at us. It's hard to describe. You can tell how envious they are by the looks in their eyes. They all wished they were us. Anyway, we went down to Santa Monica Pier and had burgers."

She reached out to touch my shoulder. "I knew it. You went out with him because he's rich and has a nice car."

"No," I objected. "It wasn't his. He was just driving it home for a guest."

"So he's not rich? You swore you wouldn't go out with him because of your stupid rule."

"It's complicated."

"Complicated. Right. What's with the dolphin?"

I held up Flipper and turned him around. "Pat won him for me."

"So it was more than just dinner, huh?"

"Yeah, we went on some rides and hit the booths." I felt flush recalling our kiss at the top of the Ferris wheel.

"You're blushing. What are you holding back?"

My flush increased as I recalled how romantic it had been atop the world in Pat's arms, with the city lights on one side and the ocean on the other. "We kissed."

"Nice first date, then?"

"It wasn't a date. Just dinner."

"Did you pay?'

"Well… No."

"What planet are you from? Just for your information, Liz, when a guy takes you somewhere, buys you dinner, and kisses you, for most women that constitutes a date."

I couldn't argue. I knew it had turned into a date.

Stacey had an old *Dancing with the Stars* episode on the DVR, and I stayed up to watch it with her. Thankfully, she quickly gave up asking me for any more details about the evening.

When the show finished, I took the dogs out, went to my room, and placed Flipper on my nightstand. My phone dinged as I prepared for bed.

PAT: Looking forward to tomorrow

ME: Me 2

PAT: I'll introduce you to the girls

ME: What girls

PAT: The chicks that stay here with me

ME: I thought u lived alone

PAT: I have a harem out back

Now I wasn't sure going over there was such a good idea, but I couldn't let Timmy down.

PAT: You can also pet my cock

I had heard of phone sex, but I wasn't ready for text sex with this guy yet.

ME: Getting ahead of yourself

PAT: He is very friendly

ME: No thnks

PAT: You can put the cock collar on him

This was getting to be too much.

PAT: I can teach you how

I laughed. I had heard of cock rings, but not cock collars, and that was not something I needed a lesson in tomorrow. I needed to cut this off before I embarrassed myself.

ME: In yur dreams

PAT: See how well you know me

PAT: See you tomorrow

I didn't want to encourage him any more, so I didn't respond.

PAT: Bet you dream about me again

I turned off the phone and got in bed. Flipper stared at me from my nightstand. Pat had been right. I couldn't get him out of my mind, and I was definitely going to dream about him again when I finally got to sleep.

CHAPTER 15

LIZ

TIMMY WAS IN THE BACKSEAT AS WE ARRIVED AT THE ADDRESS ON Myrtle Street Pat had texted me. The house was older than the others on the block. It was in need of a paint job, at least on the outside. The front yard was well kept, with a little grass and two tall palm trees to one side and a cedar on the other.

We went up the steps of the small Victorian and knocked on the door.

Timmy hugged Pat's legs as soon as he let us in. Tosca greeted me by sniffing my crotch again. I knelt to hug her.

Pat had his swim trunks and a T-shirt on. His legs were tanned and muscled. "Hey, slugger, you ready to swim?"

"Yeah, I wanna swim."

"Well, you have to wait until your mom———I mean your aunt is ready."

I caught the dig at my deception and flashed him a scowl. "I'm ready."

We went out the back door to a pool behind the house, and a

large area behind that with fruit and nut trees. The lot was huge. I put down the duffel with our towels and Timmy's life jacket. Several towels were already laid out on the lounge furniture by the pool.

Pat walked ahead. "The lot goes pretty far back."

No wonder his boss had bought this place. The lot would accommodate a much larger house.

"Timmy, you wanna meet the girls?" Pat asked.

"I don't like girls," Timmy said, scrunching his face up and stopping.

Pat took his hand and led him on. "You'll like these chicks. If they like you, they'll climb right into your lap and tickle you." Pat opened the gate and took Timmy out into the backyard.

I hurried to catch up, dreading what I was about to see.

Pat trotted away with Timmy in tow. "Your aunt wants to pet my cock."

The gate closed before I got to it. "I do not," I called after them.

How could Pat corrupt a child like that? Timmy was way too young for that kind of talk. It was a good thing he didn't know what Pat meant. It took me a bit of fiddling to figure out how to open the gate.

They were way ahead and had disappeared around a hedge. I ran to catch up.

"Do you like them?" I heard Pat ask.

"Wow," Timmy said. "They're pretty."

I rounded the hedge.

Timmy was holding a large brown chicken. "What's his name?"

Pat chuckled. "That's a girl chicken, and her name is Mazie, I think."

A chicken coop sat in the corner of the lot, behind the hedge with a fence around it. A half dozen different-colored chickens pecked at the ground.

Pat picked up the rooster at his feet. It flapped its wings a few times before settling down. "This is my cock, Mr. Busy," he said, looking at me. "And this is my harem."

I flushed with embarrassment. "I thought you meant something else."

Pat's smile melted me. "I know what you thought, Buttercup. I like how your mind works. We're going to get along just fine."

"Why do you call him that?" Timmy asked, getting me out of trouble.

"Because he stays pretty busy, keeping all the girls happy."

Timmy put the chicken down. "Too many girls is bad."

I laughed. Growing up would change that attitude before long.

Pat brought Mr. Busy over to me.

I reached for the bird. "Sure, I'll pet your cock."

He handed him to me. "See under here?" He lifted some of the neck feathers to show me. "This is the cock collar I was telling you about. It keeps him from crowing. It's called a *no-crow collar*. If he didn't have it on, he'd be too loud, and the city would make us get rid of him."

I tried petting the big bird, but he struggled to get down as I did.

Pat took my hand and showed me how to pet him. "You need to stroke him gently and pay particular attention to the head."

The heat of his touch and his words lit a fire between my thighs as I looked down and envisioned doing something entirely different.

Holy shit, I'm turning into Tina.

Pat caught me checking out his crotch. "Once you get good enough at that, I'll let you pet *Mr. Happy*," he whispered in my ear.

I must have turned ten shades of red. Lucky for me, Timmy was oblivious.

We fed the chickens, and Timmy chased them around, trying to catch and hold each one.

I tried to cool off and avoid envisioning petting Mr. Happy.

Eventually Timmy got tired of the chickens, and we went back to the pool area.

Pat pulled his shirt over his head, the way guys do. But this was not a guy in front of me anymore. This was a man. He had powerful arms, broad shoulders, six-pack abs, and back muscles that tapered to a slim waist.

The sight of him sent tingles through me. I had to look away lest I start to stare, or drool, or say something Tina-like that I would regret.

Timmy had taken off his shirt and shoes and started toward the pool.

I grabbed the duffel. "Timmy, your mom said you have to wear the life jacket."

"I don't want to. Those are for babies." He kept walking in the direction of the pool.

"Timmy," Pat said firmly.

Timmy stopped. He wasn't going to listen to me, but Pat's male voice was something else.

"House rules," Pat told Timmy. "You need to wear it until your Auntie Liz says otherwise, and only babies complain. Men just do what they have to."

I was grateful that Pat was not trying to undermine me here, but calling me *Auntie Liz* made me feel old.

Timmy accepted Pat's challenge to be a man. He put on the vest and zipped it up without further complaint.

"Is it okay if I call you Tim?" Pat asked. "I think you're old enough to be Tim instead of Timmy. What do you think?"

Timmy beamed with pride and nodded enthusiastically. He turned while I sprayed sunscreen on him.

Pat had won him over for sure.

Pat jumped in the pool with a huge splash. Timmy shrieked with joy and followed him in with his own interpretation of a cannonball.

I sat in one of the lounge chairs under the shade of the

umbrella. Tosca had parked herself in the shade near the back door of the house.

The two boys raced from one end of the pool to the other, Pat not quite letting Timmy catch him until the end, when he let Timmy win. They splashed each other and played catch the submarine, with Pat going underwater again and again.

Pat threw Timmy up in the air to splash down far away from him, and Timmy kept coming back for more. He was enjoying himself immensely, laughing up a storm and challenging Pat to throw him farther and higher.

Trent had never shown any interest in spending time with Timmy. But Pat had just the right touch with the boy. It was clearly good for Timmy to have a man to play with. Stacey had worried about the lack of a man in Timmy's life. Pat was going to be a good influence on him.

What am I doing?

A shiver rolled over me. I was imagining Pat being around for more than a day or two. Something was clearly wrong with me.

"Hey, Liz, when are you going to get in?" Pat broke me out of my trance.

I was reluctant to interrupt Timmy's fun. "Maybe after lunch."

Pat swam to the side of the pool. "House rules: bathing suits only by the pool. No street clothes." He smiled mischievously. "If you don't have a suit, Buttercup, your birthday suit will do." He kept his voice low enough that Timmy couldn't hear.

"Nice try," I shot back.

I pulled off my clothes, slowly to tease him, and ended up in the pale blue bikini I had worn underneath. I sat back in the chair and watched the two boys play some more. It had been a while since I'd seen Timmy have so much fun. No wonder my Kryptonite had failed that night outside the house. Pat was at ease with kids, and he knew how to be one himself. He would make a fine father one day.

I can't keep doing this.

I mentally slapped myself. I needed to be realistic and stop fantasizing about a carpenter, no matter how great he seemed to be. I watched as they continued to splash and swim.

"Lunch time," Pat yelled to Timmy as he clambered out of the pool. He picked up a towel and walked in my direction, dripping wet.

I couldn't avert my eyes. He had the body of Atlas. His eyes pulled me in, and time stood still.

"Would you like some?" he asked, breaking me from my reverie.

"Yes… I mean no."

I hadn't understood the question. I couldn't get enough neurons working to formulate an answer.

I would be a fool to not want some of you.

He held out his hand. In it was a bottle of sunscreen he'd picked up with his towel.

My brain started to process things again. "Maybe later," I managed to respond, trying hard to not screw up the words. Everything he did and said somehow scrambled my brain.

"Suit yourself. I'm going to start lunch. Hamburgers okay for you two?"

"Sure, can I help?"

"You can light the grill, Buttercup. I'll get the food from inside."

Timmy was drying off.

I figured out how to light the gas grill, and Pat returned with a tray of hamburger patties, buns, and the fixings.

I watched from the shade as Pat patiently showed Timmy how to put the burgers on the grill and turn them when they were ready. Pat had him help make up the plates.

We sat together under the shade, eating homemade burgers.

After lunch, Timmy turned as I sprayed another coat of sunscreen on him. He put his vest back on without complaint and jumped in the pool. He called for *Uncle Pat* to join him.

"Not yet, Tim. I have to help your Auntie Liz." He motioned to the chaise. "Now lie down. It's your turn to get some sunscreen."

I put a towel down and laid on my stomach.

He poured lotion in his hands and started on my shoulders and arms.

I moaned with pleasure. It felt so good to have his hands rubbing the slick lotion over me. I had longed for his touch without realizing it, and now he lit a dangerous fire within me——one that all the water in the pool might not be able to extinguish.

He untied my bikini string and rubbed up and down my back, stopping his fingers just at the top of my bikini bottom. He shifted down to my ankles and worked his way up one leg, rubbing my calves and then my thighs. I nearly exploded as he worked his way up my inner thigh, leaving a trail of heat, stopping just before touching me where I wanted it most. He shifted to the other leg and tortured me the same way.

"How's that?" he asked as he took his hands off me.

I closed my eyes and all my willpower melted away. "Keep it up. It feels great."

He leaned over, and I felt his breath on my ear. "Buttercup, I told you you wouldn't be able to resist me."

"Who wants to resist?" I whispered back in my trance-like state.

If Timmy weren't here, I would've been taking off my top, rolling over, and asking him to do my front right now.

He kissed my ear and stood. "Liz, is it okay if I waterproof him?"

I reached behind me to retie my suit so I could sit up. "I'm not sure what you mean."

"Trust me."

I nodded. I did trust him.

He went to the side of the pool. "Tim, ready for your swim lesson?"

Pat took the vest off Timmy, held him a few feet from the side, and had him dog paddle to the edge. The distance kept increasing, little by little, until Timmy could go from one side of the pool to the other. Then Pat did the same thing in the other direction, slowly increasing the distance until Timmy made it all the way down the long side of the pool to the other end. Pat was never more than two feet from him, constantly watching to see that he was safe.

He let Timmy jump in from the side and swim across, and eventually Timmy could jump in at the deep end and swim the whole length of the pool, all in an afternoon.

"Do that three more times and you are a certified tadpole, and you can swim in this pool without the vest," Pat told him.

Timmy quickly accomplished the task with a monster grin.

We congratulated him on his graduation to tadpole.

Pat went into the house again. This time he returned with plates of apple pie.

The pie was delicious. "This is great. Where'd you get it?"

"My sister Katie baked it for you."

"What do you mean for me?"

"I told her you were coming over, so she baked it for the occasion. I told you she makes the best apple pie in the state."

I was impressed. I had graduated to being significant enough for him to tell his sister about.

"Please tell her I agree with you. Her pie is flat out the best I have ever tasted."

Pat smiled. "Will do."

Timmy was so tired he fell asleep on one of the chaises in the shade, and Pat and I finished up the afternoon lying around the pool.

I asked for and received another application of sunscreen from the magic hands.

When it was time to go, Timmy didn't want to leave, but I had to get back in time to go to my dinner shift at The Ironhorse.

⌁

*P*AT

I<small>T HAD BEEN A FUN DAY WITH</small> T<small>IM AND</small> L<small>IZ</small>. H<small>ER EYES HAD</small>
bugged out when I'd told her she could pet Mr. Happy if she did a
good enough job with Mr. Busy. She was a lot of fun to kid with. It
was so easy to get her wound up.

And Tim was a terrific little kid to play with, very happy and
outgoing. Only once did I have to insist he pay attention to what
Liz told him to do. After that he was quite well behaved.

I, on the other hand... When I'd applied sunscreen to Liz's
back and legs, my cock went to full mast, and it took all the control
I could muster to behave myself. If Tim hadn't been there, I would
have been telling her all the things I planned to do with her, and
then I would have dragged her into the house to follow through.

This go-slow shit is murder.

I had felt the fire just below the surface as I rubbed her skin
with the lotion. She was a firecracker set to go off.

At one point, when she went in to use the bathroom, I'd asked
Tim if he knew his mother's phone number. He did, and I added it
to my phone.

By tracing Tosca's rabies tag, I'd learned that her owner had
left the state, so I told Liz I planned to keep the dog for a while
until she could find it a home.

She was relieved.

I'd sent them home with the leftover apple pie and immediately
began to plan my next move. After they left, I called Stacey to tell
her how well behaved Tim had been and to request a little information. She was happy to oblige. I had an ally.

A<small>FTER EATING DINNER BACK AT MY CONDO, WHERE</small> I'<small>D BEEN</small>
keeping my work papers, I studied the proposal on the Popovich
transaction. I had a call scheduled with them and their lawyers

tomorrow morning. My head wasn't in it, though. The more I stared at the papers, the more I saw Liz's smile, and her body in that bikini. My cock jerked to attention as I recalled rubbing lotion over her body.

Her body would soon be mine. I could feel it.

I pushed away the papers and got up to get a scotch. I poured myself a glass of my standard Johnnie Walker Blue Label. After finishing the glass and pouring a second, I decided to text my girl.

She didn't know it yet, but she was already my girl.

ME: Dinner at my place tomorrow at six

After my second glass I got a response.

LIZ: Command or request

She knew she owed me a second dinner.

ME: Whichever you prefer

LIZ: What if I have to work

I already knew the answer to that one, courtesy of Stacey.

ME: You have lunch shift I checked

LIZ: Six

ME: See you then

I had lit the fuse on the firecracker, and it was crackling. The only question was how long she could resist before the fuse reached the powder and her passion exploded. She would soon be mine.

I finished the scotch and went back to my work papers. They didn't make any more sense than they had earlier. I would have to go over them in the morning at the office. Liz-on-the-brain was screwing with my concentration.

I couldn't resist sending her my usual goodnight text.

ME: Bet you dream about me again tonight

I turned off the phone for the night.

Before she came for dinner tomorrow, it was time for my talk with that weasel boss of hers.

I'd make things *crystal clear.*

CHAPTER 16

*P*AT

THE DOORBELL WOKE ME UP. I QUICKLY CLIMBED INTO A PAIR OF pants and struggled into a shirt while I headed for the door.

A key turned in the lock, and Juanita appeared.

Living in two places had confused me, and I'd forgotten she was due this morning for cleaning.

She brought in her little tray of cleaning supplies, towels, and the ever-present grabber. After organizing her things, she disappeared down the hall and started on her hunt, grabber in hand.

She seemed almost annoyed when she'd finished her search and come up empty for the first time ever.

"Mister Patrick, you take Juanita's advice, no?"

"What advice is that?" I asked.

"You find you a nice *señorita*, no?"

She had no idea how right she was.

"Yes, very nice."

She hummed to herself as she went about her cleaning.

I grabbed my wallet and phone as I decided to get a mocha

downstairs to start the day. I checked for messages when the phone powered up. There was no reply from Liz to my final message from last night, so I decided to follow up.

ME: Was I right?

"When I meet her?" Juanita asked as I reached the front door. "Later," I replied.

I was still Pat Patterson, and Liz couldn't know about this place yet.

A very nice señorita *indeed.*

L*IZ*

AFTER BREAKFAST, I PULLED MY PHONE OFF THE CHARGER. PAT had sent a message last night after the battery died.

PAT: Bet you dream about me again tonight

He had no idea how right he was, and what a dream. A smile came to my face just recalling it.

I got through my lunch shift without any issues with Ben for a change. He had been out most of the day until just before I was off. We still hadn't had the talk he'd threatened last week, which was fine by me. Louise told me Jennie had taken my dinner shift on Saturday, and I didn't want to talk to Ben to find out why.

I arrived outside Pat's little house on Myrtle Street late. The traffic over the hill had been worse than usual——not that I drove it often, but that's what the radio had said.

I handed Pat the bottle of wine I'd brought as he ushered me inside. "Sorry I'm late."

He kissed me on the cheek. "No worries, Buttercup."

I rolled my eyes, but it was better than Cupcake.

"Just having you here makes my day. I'd give you a tour, but from here you pretty much see the whole place."

We'd spent all day outside yesterday, and I hadn't realized how spartan the house was. I could see a table with chairs, a couch with a coffee table, a chest of drawers, one overstuffed chair, and an end table. The walls were bare, with no artwork or even posters. The interior was even more in need of paint than the outside, with areas of bare spackle where the walls had been repaired.

Pat carried the wine to the kitchen and started checking drawers. "I don't know if I have a corkscrew here." He located a screwdriver. "Hope you don't mind the brute-force approach." He pounded the cork into the bottle with the screwdriver and poured wine into two plastic water cups. He handed me one. "Living in one of these remodels is akin to camping sometimes. I don't bring much with me."

"No problem. I like camping. Are we doing s'mores as well?"

He shook his head. "Sorry, just ice cream." He sipped his wine, then held up the cup. "You have good taste."

"One of the perks of waitressing at a high-end restaurant. Quite a few of our regulars are wine snobs, and hearing their complaints and compliments gives me an education."

He started to pull food out of the fridge. "This meal may be a step down from what you're used to."

"I doubt that. Eating baked beans straight out of the can is what I'm used to."

He closed the fridge. "How does Chicken Piccata sound?"

"Heavenly," I replied. I caught myself checking out his ass.

He had me slice the chicken breasts while he prepared the sauce and heated water for the noodles. He didn't have a mallet, so I used the back of a frying pan to pound the meat thin. Every time I walloped the defenseless little pieces of bird, I imagined it was my boss's head.

Pat heated olive oil and butter in a pan. "Easy there, Buttercup. It's already dead."

I giggled and reluctantly stopped banging the chicken to prepare the flour and Parmesan for dredging the pieces.

A half hour later, we had plates of Chicken Piccata over linguine on the table. He produced a bowl of green salad from the fridge, and we sat down to eat.

Pat raised his plastic cup, and I tapped mine against it.

I took a sip. "Hardly camping."

"Special guest calls for a special meal."

As I glanced up, a warm smile crested his lips.

"You forced me here," I reminded him. "Dead battery, remember?"

"So you aren't here of your own free will?"

I blew out a breath. "Of course I am."

His eyes brightened. "I knew it. You can't resist me."

I threw a piece of cherry tomato from the salad at him. It hit him in the chin and dropped to his lap.

He smirked. "Being naughty is going to cost you, Buttercup. You're asking for a spanking or more." He winked.

I couldn't hold back my smile, though I managed not to repeat my *"What if I like it?"* line.

"If you say so, but don't forget that I'm going to pay you back for the battery."

"These evenings with you are payment enough."

His words warmed me. He said the nicest things. I *was* going to pay him, but there was no sense in arguing before I had the money in hand anyway.

As we ate dinner, he had me fill him in on my day at the restaurant. How anybody could think a day in my boring life was interesting was beyond me.

"Now tell me about this carpenter phobia of yours."

I wasn't ready for that. "It's just one of my rules."

He reached out to touch my hand, which yielded warm tingles.

"Like I told you before, to vanquish your fears, you have to face them straight on."

He had been right about my fear of falling on the plunge ride, so I decided to elaborate.

"I've had two serious boyfriends." I cleared my throat. "Both of them worked construction. They didn't have steady work, which I guess is sort of the nature of the job. They both also turned out to be irresponsible, lousy dickheads," I spat.

I hesitated to admit the obvious. "Things didn't work out. The first one left when his work ran out."

The concern on Pat's face was genuine. "I'm so sorry, Liz."

"And he drained my bank account on his way out the door," I added.

"Give me his name, and I'll go find the schmuck and get you your money back." He sounded like he was mad enough to actually do it.

I sipped my wine. "That's in the past. I really don't want to revisit it."

"If you change your mind, the offer stands. I can find dirtbags like him."

I considered revenge for a moment before I shook my head. "The last guy, Trent, stuck me with…" Tears pricked my eyes. It was hard to admit I had been so stupid. "Well, I was left holding the bag for his bills too when he bugged out."

"Tell me his last name."

I sat up straighter. "Why? So you can go beat him up?"

"See how well you know me?"

"You can't solve everything with your fists," I said.

"Maybe not, but it's a good start."

I giggled at the thought of Trent getting half the treatment that biker had gotten on Saturday. I re-crossed my legs. The idea of Pat fighting for me was hot.

He mouthed a kiss in my direction. "Tell me what he did. I bet I can help."

"It's really my fault. I co-signed a loan for his truck, and he's not paying, so now they're going to start garnishing my wages." Tears rolled down my cheeks as I started to cry.

He reached out and rubbed the back of my hand. "It's not your fault, and they can't do that on a car loan, I don't think."

His touch was distracting, sending signals to my lady parts that confused me.

I shook my head. "The letter I got says they're going to start taking part of my check."

He continued to rub the back of my hand. "And that makes you think being an irresponsible dickhead is part of being a carpenter, is that it?"

It sounded stupid when he put it that way.

"My rules keep me safe."

"Were they both under six feet tall?"

I thought for a moment as I stabbed the last piece of chicken. "Yes, but what does that have to do with it?"

"It just proves that your rule is not specific enough. You need to change it to no carpenters——"

"Non-professional guys," I corrected. I threw a crouton at him.

"Be careful, Buttercup. You're playing with fire." He paralyzed me with his stare. "Your rule needs to be no non-professional guys under six feet, simple as that."

I threw another crouton at him, hitting him on the arm. "I make my own rules."

I could be naughty if I wanted to.

"I warned you," he said, standing.

I huffed and crossed my arms. "You can't——"

"I warned you, and you've been naughty for the last time." He came around the table and pulled me to my feet.

I shrieked and put my hands behind me to cover my backside.

CHAPTER 17

Liz

Instead of a spanking, Pat grabbed my shoulders, and his mouth claimed mine.

I gave in as my hormones overrode my petulance. I wanted this more than I had admitted to myself. I wanted *him*, and I needed him to want me too.

Our tongues jousted for position, and he grasped my ass and pulled me tightly to him, rubbing me against the bulge of his growing arousal. His other hand fisted my hair. I grabbed the back of his neck and pulled myself up to him.

"Close your eyes," he commanded sternly as he broke the kiss. I complied.

He left me standing by the table, all alone.

I heard him walking around the room as I stood still, tingling with anticipation. I peeked.

He turned off the lights and approached me again.

His breath was hot on my face, my mouth becoming dry as my

pussy became wet. So many thoughts were running through my mind.

He fisted my hair again and pulled me in for a kiss, our lips brushing lightly against each other at first, followed by searching tongues. He broke the kiss with his hand still knotted in my hair. His other hand moved to the hemline of my dress, the tips of his fingers brushing against the skin above my knee. His eyes held mine as he slowly inched up my leg under my dress. A wildfire built inside me as he teased, slowly approaching where I most wanted his touch.

I tried to move closer, but his hand in my hair prevented it. I stared into his eyes in the dim evening light coming through the windows. His lips brushed against mine, his stubble slightly scratchy. His finger traced the contour of my thong. I bucked my hips toward him, aching to have his hand on me.

He reacted by pulling his hand away and yanking my hair. "Stand still," he commanded.

I was powerless to resist. I had no will to resist. I wanted more, not less.

His hand moved under my dress again as he slowly backed me against the wall. His fingers gently ran across the fabric of the thong that separated them from my drenched folds, sending the electricity of anticipation surging through every nerve in my body. He kissed me lightly, lips only, no tongue.

"Please," was all I could manage to say.

His breath was warm, the pine and spice scent of his hair strong.

"Patience," he said.

His fingers again moved back and forth across the fabric of my thong. He pulled it to the side and brushed his fingertip over my soft folds, his light touch making my brain stop. Slowly, his fingers traced inside my slippery folds to my entrance.

"You're so fucking wet," he said hoarsely.

His fingers went back and forth, over and between, teasing my clit and my entrance.

I wanted to ask him for more, but I couldn't. I wanted to tell him how much I wanted his cock inside me, but I didn't dare.

He was in control. He turned me around toward the wall. "Take off the dress," he commanded.

I reached behind me for the zipper.

"Slowly," he said.

I carefully pulled down the zipper and slid the dress off my shoulders, pushing it past my hips to pool on the floor. I lifted my feet one by one and kicked it to the side. I started to turn to face him, but he stopped me.

"Now the bra," he whispered.

I undid the clasp and slowly slid the straps off my shoulders, throwing it to the side with my dress.

He moved up behind me, tracing his fingers over my shoulders and down my sides, leaving a trail of sparks. A shiver rolled through my body.

I moved my hand behind to reach for him.

He grabbed my wrist and stopped me. "Behave yourself."

Behaving myself was the furthest thing from my mind right now.

He moved closer, and the bulge in his pants pressed up against me.

I slid my hips back and forth against his hardness.

He moaned and slid his hands around me. One hand dipped between my soaked folds and entered me like a hook, pressing a fingertip to that sweet hidden spot inside. The second cradled my breast and tweaked the hardened knot of my nipple.

I moaned each time he pressed harder against my G-spot. I had no idea how I managed to stand with all the sensations running through me. I spread my legs farther to give him more access.

He released my breast and moved to my clit, tracing circles

around the sensitive nub, working my pleasure spot as his chest pushed my breasts against the cold wall.

The avalanche of sensations raging through me was like a wildfire out of control.

I tried to give him more by rocking my hips against his cock.

He continued to move his finger in and out, caressing my G-spot, while the other hand played music on my sensitive clit, bringing me closer and closer to the edge.

With a single word, he pushed me over.

"Come," he whispered as he brushed his lips against my ear. "Come for me," he demanded.

Just like that, I lost control. My eyes clinched closed, and I breathed hard against gritted teeth. All the muscles in my body became tight, and I constricted around his finger. Uncontrollable tension pooled in every cell of my body, and like a bomb, the pleasure exploded inside of me. I let go of everything as a scream escaped my mouth. I quivered as he pulled his finger out and pressed it hard against my clit, rubbing with the mastery of a man who knew women all too well.

His lips were against my ear. "You're mine, naughty girl," he whispered.

He turned me around, bringing his finger to my lips, my scent filling my nostrils.

I opened my mouth and took his finger inside, sucking it clean of my juices. Tasting myself, I grew even wetter——if that was possible.

If he could make me feel this way with just his fingers, what could he do with the monster imprisoned in his jeans?

I hoped to find out. I grabbed for his crotch again.

He stopped me, grabbing my wrist. Denying me.

"You want it?" he asked.

I licked my lips and nodded, no longer denying what I wanted.

He stepped back and started unbuttoning his shirt, eyeing my breasts.

I watched intently, expectantly, frozen still, as if this were the first time. He slowly undid all the buttons, and the shirt dropped to the floor.

His eyes took in my body from head to toe. I could sense him devouring every inch of my naked skin, only the fabric of my thong covering me. The grin on his face and the fire in his eyes showed the appreciation I longed for.

"You look so fucking beautiful, Buttercup." His voice was intoxicating, thrilling, and ominous. "Turn around."

I turned, and he pushed me back up against the wall.

I felt the heat of his chest against my back, the bulge in his pants against my ass cheeks, my breasts pressed against the cold wall. He rocked his hips, the bulge of his cock teasing my ass.

"You want this?"

I reached behind to show him how much I wanted him, but once again he stopped me, taking my wrist and pulling my arm up behind me.

I couldn't get free. He was just too strong.

He released my arm and with a sudden jerk snapped my thong. The scrap of garment fell away. He spun me around, fisted my hair, and brought my mouth to his to claim me with another kiss——a feral kiss, full of lust and want and need.

"Tell me," he demanded.

"I want you," I told him, reaching for his pants, running my fingers over the bulge of his cock.

He slowly unbuckled his belt. He undid the button, followed by the zipper, slowly, very slowly, torturing me with the wait.

I hooked my thumbs in the sides of the jeans and pulled them down.

He kicked them to the side.

I ran my fingers down his abdomen to his thighs, careful not to touch his erection. Two could play the teasing game. Payback was a bitch.

I traced my fingers down and up again several times, watching the increasing tension in his face, before pulling at the waistband of his boxer briefs and releasing his cock to spring free. As I took in the sight in the dim light, my heart skipped a beat. To feel it through his pants was one thing, but seeing it was another completely. His cock was perfect, thick, and beautiful.

I ran a finger along the velvety underside, from the root to nearly the tip. It jerked upward as I did. I knelt and moved my mouth close, then licked the light drop of pre-cum from him, savoring the saltiness. I cupped his balls, feeling their weight by rolling them around in my hand. I grasped his shaft with two fingers near the base and squeezed.

He rewarded me with a moan.

I ran my tongue from the tip to the root as I gazed up at him. Our eyes met, and my pussy clenched at the primal lust in his eyes. I licked the tip, around and around. I opened my mouth wide, wrapping my lips around him as I grasped the shaft with my full hand and started to work it up and down. My other hand cupped his balls and held them as my tongue worked around his crown inside my mouth.

The groans of pleasure I elicited were like an aphrodisiac, urging me on. Knowing that I had the power to turn him on was exciting, intoxicating.

I took more of him in my mouth, as much as I could, to the back of my throat. I started to move him in and out, stroking him with my hand in tandem with my lips. The look of pure pleasure on his face was my guide. I worked him faster and deeper, as much as I could take. I let go of his balls to put both hands on his length, pulling tightly and twisting every time I withdrew him from my mouth.

His groans increased as his legs trembled. Suddenly he grabbed my hair and pulled my head back, away.

What had I done wrong? I was sure I'd opened my mouth wide enough to not scrape him with my teeth.

He retrieved a condom from his jeans, ripped open the packet, and handed it to me.

I slowly rolled it down his length, working it lower and lower, all the while looking up to catch the desire in his eyes.

He leaned over, put his hands under my arms, and lifted me up against the wall in a single move.

I wrapped my legs around his waist as he lowered me onto his cock. I snaked my arms around his neck and pulled my chest to his.

He was huge and tight as he slowly entered me, expanding my walls as they'd never been before. When he'd lowered me fully, he moved his hands to support my ass and began to pump in and out of me. He thrust forcefully, fully into me, banging my back against the wall. My breasts rose and fell against his chest, my pebbled nipples scraping his skin. One hand moved to my breasts, while the other strong arm held me up.

My heart pounded, the blood rushing in my ears louder than our grunts and groans. The waves of pleasure built inside me again, to the vision of the shoreline, the waves beating against the sand. The sensations became uncontrollable as he pounded into me, filling me, forcing me over the edge once more.

The surges of pleasure rolled over me in spasms. My fingers dug into his back, my legs were like a vice around his waist, and my core clenched his cock as the starlights came and I screamed out my pleasure again.

With a final thrust, he pulled my hips down and went deep. He tensed and groaned as he came.

I hung around his neck, still pressed up against the wall. I went limp with a combination of satisfaction and exhaustion.

The pulses of his cock inside me slowly dissipated as his panting slowed to more normal breathing. He repositioned his hands under my ass, supporting me as he pulled away from the wall, and he carried me——still impaled on him——into the bedroom. There, he lifted me up and off of him and laid me down on the bed.

I pulled the covers down and got under them as he went to the bathroom to dispose of the condom. He returned quickly and climbed into bed with me.

His arm came around me, and I rested my head on his chest, listening to the thump of his heartbeat.

"So you're a screamer." He chuckled. "I guess that means we won't be doing this in public."

I didn't know what had gotten into me. "Sorry, I've never screamed before."

Actually, I knew exactly what had gotten into me. The difference was him. He was a real man. No, that wasn't exactly right. He was more than a man, perhaps a different breed——half man and half animal, and he brought out something primitive in me. Something that couldn't be denied, couldn't be quieted.

He kissed the top of my head and held me tight.

We snuggled, my man holding me, warm, possessive, and protective. He had claimed me, and I was his.

I hoped.

"Can I stay?"

He squeezed me. "I'd like to see you try to leave."

I had broken my rule, but there was no resisting him. I simply couldn't control myself. He had doggedly pursued me, and the more I tried to escape, the more I felt drawn to him. I blamed it on hormones or pheromones or one of those chemical things that couldn't be explained or counteracted. His pull was too strong to overcome.

I am his.

HIS PHONE RANG, WAKING US BOTH UP. HE PULLED AWAY.

I grabbed his hand. "Just let it go," I pleaded. The dim red numbers on the bedside clock read ten-twenty.

He got up. "I can't. One thing you'll learn about me, Buttercup, family always comes first. The phone's on do-not-disturb. The only calls that can get through are my family." He picked up the phone. "And you, of course."

And me of course? Wow.

He answered the phone. "Yeah, Steven, what's up?" He was on for only a minute. "Text me the address and tell her I'm leaving right now." He hung up the phone and turned on the light.

I blinked to see.

Distress was etched on his face. "My sister-in-law thinks she's being followed, and she just had her tires slashed while she was getting something to eat." He didn't bother with underwear, he pulled on pants from the dresser and reached for a shirt.

I sat up. My clothes were in the other room. His sister-in-law was in serious trouble if someone had slashed her tires.

He was moving quickly. "I have to go get her right now." His eyes held a steely resolve.

God help anybody that got in his way.

"Can I help?"

"No, just go home. I'll be in touch." He leaned over and kissed me briefly before bolting for the door. His truck roared off down the street as I went searching for my clothes. I stuffed my broken thong in my purse.

CHAPTER 18

PAT

STEVEN'S CALL COULDN'T HAVE COME AT A WORSE TIME, BUT family always came first, and I had to answer the phone.

He told me Emma had pulled into a Wendy's for a bite to eat and come out to find all four of her tires slashed. She had called him back home in San Francisco, and he'd called me because Bill and Uncle Garth had both left town this morning on business.

I raced on to the freeway as fast as I dared in the big pickup. Getting stopped by Highway Patrol would not help. I dialed Emma as soon as I got settled on the freeway. My phone showed thirty-five minutes to reach her address. I nudged the truck up to eighty-five.

She answered on the first ring and started babbling a mile a minute.

"Emm, slow down. Are you still inside right now?"

"*Yeah. Patrick, I'm so scared.*"

"Did you call the cops?"

"*Yeah, but they said it might be an hour on a vandalism call. I'm scared, Patrick. I can't just stand outside after they close.*"

"Tell me how many people are in the restaurant."

She paused. "*Three other customers and a few behind the counter.*

I put the phone on speaker so I could keep both hands on the wheel. "How's your phone battery?"

A few seconds later she responded. "*Fifteen percent. It won't last long.*"

"Okay, listen carefully, Emm. I want you to hang up now to save your battery. We can't have it go dead. You'll be safe inside for a little while. I'll call you back when I get close. Don't let them force you out of the restaurant until I get there. Got it?"

"*Okay.*" She sobbed. "*Patrick...*" The call dropped.

I didn't know if she'd hung up or the phone had died. My heart pounded. She might only have one call left, so I couldn't call her back until I got closer. I took the truck up just past ninety where the numbers on the speedometer stopped. I watched the taillights ahead of me for any sign of the cops.

When the sign appeared saying the exit was six miles away, I took the pickup up past the end of the speedometer. My mouth was dry. I kept my eyes focused on the cars ahead. I guessed I was going well over a hundred. I was glad Phil had opted for the monster V-8 in this truck. I had to keep switching lanes at this speed, and I passed some cars on the right. The steering wheel was slippery under my sweaty hands.

I braked hard for the exit. The Wendy's was only a half dozen blocks away. It was a little past closing time now. I hit call-back.

"Patrick, they're closing." The fear in her voice was palpable.

"Emm, go to the bathroom and lock yourself in for a few minutes. I'm almost there. And keep the phone on."

"*Okay.*" A moment later the sound of her latching the deadbolt came over the phone. "*I'm inside.*"

I hit a red light. I slowed and looked both ways. I picked a gap in the crossing traffic and gunned the truck through the intersection. The sign with the red-haired girl was two blocks away.

Over the phone I could hear them yelling through the door for Emma to come out of the bathroom. I pulled into the parking lot and straddled two parking spaces next to Emma's car with the flat tires.

"Emm, I'm here. You can come out now."

Moments later Emma emerged, trailed by an irate man in a Wendy's uniform.

I took her into a bear hug.

She shivered in my embrace. "Patrick, I'm so scared."

"It'll be okay. I've got you." I walked her to the passenger door of my truck.

A minute of explanation and three Benjamins later, I'd calmed down the Wendy's shift manager. I joined Emma in the truck.

"Who did that?" I asked her as I pulled out onto the street.

"I thought maybe I was being followed by a Mustang, so I called Steven, and he told me to pull in here. He said if the car followed me after the stop, to head back to Bill's condo. But when I came out, my tires were all flat. That's when I freaked out."

I put a hand on her shoulder to reassure her as we stopped for a red light. I checked the rear-view mirror. A white mustang with pink racing stripes was two cars behind me. I turned right and circled the block. The Mustang followed.

"Is that the car behind us?"

Emma turned to look back. She gasped. "That's it. I recognize those ugly stripes."

He was two cars behind us again on the main road back to the freeway. How many Mustangs with those god-awful pink stripes could there be in LA? I got my chance when we stopped at another red light and the car between us switched lanes. The Mustang stopped a few car lengths back. "Hold on, Emm." When the light turned green, I put it in reverse, looked back, and floored the big V-8. We hit the little car hard, and I shifted into drive and roared away.

In the rear-view mirror, I could see that the Mustang's front end had been no match for the solid steel bumper and trailer hitch on Phil's heavy-duty pickup. The lights were shattered and the hood peeled way back.

Emma laughed like a little kid. "Why didn't I think of that? Let's do it again."

I was tempted. "We caught her by surprise once. It won't happen again. I'm not taking the chance that she has a gun."

"She? I thought it was a man."

"Nope." In the backup lights before we'd rammed the car, I'd made out that the driver was a woman. Wearing a baseball cap, but definitely a woman.

I stopped for another red light before the freeway entrance.

Emma relaxed into her seat. "I'm just glad it's over."

I glanced at her. "Who would want to follow you like that?"

Emma paused for a moment and shook her head. "I live a pretty boring life. The closest I come to making an enemy at the museum is when I tell a kid to spit out his gum."

Emma shrieked as the crunched Mustang pulled up beside us on her side.

The light turned green, and I gunned it to get across the inter-section to the freeway on-ramp. The sports car matched us. On the other side, I cut right and forced the banged-up Mustang off onto the shoulder. Its horn blared as it hit the bushes and came to an abrupt stop. I continued onto the freeway, watching my rear-view mirror. No sign of the little car with the stupid pink stripes.

"I know who that is." Emma's voice was quaking. "That was Cruella, Steven's old boss. She blames us for everything that's happened to her."

Emma slowly calmed herself enough to tell me what had

happened between her and Steven and this lady, Monica Paisley, and quite a story it was.

"It sounds like she had it coming to her, but crazy does what crazy wants sometimes. And I dig the nickname."

Emma laughed. "It fits her." She took my phone and called Steven, filling him in on the excitement. "I can be on a flight home tomorrow," she told him. She handed me the phone. "He wants to talk to you."

"*Whatever it takes, Patrick. Keep her safe,*" Steven said.

"No problem. What else are big brothers for? She's family. But listen, Steven, I think she should stay down here for a while 'till we get this sorted out. Between me and Bill and the Hanson firm, we have a lot more resources to keep her safe here in LA than you do up there. And with your broken leg, even Monica could probably whoop your sorry ass."

"But I need to get back to work," Emma complained.

Steven heard her. "*Put me on speaker.*"

I toggled the phone's speaker.

"*Emma, stay there until Patrick says otherwise, and do everything he tells you. Everything.*" His tone left no room for disagreement.

Emma nodded reluctantly. "Okay."

She took the phone again, and they traded lovey-dovey goodbyes.

I pulled off on the exit leading to my condo building, which Lauren liked to refer to as the Battlestar Covington. Bill and I had the two condos on the top floor.

After we'd parked, the ever-present Oliver greeted us at the door. "Good evening, Mister Patrick and Miss Emma."

I could never figure out when this guy took off to go home. He always seemed to be here.

I instructed Oliver that absolutely no one he didn't recognize, especially a woman, should be allowed up to see Emma. He wasn't armed, but he did have pepper spray and a Taser behind his podium, just in case.

He agreed and noted the instructions in his pass-down log for the other doormen.

Once upstairs, I called Bob Hanson of Hanson Security to request a protection detail for Emma. He agreed to send people over, starting with my buddy Winston Evers tonight. An ex-FBI agent, Winston was someone I could count on to keep Emma safe.

"Shit," she said. "I forgot to get my suitcase out of the car."

My phone dinged with a text.

LIZ: Is everything ok?

"Is that her?" Emma asked.

"Her who?" I said innocently.

"Liz, the her you've been lying to for a week or so. The one you pretended to be a security guard for on Saturday so you could be around her. Ring a bell?"

My smile gave me away.

Emma opened the fridge and took out a water. "She has my seal of approval, by the way. I like her."

Not that I needed her approval, but it was nice to have.

"Thanks, and you can take the spare bedroom. We can get you some clothes tomorrow, but for tonight all I can offer you is a shirt and clean panties."

She turned beet red. She'd been so scared tonight, I could see she had wet her pants.

She nodded, and I retrieved a cotton button-up shirt of mine and a pair of blue hip-hugger panties from my drawer.

"You stock women's underwear?" she asked skeptically as she took the clothing.

I smirked. "More like collect. But they're clean."

She examined the panties, shaking her head. They passed her inspection. "You Covington boys are something else."

She left for the guest bedroom.

I took out my phone.

ME: She is safe with me tonight

LIZ: Yur a good man Pat

ME: What you going to dream about tonight

LIZ: A good man

That's my girl.

Winston arrived a half hour later, and I filled him in on the evening. I left it for Emma to explain the lady stalker in the morning.

I set him up with a blanket and pillow for the couch.

I know who I'm dreaming about tonight.

THE SMELL OF FRESH COFFEE GREETED ME WHEN I OPENED MY door.

Winston was already up and at the coffeemaker.

"Coffee's ready, Mr. Bossman."

I joined him in the kitchen to grab a cup of the brew. I added some mocha powder to mine.

"Couch okay last night?" I asked.

"Little on the short side for me, but I'm used to it."

"That's what she said," I kidded him.

He punched me lightly in the shoulder. "Maybe your women, but not mine."

I went to the laundry where I'd put Emma's clothes from last night in the wash. I moved them to the dryer.

Emma wandered out in a bathrobe.

Together the three of us fixed eggs, sausage, and English muffins with some of Katie's homemade orange marmalade.

The phone rang, and I picked it up. It was the doorman checking to see if it was okay to let a Constance Collier up. Winston confirmed Constance was with him, and I cleared her.

She arrived a minute later and introduced herself. She was short, but entered with a firm, assertive handshake. Dressed in jeans, tennis shoes, and a leather flight jacket, she didn't look like much, but Winston assured me the diminutive ex-Secret Service agent was the real deal.

"Mrs. Covington," Winston said. "Constance here will be your daytime shadow for a while."

Emma gave him an uneasy look.

"Mrs. Covington, Constance is ex-Secret Service. She's top notch."

Relief flooded Emma's face. "It's Emma, and when do you go lock the bitch up?"

Constance cleared her throat. "Mrs... Emma," she corrected herself. "It's not that simple. I've been to the restaurant this morning. I have bad news and worse news."

We waited for the punch line.

"The bad news is that they don't have surveillance video in the parking lot, so we don't have proof of who slashed your tires."

"And the worse news?" I asked.

"I'm sorry, but your car was torched some time last night, so this has escalated to a major threat."

Emma gasped. "You mean my car... Can't the police do something?"

"Emma," Constance continued. "I've confirmed that Miss Paisley does own a white, late-model Mustang, but that's not enough to go to the DA with. Even if we confirm that her car followed you last night, your statement, Mr. Covington, is that you backed into her and then left the scene?"

I nodded.

"To the police, that's leaving the scene of an accident, and they could end up charging you and not her. Clearly not a desirable outcome."

Winston spoke up. "The hard part now is deciding what to do. You have a few choices, but none of them are good."

Emma's brow creased. She nodded, waiting for more bad news.

"We can try to get a restraining order against this lady," Winston told her.

Emma coughed. "What good does that do?"

"It makes it an issue you can call the police on," Winston continued, "if she violates the order and gets too close. But as you can imagine, if she wants to hurt you, she may not care about a court order."

"Duh," Emma responded. "We see that all the time with the crazies that stalk the Hollywood types. There has to be something else."

"There are a few other things," Constance said. "We could try to scare her off by threatening her. We could try to get her in a sting, or we could just provide security and see if she gives up. The last option is that you go back to San Francisco, and we surveil her and do nothing if she doesn't follow you."

"I'll have to talk to Steven," Emma said.

None of the alternatives sounded very good to me.

"In the meantime," Winston said, "we'll investigate to see if we can turn up any other evidence that she was the one who vandalized and torched your car, but it will take a few days."

With a nod, Winston departed to start their investigative side of things.

Emma called Steven, who was not at all happy to hear that things had heated up via a match to Emma's car.

When the laundry finished, Emma got dressed, and Constance escorted her out on a shopping trip, since her clothes were now a pile of ashes.

CHAPTER 19

Liz

I hadn't gotten to see Pat yesterday. He had been understandably busy taking care of his sister-in-law, but we had still exchanged texts, including his normal goodnight one about my dreams.

I had dreamed about him, but I didn't tell him that.

Ben, our terrible manager, wasn't at The Ironhorse when I showed up for the lunch shift. When I asked Louise about it, she said he hadn't been in last night either, but that was all she knew.

Lunch started with a bang as several large groups arrived shortly after opening. Luckily, I got the biggest one seated in my section. They were celebrating landing some big account, from what I overheard, and had brought big appetites. The man in charge ordered several bottles off the upper end of the wine list, which was unusual for lunch, but I was not complaining. The tip for this group was going to be a monster.

PAT: Call when you have time

I was gathering up salads to bring out when Tina came up.

"I hear carpenters really know how to work their tools," she said.

"Tina," I said in a hushed tone. I leaned in close and touched her shoulder. "Oh my God. Between the great hands, the big tool, and the tight fit, you were so right. You just have no idea." I went back to my table with a spring in my step.

Tina was speechless for once.

About halfway through my shift, I saw Ben come in, but he went directly to his office, which was fine by me. The less he was around the better, and I was too busy to worry about him anyway. As the end of my hours approached, I realized today's tips were about double my usual lunchtime total.

As my last lunch customer settled up, Louise found me. "Stay clear of Mr. Perham. He's in one hell of a mood today. Nearly bit my head off when I asked who was making the cash drop at the bank today."

"I'm not looking to talk to him," I assured her.

On my way back to the break room, I found Ben resetting the registers again. These new machines sure took a lot more looking after than the old one had. I'd turned to take the other way around when he called to me and told me to see him in his office. I cringed, then followed him to his cave.

He sat down behind his desk. He had a bandage on the side of his forehead, and rage wrote its ugly mark across his face. He eyed me, his gaze coming to rest on my chest. "Your boyfriend is not allowed in the restaurant any more, or even in the parking lot. Period."

I crossed my arms. I couldn't understand what Pat could have done to warrant this sudden banishment, and then it hit me. Pat had beat him up. I had told the brute I could handle it, but he had ignored me like the Neanderthal he was.

"And, Elizabeth, I'm going to have to rearrange your schedule," Ben continued. "You and Jennie are going to switch dinners and lunches on Tuesday and Thursday."

This can't be happening.

"But, Mr. Perham——"

"That's final." He was talking to my boobs again. The pervert couldn't hold eye contact.

My stomach tightened. "But I need those shifts, and I'm senior to Jennie." I wanted to tell him to stop staring at my boobs, but I needed this job too much.

"You talk back to me one more time and you're fired. Now get out of here, and don't come in tonight either."

A chill raced through me. I turned and left the office, crying.

How could Pat do this to me?

I walked right past Louise with watery eyes, gathered up my purse, and left.

I sat for a moment in my car, contemplating what had just happened. I tried to control my rapid breathing and calm down. There was no way fewer shifts and less money would work. I could try to get extra weekend catering work, but they didn't pay much. How could I tell Stacey? I banged on the steering wheel, but that hurt my hand more than the car.

My fingers trembled as I typed out the text.

ME: What did u do to my boss?

I waited for the reply, knowing that it wouldn't help.

PAT: Warned him to leave you alone

I shouldn't have bothered. It didn't help. Nothing could help me now. I had seen the fierceness in his eyes that first night he threatened to *warn* Russ. I had told him I could handle it. Now he had fucked it all up.

I blinked back my tears and turned the key, turning to look behind me as I backed out. I stopped.

Ben was walking through the parking lot, and he had Jennie with him. She got into his car.

The tramp.

But she wasn't the real problem. Things had been tolerable until Pat fucked it up for me. Pat was the problem. He didn't understand that he couldn't fix everything with his fists. I trembled with anger, and my fingernails dug into my palms. I wanted to scratch his eyes out right now. I closed my eyes and took a few deep breaths. It didn't help.

"You fucking asshole," I screamed in the empty car.

There were actually two assholes: my creepy boss, and the hothead who couldn't leave well enough alone. He just had to go and fuck up my life.

It seemed like forever before I felt in control enough to drive.

Fucking hothead.

I started my car. The fact that it turned over right away only reminded me that I owed Pat the money he'd paid to get it fixed. I owed money for Trent. I owed Pat. And now because of Pat, my tips were going to be shit.

Asshole.

If he had been a doctor or whatever, he wouldn't have done that. I told him I could handle it myself. Why hadn't he listened? Because he was a dumbass construction guy, not a college graduate with some sophistication——not a doctor, not a lawyer, not a cop or a fireman, or even a boring accountant for that matter. Just a dumbass bundle of muscles and fists with a pea brain. How did the saying go? *To a man with a hammer, every problem looks like a nail.*

Asshole with a fucking hammer.

I had never asked him, but he probably didn't even graduate from high school, just like Mike. Trent had graduated, but you couldn't tell it sometimes. High schools didn't have majors, but if they did, his would have been sweet-talking girls. He did it so well that I fell for him when I should've known better.

After Mike, I should have known better, and after Mike and Trent, I definitely knew better. I knew enough to make a rule, but I was stupid enough to ignore it.

When I got my DVM degree, Pat would still be swinging his hammer. I would be the brains, and he would be the brawn. Maybe I could have had coffee with Ben——gagging if I had to. Sometimes you just have to do unpleasant things to protect those around you.

I could do what I had to and take care of Stacey and Timmy.

Tires screeched.

A car honked.

I skidded to a stop, just barely avoiding an accident.

I shivered with fright.

My heart raced.

My hands trembled. I'd been so wrapped up in my misery, I hadn't paid attention to the road.

I started to breathe again and waved apologetically to the other driver. He flipped me the bird and mouthed much worse through his windshield.

I started again, watching the road this time. My hands still trembled as they held the wheel. I tried to swallow, but my throat was too dry. How much good would I be to Stacey and Timmy if I got killed on the road?

This was all Pat's fault, the A-hole.

No, it was my fault, too, for ignoring my rule. My rules kept me safe. I ignored them at my peril. This was just another lesson.

When I opened the front door, the house was as empty as I felt. Cold and empty. Timmy was at school, and Stacey wasn't home yet. A vase of flowers sat on the table. Candy walked up to rub against my leg. The dogs were out back.

More than a dozen red roses. I inspected the card. It was from Pat, hoping I felt better today.

He had no clue.

I checked the fridge and found a mostly full bottle of Chardonnay. Stacey had used a little for cooking last week. I poured a glass and parked the bottle on the coffee table, my butt in the couch.

I let the dogs in and turned on the DVR. *Judge Judy* was too serious. I choose *The Bachelor*. It was an episode I'd seen a long time ago. I finished my glass of wine and poured another. I wondered if it would take three or maybe four glasses for me to forget enough of the episode to make it worth watching again.

I decided three should do it and chugged my second glass, pouring another as the show started. The Bachelor had a double degree in accounting and supply chain management.

Now there was my kind of man: a professional with not one college degree, but two. Why couldn't I meet a man like that? Someone who didn't spend every Sunday getting drunk and yelling at the television, surrounded by a bunch of other morons swilling beer.

The bachelor was on a date with a beautiful blonde in a low-cut dress, showing a lot of cleavage, with nice jewelry, nice shoes, nice makeup.

My answer was obvious. She looked perfect, and I looked, well, at best normal. I wished I could be the girl on the show, having dinner with the good-looking professional guy with the two college degrees, nice manners, and a future——most of all, a future.

"Auntie Liz, Auntie Liz, wake up." It was Timmy jostling me awake.

"Let her sleep," Amy told him.

"But she'll be late for work if she doesn't wake up."

Work? I had fallen asleep on the couch. *The Bachelor* was still playing on the TV. My neck was sore.

"I don't have work tonight," I told Timmy. "But thank you for trying to help." I got up and stretched while Amy took him into the kitchen for some juice.

"Nice flowers," Amy noted. "Looks like you have an admirer."

"Had," I responded.

She didn't dig for any answers. It was nearly dinner time, and Stacey would be home soon.

I let Amy go while I fixed us something to eat. I found a package of chicken nuggets and some French fries in the freezer. One baking sheet into the oven, and dinner was cooking.

"And Jerry's big sister, she has a job walking people's dogs," Timmy told me as I was setting the table. "She gets rich doing it." He sipped on his juice. "I think I can be a dog walker when I'm older. Then I can make some money, and I can buy Mommy things. She says she gets the jobs with an app on her phone. That sounds cool, don't you think?"

Dog walking——now that might be an idea for bringing in more money. I had spare time during the day most days. I was responsible, I loved dogs, and they loved me.

Stacey arrived, and we all sat down to dinner, such as it was, and heard about Timmy's day in school. That was a good break from thinking about my shitty life and worrying about how I was going to pay the bills next month.

Dog walking?

After dinner, Stacey sent Timmy to do his homework, and we sat on the couch.

"Tell me about the problem, Liz," Stacey said, pointing to the empty wine bottle on the coffee table and the mostly empty glass. "You don't drink in the afternoon unless something is wrong."

She knew me.

I needed to vent. "It's Pat, and work, and… Pat beat up Mr. Perham."

Stacey perked up. "No shit? That's great. What did he do?"

"I don't know, I wasn't there. Mr. Perham came in late today, at the end of lunch, and called me into the office. He had a bandage on his head, and…"

"And what?"

"He told me that Pat hit him and wasn't allowed in the restaurant anymore."

"Well, that's no big deal, and it gets Mr. Creepy off your back."

I shuddered. I didn't know how to tell her how bad the money problem was going to get. I always sheltered her from that.

"Then he switched some of my dinner shifts to lunch and cut me back. He canceled my shift tonight." I started to sob. "This is really going to hurt my tips. Dinner is so much better than lunch."

"That ass," she said. Her eyes shared the rage I felt at Pat. "I'd like to give that asshole boss of yours an anatomy lesson with a dull scalpel."

"But you're missing the point, Stace. This happened because Pat went all Neanderthal and beat him up."

"So? Since when is it bad to have a boyfriend that sticks up for you? Huh?"

"He's not my boyfriend."

"The hell he's not. What about the flowers? Just like dinner the other night in Santa Monica was what we on Earth call a date. You can kid yourself all you want, Liz, but don't try to kid me. He's your boyfriend, and you like it."

I had liked it up until now. "But he's screwing up my life."

"So? Relationships are messy. Most girls would die for a guy like him. Maybe I'll call him if you don't want him."

She wouldn't do that.

"I saw the way he looked at you, Liz. He is hot for you. He likes kids, and he just gave your asshole boss what he deserved. If you don't see that as top-notch boyfriend material, you need your stupid head examined."

"I have to be responsible, and he's messing up my work."

"Then pick up a shift or two back at Olive Garden. They loved you there."

I hadn't considered the Olive Garden. It was a step back, but if I was willing to do dog walking, what the hell? I got up.

"I'm going to take a bath."

"Yeah, just run away like you always do."

"I do not."

"Do too. You ought to talk to him. You have a good thing going there."

I shut my bedroom door behind me.

*P*AT

WHEN I WALKED IN TO CARDINELLI'S, BILL'S RESTAURANT, KATIE and Emma were waiting for me at the table. Katie loved the food here, and it didn't hurt that she was Bill's little sister, so the staff treated her like royalty.

"Hey, Patrick, you didn't have to dress up for me," Katie said with a laugh.

I was wearing my Pat Patterson outfit. "Very funny, Katherine."

I got hugs from both of them.

"Where's your shadow?" I asked Emma.

She nodded toward the far wall. "I asked her to join us, but she said it wasn't protocol."

Constance stood guard against the wall at a table by herself, scanning the room and keeping a clear line of sight to the entrance. She was the consummate professional. Emma was in good hands.

Katie was swirling her glass and contemplating it, a trait that always indicated something was bothering her.

"We missed you at the Children's Hospital event on Saturday," Emma said.

Katie sighed. "Yeah, I know. I got stuck with a Saturday audit job in San Diego and got back late."

"That sucks," I lamented. Her job had terrible hours. Even worse recently than before.

"It's just the penance we all have to pay to get a CPA."

Katie was determined to get her CPA and strike out on her own. But the big firms pretty much controlled the route to getting certified. Not only did she have to have the degree and all the coursework in college, she had to pass five tests after that, which she had done, *and* get the firm to sign off on her practical experience hours.

"How much longer below decks?" Emma asked.

Below decks was the term Katie had coined for working as an indentured servant at the big accounting firm she'd joined. She likened the work to being a Roman galley slave, pulling the oars. While the partners enjoyed the fresh air on the top deck, the first- and second-year accountants did all the heavy lifting.

"'Till September roughly. Then I should get signed off and be able to apply. It can't come soon enough. I swear, this year I think they're going to lose even more of us second years than they expect, and my boss seems to have it in for me recently."

She'd told us before that only a few stayed at the firm past the second year in hopes of making it on the partner track.

"That's the Covington curse," I offered. "He's probably just jealous and wants to make an example of you, to show everybody he can't be bought or intimidated."

Katie contemplated her glass some more. "That's not it. He's just a pig."

I put my glass down. "He's not hitting on you, is he? That I can fix."

"Nothing like that," Katie said. "No, he just keeps piling more work on every day. I swear he's trying to get me to quit. Like I said, he just has it in for me for some reason."

Katie raised her glass in my direction. "To you and your new girl."

We all clinked glasses.

"Thanks for the pie. It was a real hit," I told Katie.

"When do I get to meet the mystery woman?" she asked. "I understand you had quite a date."

I stared at Emma. "Somebody's been spreading rumors."

"Don't blame me," Emma said. "You go to a family function undercover as a stealth date? I think that's romantic."

"It wasn't a date," I protested.

Our waiter arrived to take our orders, interrupting the inquisition for a minute.

Tony Soldano had been with the restaurant since Marco and Bill opened it. No matter where we sat, he was invariably our waiter. I had yet to find an evening when he wasn't here.

"Tony, how goes the search?" I asked.

"Slow. Still haven't found the right place yet, but I will."

Tony had been looking for a restaurant to buy or manage for months now. He had saved for years, and Marco was encouraging him to spread his wings. I thought he would do great.

My respite from the girls' interrogation ended as soon as Tony departed.

"So tell me about her." Katie asked.

"Just a girl I met after the last Habitat weekend."

Emma interrupted me. "You should have seen him. It was hilarious. He comes to the polo field dressed up like a security guy and follows her around like a little puppy dog."

"I did not," I protested.

Emma pointed her finger at me. "Did too, and at the end of the day, the valet guys told me he drove her home in Gordie Mossbacker's Ferrari when her car wouldn't start."

"Patrick," Katie said. "Please tell me you didn't sabotage her car so you could save the damsel in distress."

I put up my hands. "I'm innocent."

I was rescued by Tony returning with our meals.

Katie sipped her wine. "So what's the deal with the security getup then?"

I put a forkful of pasta in my mouth to avoid the question.

"I should let Patrick fill you in," Emma answered.

"It's like we were saying the other weekend," I said after chewing. "Once a girl hears my last name, I'm no longer me; I'm a Covington, a guy with money and a name, and well, it's just impossible to know how attracted she is to just me without the other stuff."

Katie's mouth gaped open. "So you just lie to her and expect to start a relationship that way? Are you crazy?"

My plan didn't sound so smart when Katie put it that way. "It's just until I'm sure it's me she's into."

Katie shook her head. "Patrick, you have your head up your ass."

"That's what we all told him," Emma agreed.

Katie stared at Emma. "So you knew about this?"

"He only told us after he'd started the charade. We just agreed to let him hang himself."

Katie finished another bite before renewing her attack. "Put me down as opposed. If this blows up in your face, don't come crying to me."

I waited for the next insult, but she seemed to be finished for the moment.

"Understood. I'm just sick of having the family name poison every relationship for me."

Katie waved her fork at me. "Have you ever stopped to think that maybe you have something to do with that?"

"Now what is that supposed to mean? Like, now it's my fault?"

Katie continued. "Patrick, you know you don't have the best reputation in town. The way you go through women like they're Kleenex and the way you flash your money around, showering them with gifts and expensive dates? Well, no wonder you attract the wrong kind of girl."

I swirled my wine in the glass and peered into the red liquid, hoping for inspiration, but a response was nowhere to be found.

We ate in silence for a few minutes as Katie let me stew.

"Look at your brothers. They found fine women without having to deny the Covington name," Katie said.

Emma smiled. We all knew she was a rare find, and Steven was a very lucky man to have her.

My fault, my ass. Katie has no idea what she's talking about.

I was done being beaten up by my sister, at least for this evening. "For right now, I'm still Pat Patterson," I told them firmly. "I'll tell her when the time is right."

Luckily for me, Emma wanted to get off the subject. "I feel safe right now, but I have to get back home to Steven," she said. "I can't just stick around here forever." She looked pained.

And she was right. The current situation was not sustainable. We had to solve this psycho Monica problem and get her back home.

CHAPTER 20

LIZ

AFTER A RELAXING BATH, I WAS READY TO JOIN THE WORLD AGAIN. Stacey was in front of the TV with another season of *Survivor*.

I joined her. My phone rang on the counter. I ignored it.

"Aren't you going to get that?" she asked.

"No, if it's work, I don't want to talk to them, and the same if it's Pat."

Stacey got up to check the phone anyway. "It's your boyfriend," she said with a smirk.

I scowled at her. "Not interested."

The ringing stopped.

The tribal council was voting. My phone rang again.

Stacey lunged for it and answered before I could stop her. "Hello? Liz's line... Who may I say is calling?" She handed the phone over to me, whispering "Blaine."

"Hello?" I said tentatively.

"*Is this Liz?*" he asked.

"Yes."

Stacey was giving me the evil eye, and she didn't bother to mute the television.

"This is Blaine from the charity event on Saturday. I hope I haven't caught you at a bad time."

"No, it's okay. Just give me a sec." I retreated to my bedroom for some privacy and to escape Stacey's accusatory stare. "I needed to get away from the noise. How are you?"

"Pretty busy at work, but otherwise fine. Look, I'm calling because I thought we might get together for dinner."

That shook me. I hadn't prepared an answer. "Sure, that would be nice. Something casual, if that's okay with you."

"No problem. How is tomorrow for you?"

My dinner shift for tomorrow had been canceled. "Tomorrow works. How about seven?" Starting late would keep it short.

"I'll pick you up at seven then."

Riding with a guy on the first date was a no-no for me, in case it didn't work out.

"You pick the place, and I'll meet you there," I said.

"And miss a chance to ride in my Ferrari? A gentleman drives a woman. Just tell me where to pick you up. Anyway, I want it to be a surprise." He was insistent.

Pat was the one who'd said I needed to face my fears head on. And it was a chance to ride in a Ferrari again, this time with the owner. "Okay."

"Where do you live?"

Somehow I wasn't prepared for that question either. "I have to check to see if we can get a babysitter for my nephew. I'll call you back in a bit."

Why was I skittish about taking this step? Was it that he was a lawyer and Pat had been so negative on lawyers?

I returned to the couch with Stacey, expecting an inquisition. I put the phone on the coffee table.

She didn't disappoint. "So?"

"He's just a guy I met on Saturday at the charity thing, a lawyer. I'm going to have dinner with him tomorrow."

"Where's he taking you?"

"Don't know yet."

"So quickly we forget. What about your dating rule number three? Never go out with a guy unless you know where he's taking you?"

I swallowed. She was right. I had screwed up. "I'll text you tomorrow when we get there. Is that okay, Mom?"

Stacey shook her head.

I dialed Blaine back from the couch. I wasn't going to let Stacey intimidate me.

"Okay, we've got a babysitter." I wasn't going to violate my rule number two, though. I gave him the address of The Ironhorse to pick me up instead of my home address. "See you at seven."

My first real date with a professional man——one with a stable job and a good income. One I wouldn't have to support or serve beer to on Sundays.

"I think you're making a mistake," Stacey said.

I ignored her. I was a grown woman, and I could do what I damned well pleased.

"You're making a mistake," she repeated.

My phone dinged again. She grabbed it before I could.

"Give me that."

The words had no effect on her. She giggled and handed me the phone.

PAT: Bet you dream about me again tonight

"I bet he's right too," she said.

I huffed and left. I didn't need any more abuse from my little sister. I slammed my bedroom door.

"I bet he's right," she yelled again from the other room.

I composed my reply.

Asshole Neanderthal.

P_{AT}

Later, back at the condo, I still hadn't gotten a call back from Liz, so I sent my standard text.

ME: Bet you dream about me again tonight

I didn't get a response for a few minutes.

LIZ: Don't call don't text don't come over

Something had gone wrong, but I had no idea what. This was not good.

ME: What's wrong?

That turned out to be the wrong approach.

LIZ: Leave me alone

My instinct was to drive over to talk to her, but Emma didn't want me to leave.

"Give her a day or two to cool off first. Maybe send her flowers," she advised.

I got online and arranged a delivery for tomorrow.

Why do women have to be so difficult?

CHAPTER 21

Liz

THE NEXT EVENING I HAD PICKED OUT A PALE PINK BLOUSE WITH A dark skirt and heels, and a thin white sweater for my dinner with Blaine. I didn't get to wear heels often because of work, so this was a treat. I went for some more makeup——mascara, eyeliner, a touch of blush, and just a hint of eye shadow. It was like playing dress up. Simple jewelry and I was done.

"Don't forget to text where you are, just to be safe," Stacey reminded me as I walked to the door. "I'll be on shift at Memorial, but you can reach me if you need to."

"Sure, Mom." I closed the door behind me.

Blaine pulled up to The Ironhorse a little early, but I was ready.

I had a twinge of angst, but it was too late now for second thoughts.

He was in a suit and tie, and his tie was pulled up, not loose the way so many men wore them after work. He looked nice.

"Bet you've never ridden in a Ferrari before, huh?"

I didn't want to hurt his feelings. "No."

His was yellow, instead of red, but to my uninformed eye, it was pretty similar to Pat's. Well, not Pat's, but the one Pat had driven me in.

"Wow, this is low."

Blaine made a show of peeling out.

"You might want to go a little…"

He turned the corner and hit the brakes. A high schooler was crossing the street with his dog.

I finished my sentence. "Slower around here."

He didn't say anything, probably upset that his showing off hadn't gone as planned. Why was it guys always hit the gas extra hard the first time they got a girl in a car? Maybe the noise was a testosterone rush or something.

The rest of the drive was uneventful because it was still the tail end of rush-hour traffic. A sleek yellow Ferrari didn't go any faster than a rusty yellow Chevy in LA traffic. Kids on skateboards were passing us on the sidewalk.

Blaine wore quite a bit of cologne, and the scent wasn't particularly appealing. I cracked my window for a little fresh air. *Pat doesn't wear cologne.*

We eventually parked, and Blaine walked me into the restaurant——not any restaurant, but Le Papillon Bleu, one of the most expensive places in the LA basin. Nobody with my kind of income could afford to eat at a place like this. I'd checked out the menu once. It ran about two hundred per person once you added wine, and they had quite a wine list.

We passed a wall with multiple Forbes five-star plaques on it, seemingly one for every year.

"This is your idea of casual dining?"

He smiled. "I thought I'd take you to a place you hadn't been before."

This would be a good opportunity for me to see how the elite competition operated, beyond the fact that they probably put an extra zero at the end of all the prices. Given that there were only about a half dozen Forbes five-star restaurants in all of California, this was going to be a great meal.

"You're right. This will be my first time. You've been here before?"

"Pretty regularly. It's one of only three places I frequent," he said. "I only eat where I can get Aglianico with dinner."

I cast him a quizzical glance.

He explained that Aglianico was believed to be the oldest cultivated variety of wine grapes. "It's the variety of grape that was used to make wine for the Roman emperors."

Great, a snob. Strike one.

I texted Stacey while we waited to be seated and put my phone on silent.

When our table was ready, they required us to drop our phones in a metal box outside the dining room. The maître d' closed the lid to the box before he showed us to our table.

"The box blocks the signals so the phones won't ring and disturb us during dinner," Blaine explained.

Pretty sophisticated, but not a policy we would want at The Ironhorse. It would probably drive half the customers away.

The room was small compared to The Ironhorse, but it had to be hard to fill a room at the insane prices they charged.

Before I could pick something, Blaine pulled the menu from my hands and folded it on top of his. He seemed to have decided I wasn't capable of picking my own food. When the waiter came over, he made a point of ordering without opening the menu, trying to impress me by having it memorized. In French no less.

Strike two.

When the wine came, it was quite good.

He started to tell me about his day, with a voice lacking emotion. When he smiled, there were no dimples and it lacked something, or perhaps it just looked forced. There was something odd about him that I couldn't quite place. Something artificial.

Something hidden. His sleeve rode up as he took a drink from his water. He had a tattoo on his wrist.

"What's the story with the ink?" I asked.

He pulled his sleeve up a little farther to show me the tattoo.

"BW," he said. "My sister and I got drunk——a little too drunk ——down in Mexico. We were both going to get our initials tattooed on our wrists. It seemed cool at the time. But when it was her turn, the margaritas had worn off, and she backed out." He laughed.

He asked if I had any tattoos.

I told him I'd never had the urge. "Tell me about your family," I suggested. "You said you have a sister?"

"Yeah, and also a brother out east. Long line of lawyers in the family. My father was a lawyer, my sister's a lawyer here in LA, and my other brother is a lawyer out in Boston. It just runs in our genes."

I told him about Stacey and Timmy, but didn't go in to my parents.

A short while later, he asked about the Covingtons.

I told him I didn't know them well.

That didn't stop him from continuing to ask for some reason. He thought I was being coy. He had seen me with them at the polo grounds and had obviously mistaken their friendliness for closeness.

I found his repeated questions annoying. Some people were just overly interested in rich people, which sort of explained the Kardashians. I tried to turn the conversation by asking him to tell me more about what he did for a living.

That helped for a while until I remembered Pat's two categories of lawyers. It was clear Blaine was in the shifty category since he handled criminal defense.

"But what if your client is really guilty?" I asked.

"Look, I'm not Santa. It's not my job to figure out who's been naughty or who's been nice."

Strike three, the morals of a snake.

The dinner improved when the food arrived. It was tasty, but sparse. They were quite minimalist here when it came to portions, although the presentation of the food was the best I had ever seen. The food kept Blaine busy as he both ate and made a point of explaining the meal, as if elegant French cuisine was beyond someone like me.

Strike four.

I shouldn't have, but I found myself comparing him to Pat. He wasn't winning. Not even close. Maybe he was the kind of guy that grew on you. I could hope. Maybe I was being too harsh.

When he suggested for the second time that he would take me back to his place for an after-dinner drink, I knew this had been a mistake.

The first time he'd said it, I'd laughed it off as a joke, but now it was obvious he was serious. I should have driven. I shouldn't have violated my dating rule.

Strike five.

"This was a mistake. I'm not ready for this," I said as I folded my napkin and stood.

"Sit. I'll drive you home."

"No thanks, I'll call a ride."

His mouth gaped open. He was apparently not accustomed to being told no.

I turned and left, retrieving my phone from the little metal box on the way to the door.

He was trying to get the waiter's attention as the door closed behind me.

The app told me there were lots of Ubers nearby. I typed in the address of The Ironhorse, and one arrived right away.

A little green Prius pulled up at the curb, and I got into the backseat.

The short girl behind the wheel greeted me cheerfully. She looked like she was barely out of high school.

Blaine exited the restaurant just as we pulled away from the curb, a shocked look on his face.

I turned away and didn't bother to wave.

I was safe in this little steel cocoon.

THREE INTERSECTIONS LATER, WE HIT A RED LIGHT.

A yellow Ferrari pulled up next to us, and the driver grinned at me through the window.

Blaine.

He motioned for me to open the window.

I almost peed in my pants. I looked straight ahead, pretending I hadn't seen him, but it was too late. I was shivering.

A chill rolled through me, all the way to my toes. The young girl driving me wouldn't be any help. Once she dropped me at The Ironhorse, Blaine could follow me and find out where I lived, where Stacey and Timmy were too. This was full-on, red-alert bad. What could I do?

I'm so fucked.

I had no other choice.

My fingers trembled as I selected his contact. I hesitated before pressing the phone number.

"Hi, Buttercup."

I composed myself as best I could. My throat was so dry I could barely speak. "Are you home?" I squeaked out.

"I'm out. What's up?"

"I need your help." Understatement of the year.

"Anything for you."

I gulped. "I'm being followed, and I'm afraid to go home."

My statement caused my driver to start checking her mirrors, and she threw a concerned look my way in the rear-view mirror.

"Where are you now?" he asked instantly.

I was cold. I gathered my sweater around me. "In an Uber, northbound on the freeway before the hill."

"*Turn around. Go to my house. I can be there in ten minutes. Don't let the driver stop for anything, and I mean anything.*"

"Okay, let me call you back in a minute."

I hung up. "We need to change the drop off," I told the young girl.

Serious concern tinged my driver's voice. "Followed? What's going on?"

I did my best to calm her down. "Just a guy I don't want to talk to." I worked the app on my phone again to cancel the ride and request another, to Pat's address this time.

Her phone buzzed in its holder. "So now you want to go south?" she asked, squinting at the display.

I assured her I'd entered the right place, and she exited the freeway to reverse course. I looked back, and Blaine's yellow car followed us off the exit.

I called Pat back. "We're on the way. I'm in a green Prius Uber."

My driver seemed more nervous by the minute.

Pat assured me he would be there and ready for me. He told me to wait by the front door. He would be on the street to talk to my pursuer. I didn't tell him it was Blaine.

We made it uneventfully to Myrtle Street, and my driver pulled up at Pat's little house. The poor girl was about at the end of her rope; she might not stay an Uber driver for long. The Prius left in a hurry the instant I closed the door.

I ran up to the front door. I didn't see Pat anywhere, but I tried the knob and it was unlocked, just as Pat had said it would be. I stood by the door, shaking.

Pat, where are you?

I froze and nearly shit in my pants when Blaine came to a screeching halt in front of the house.

⌇

PAT

I HADN'T HEARD FROM LIZ SINCE THE TEXT TO LEAVE HER ALONE last night. My heart pounded as I hung up the phone, grabbed my jacket, and announced to Emma and Winston that Liz needed me. I refused Emma's offer to come along and left her behind at my condo.

I was in Phil's truck two minutes later and pushing it to the limit on my way back to Myrtle Street.

A minute later, my phone lit up with Liz's bright face on the display. I put it on speaker.

"*We're on the way. I'm in a green Prius Uber,*" she told me.

I floored it through the intersection as the light turned yellow. "Just go up to the front door and wait when you get there. I'll be out front, but I don't want you anywhere near the street. Got it? The door will be open. Go inside if he stops anywhere near the house."

She told me she understood as I rounded the corner a few blocks from the house.

I parked in front of the neighbor's lot, leaving room for her ride to drop her off in front of my house, and waited. I tried to slow my breathing. I had made it in time. But I was more jittery than at the beginning of a judo match.

Her Uber arrived a few minutes later and instantly sped off. Liz ran up to the door and waited.

I crouched down in the seat of the truck.

Right behind her, a yellow Ferrari stopped at my house. The driver climbed out and rounded the back of his car.

That was my cue. I climbed down from the truck and closed the distance between us with a few quick strides, balling up my fists. It was the scrawny-ass fucking lawyer from Saturday.

"I know you. You're Blaine Willey, the scumbag lawyer that stalks defenseless women."

He took a step back.

I spit on the stupid yellow car.

"Do I know you?" Willey asked, stepping back again. The fear in his voice was palpable.

I advanced on him. "I know you, and that's all that matters, dirtbag."

He backed up and shrank another few inches, if that was possible.

"That's my girlfriend you're chasing halfway across town, you little shit. I'm gonna cut off your pathetic little dick and feed it to you." I kicked his car.

The little dickhead ran around the Ferrari, mumbling he'd sue me if I laid a hand on him.

What a pathetic excuse for a threat. Only a motherfucking lawyer would say something so dumb.

He dove into his car and slammed the door.

I jumped to the sidewalk as he left, flipping me the bird out his window.

If he came back, I would reward him with a serious need for emergency dental work, the fucking little prick.

I looked up and saw that Liz had forgotten to go inside when he drove up.

"That's one scrawny little slimeball that won't be bothering you again," I called to her.

I found her trembling terribly as I hugged her. "Buttercup, you're shaking like a leaf." I chastised her for not going inside and following the plan.

She merely nodded and pulled herself into me.

CHAPTER 22

LIZ

PAT COMFORTED ME WITH A TIGHT HUG AFTER USHERING ME INSIDE.
"What was he doing following you at this time of night, anyway?"

I cringed. "He took me to dinner."

His sigh clearly indicated disappointment. His finger lifted my
chin as he held my eyes.

Tosca was trying to shove her nose between us to sniff me once
again.

"You have shit for brains, girl? I told you lawyers only come in
two flavors, boring and slimy."

Most guys would have yelled at me. Pat merely made fun of
my giant fuck-up.

"You said shifty," I corrected him.

"Slimy, shifty——same difference. They're all worthless." He
pulled me tighter and whispered into my ear. "You should know
better, Buttercup."

His embrace had calmed my jitters and now heated me up in all
the wrong places. I had to remind myself that this was the man

who had personally destroyed my finances by beating up my boss, right when I needed the money the most. I had only called him because I didn't have any other alternatives. I couldn't lead Blaine to my house and put Timmy and Stacey in danger.

"I'm sorry, I didn't know what else to do…"

He put a finger to my lips. "Hush, Buttercup. You did exactly the right thing——not the dinner with a scumbag lawyer part, but the calling me part." He kissed my forehead.

In the same circumstances, Trent would have been mad, and Mike, well, he would have been even worse. He would have found a way to call Blaine back and hand me over for the insult to his pride.

Pat released me and took off his jacket, laying it over the back of a chair. "Why don't you sit down for a minute."

"No." I didn't want to stay. "I need to go."

"Sit down. It seems like you owe me again."

Last time it had cost me two dinners. "No, I will not sit down. A gentleman wouldn't ask for anything in return for helping a lady out of a jam."

"Why does everything with you have to be such a battle? Want me to call the blood-sucking lawyer friend of yours back here?"

"You wouldn't dare." Had I given him credit for being better than Trent or Mike a little too quickly?

"No, I wouldn't. Because I'm a gentleman, and a gentleman wouldn't place a lady in such obvious danger. The slimy fucker would probably have had you chained naked in his basement by now if I hadn't saved your ungrateful ass."

I cringed. He might be right about the basement part. And he was absolutely right that I was being an ungrateful bitch.

"Sorry."

I took off my sweater and laid it on top of his coat. As much as I didn't want to, I did owe him big time. Whatever he made me do had to be better than the alternative of being with Blaine right now. Reluctantly, I went over to him.

"Okay, so what do you want?" I dreaded his response. Mike would have had me on my knees right now, unzipping his fly.

His eyes pierced me. "Buttercup." He pulled me closer, grasping my shoulders. "I want you to do what I ask tonight without arguing."

I nodded silently. What choice did I have?

"And I want you to listen." He spun me around. "You can start by cooking us dinner."

"But I already ate," I shot back before I realized how bitchy it sounded.

"Is this you not arguing? Cuz you suck at it."

I opened the fridge. "Yes, master. I take it you didn't eat yet?"

"Barely a bite before you called."

"What would you like me to fix?" I managed a civil tone.

"Whatever the chef desires." He was infuriatingly polite.

I located asparagus and some grated parmesan cheese that would do for a vegetable. I turned the oven up to 400.

"Do you have any olive oil and spices?"

"Boxes in the pantry."

The pantry contained a half dozen cardboard boxes filled with spices and all the miscellaneous pantry items a well-stocked kitchen needed.

"Still unpacking or don't plan to stay long?" I asked.

He got up, grabbed the asparagus, and started washing them. "I just brought those over, and I've been a little preoccupied with this one infuriating blonde." He snapped the stalks of the asparagus and set them down.

I wasn't settling for one backhanded compliment. "So your Neanderthal brain can't handle two things at once?"

He glared back at me. "What is your problem anyway?"

I located the olive oil and greased a baking sheet for the oven. He knew perfectly well what he'd done.

I pointed my finger at him and sniffled. "You."

I pulled chicken breasts out of the refrigerator.

A look of puzzlement clouded his face. "And what does that mean?"

I pulled a knife from the block and opened the package of chicken. I waved the knife at the ceiling. "You fucked up my life is all." I sliced two chicken breasts into thin filets, tears pricking my eyes.

"Well, pardon me for answering your call and breaking up your wonderful lawyer date tonight."

"Not that."

I was in danger of losing it, thinking about everything that was going wrong. Tears welled in my eyes.

I put down the knife and gave it to him with both barrels. "You waltz into my life and treat me so nice that I break my dating rule. Then you fuck up my life so I can't pay my bills," I yelled. Tears rolled down my cheeks. "I'm going to be late with the rent, and I won't be able to pay Stacey's tuition bill, all because you have to go all Rambo on my boss." I sobbed.

My predicament sounded even worse when I said it all out loud.

Pat approached with his hands out.

I pulled back. "Don't touch me," I warned him.

He ignored me and grasped my shoulders.

I tried to squirm away, but he held me firmly. "Look at me."

I looked down and sniffled. I considered kneeing him in the balls, but I had no car outside to escape with.

He held me firmly before pulling me in and hugging me. "I can fix this," he said. "Whatever you think it is, I can fix it."

I hated that he was the cause of my troubles. Being in his embrace with him saying those things made me feel so protected. I should have been enraged.

"What? You going to beat him up again?" I tried to push away, but he held me.

He rocked us side to side, like a slow dance. He whispered in my ear. "Buttercup, we need to talk. Things aren't the way they seem. I didn't beat up your perverted boss. I went to warn him to leave you alone. He got so scared he backed into a curb and fell down. I didn't lay a hand on him."

"You didn't hit him?" I asked.

Ben hadn't actually said that Pat hit him. I'd just assumed so from the bandage on his head and his banishing Pat from the restaurant.

Pat kissed the top of my head. "Of course not. I don't hit people, remember?" He continued to rock us back and forth. "Liz, I promise you, this will be fixed in a week or two."

I had no idea how he could fix anything with Ben in a week or even a month. "But I saw you beat up that biker."

"I didn't hit him, though. We talked about this. He came at me, and I defended myself. I just made sure he hit the ground hard enough to regret it. Now, will you settle down and listen if I let you go?"

I sniffled and nodded.

He stepped back, lifted his shirt, and pulled down the waistband of his jeans. He took my hand and placed it on the side of his stomach. "You see this scar right here?"

I ran my fingers over the ridge of scar tissue. It was over an inch long and quite distinct. It sat just below belt level, which is why I hadn't seen it at the pool.

"I haven't hit anybody since I got this."

I waited for him to continue as I traced the outline of the ridge on his warm skin.

"A few years ago, my brother Steven and I were called to rescue a friend's sister. A bunch of bad dudes had her almost naked when we got there. Any later and it would have been really bad for her."

I shuddered. "My God."

"We got her out of there safely, but in the process, Steven and I beat a few of the guys to a pulp. Steven broke one guy's arm, and I put another in the hospital in a coma. He came out of it okay about a week later, but it was scary for a while thinking I'd almost killed the guy."

I pulled my hand back. I had been rubbing his scar this whole time.

"Steven got convicted of assault."

"That's not fair."

"The guy with the broken arm turned out to be the brother of a cop, and when the police arrived, they took his word over ours. Anyway, the conviction nearly ruined Steven's life, and the only reason I didn't get the same treatment was this wound." He touched his scar. "When the guy stabbed me, it made it pretty hard for them to say I was the aggressor."

I nodded silently, taking the story in.

He put his shirt back down. "That's why I stick with judo now. I won't hit anymore. I'll use judo to defend myself if I have to. I find that most of these creeps like your lawyer boyfriend or your fucking boss are cowards, and if I come on strong enough, loud enough, and crazy enough, they just back down, and I avoid a fight. It worked with two of the bikers at the fundraiser."

The Neanderthal I had pictured him to be was morphing into a strong, thoughtful protector.

"I didn't beat up your boss," he said again. "Anyway, I'll get this all straightened out. Just give me a little time and trust me. If I don't have it fixed in two weeks, then you can be mad at me. Okay?"

I nodded. I still had to process all this, and dinner wasn't making itself.

"Let's get you fed." I went back to the kitchen island.

"Us. I'm having dinner with my girl."

"Is that what I am? I thought I was just someone who owed you something." I regretted how bitchy that sounded as soon as I said it.

"You really suck at not arguing, don't you? Are you going to be obstinate and deny that you want to have another dinner with me?"

My smile gave away my answer as I started fixing the chicken.

Pat opened a bottle of wine, and we drank while preparing the food.

After some flour, eggs, breadcrumbs, pizza sauce, olive oil, and cheese, I was ready to put my interpretation of chicken parmesan and roasted asparagus in the oven.

He located some fettuccine and heated water for the pasta. He brought some wood in from the back and lit a fire in the old brick fireplace. Evidently he hadn't checked the chimney, so the first few minutes gave us a smoke-filled room before he got the flue properly opened.

The place lacked smoke detectors, which kept it quiet, but he said he would get that changed.

"You know you're going to smell this smoke for a month," I told him.

He shrugged. "I should have checked." He opened a few windows, and the slight breeze had the smell mostly under control by the time the meal was ready.

We finished off the first bottle of wine and opened a second. Pat turned off all but one of the lights, and we sat down to our fireside dinner. The flickering light played on his face and in his eyes as we started to eat.

Tosca positioned herself at our feet, waiting for scraps.

This was so totally unlike the earlier part of my evening with Blaine. Pat was so natural and unassuming and kind with his words and questions. He had me talking the whole time——explaining my desire to be a vet, how we had accumulated so many pets, and how I wanted to start a ranch for retired horses.

"So when Mom passed away, I took a leave from UC Davis and got whatever jobs I could. Without a degree, waitressing seemed to be the best fit hours and income wise if I could get into a place with good enough tips. When I moved from the Olive Garden to The Ironhorse, it helped a lot, and Stacey was able to enroll full time so she can finish sooner."

"Go on," he encouraged me.

"The plan is for her to finish this year, and with the nursing shortage, she should be able to get a job right away. With two of us working full time, we should be able to save enough for me to go back to Davis a year after that and finish up. I'm hoping my scholarship comes through to make it easier."

"Very impressive, Doctor Turner."

"Not yet. I still have a lot of school to go."

We opened another bottle of wine and moved to the couch.

I shook off my shoes and nestled in next to him. It was warm and comfortable leaning in to him, his arm draped over my shoulder. The wine was getting to me. I started to draw circles on his thigh with my finger.

"Tell me more about this horse retirement ranch idea," he said as he stroked my hair.

I took another sip.

~

P*AT*

SHE CONTINUED TO STROKE MY THIGH, MAKING IT ALMOST impossible to stay the gentleman. My cock was so hard it hurt, trapped in its denim prison.

"When we were little girls, Mom and Dad leased a horse for us," Liz explained. "Well, really he was a Welsh pony. We couldn't afford to buy a horse, much less two, so Stacey and I shared the pony for two years. His name was Tigr. He wasn't as well behaved as he should have been, but that's just how ponies are. We learned to ride, and we had the most wonderful time."

Liz stopped and swallowed the last of her glass. She was beaming, with misty eyes. "Those were two of the best years of my life, I think."

I poured us both some more wine.

"Have you ever ridden?" she asked.

"No. As boys we rode dirt bikes, but not horses."

She cuddled up to me. The wine was obviously getting to her.

"Anyways, Tigr was a great little pony, but at the end of the second year, Mom couldn't afford to lease him again, so we stopped riding. He was getting old, and the family we leased him from couldn't afford to put him out to pasture, so they sold him." She started to sob.

I pulled her in tighter to comfort her.

"Later," she managed, her voice cracking, "we found out the man that bought Tigr sold him to a Mexican packing plant." Liz started to cry uncontrollably.

"That's terrible." All I could do was hold her as she worked through the pain.

"So I want…" She sniffed. "To provide an affordable place for some of these horses to retire, so they don't end up like Tigr. You have no idea how hard it is for the owners of these horses to find a good place to retire them. And if I can give a hundred or so a good place to live out the rest of their lives in comfort, that's what I want to do. Along with being a vet."

Liz truly cared. Her passion was palpable, and her motivation so noble it hurt just to think about it. She didn't deserve the shitty hand life had dealt her——losing her parents and having to deal with that crap boss of hers screwing up her life.

"I gotta pee," she announced.

On her trip back from the bathroom, it became apparent how drunk she was. She wobbled her way to the couch and grabbed the bottle to pour another glass of wine, but I withdrew her glass before she got the chance.

"Hey, I want another," she complained.

"Looks to me like we've had enough for tonight."

I got up and took the glasses to the sink. I turned around to see her chugging directly from the bottle and finishing it off.

"I had such a shitty day. I deserve this."

No doubt that was true, but she was clearly past her limit. She held on to the back of the couch for support before settling back into it.

"Got another bottle? Thas good stuff."

"Bar's closed for the night, Buttercup," I told her and went to use the bathroom myself.

I returned to find her holding my bottle of Red Label and working on a glass of the scotch.

"I can't leave you for a minute," I said.

She finished it before I reached the couch.

I snatched the glass away.

Looking at what remained in the bottle, it seemed she had poured more than one shot. This was not good.

"How much did you have?"

She held up two fingers. Her eyes were heavy and her movements sluggish. She raised a third and then a fourth. She slouched back into the couch.

"You're going to regret this in the morning, Buttercup." I took the scotch and put it up on a shelf in the kitchen that I hoped would be beyond her reach.

"Nope, I don't get hangovers." She slumped down farther.

I sat down with her.

"I think you're hot," she said.

"You're drunk."

"Juss a little."

She was certainly drunk enough to be off limits. It was my fault for not cutting her off earlier.

"I still think you're hot." She leaned over and cuddled against me, putting my resolve to the test. I wanted her so badly I ached. At least she wasn't stroking me anymore.

"Does Mr. Happy want to play?" she asked.

My cock was stiff as a board. I ignored her question. I held her and stroked her hair and her shoulder as we watched the fire.

Her breathing slowed, and a few minutes later she was out. At least she wasn't a mean drunk.

I laid her down on the couch as I got the bed ready and pulled down the covers. I returned and picked her up as gently as I could, supporting her head. She was completely out of it. When I got her to the bed, I pulled off her skirt and blouse. The sight of her in the black lace panties and bra nearly sent me over the edge. I folded her clothes on the bureau and pulled the covers over her.

She snorted a few times. She was out cold.

I grabbed a pillow off the bed and a comforter from the closet, turned off the lights, and closed the door as I left.

The fire was dying down. I took Tosca out for a minute before I shed my shoes and turned off the lights. I wasn't meant to sleep on this couch. It was too short for me to fit. I cursed myself for letting Liz drink so much tonight and ruining my chance to sample all she wanted to offer me.

An hour or so later, unable to get any sleep, I gave in. I got up and opened the door to the bedroom.

She was breathing evenly and peacefully.

I closed the door behind me, stripped down to my boxer briefs, and then removed those too. I had slept in the nude forever. I could never get used to the elastic waistband strangling an overnight hard-on.

I slipped under the covers with my girl.

CHAPTER 23

Liz

I WOKE IN THE MIDDLE OF THE NIGHT WITH AN URGENT NEED TO pee. I slipped off the side of the bed, disoriented. The floor was cold. I shivered lightly and scraped my shoulder against a wall that shouldn't have been there. I forced my legs together to keep from leaking and rubbed my eyes. I looked around. Only the dim red numerals of the digital clock illuminated the room. Three-thirty in the morning. The large shape under the covers could only be a man in my bed. I found the entrance to the bathroom and went.

My memory was more than a little foggy, but I recalled getting to Pat's place. I'd been drinking——a lot, if the dry mouth and fur coating on my tongue meant anything. I couldn't recall anything after that.

Feeling my way around the wall that had attacked me earlier, I found my way back to the bed. It wasn't mine.

I'm sleeping in Pat's bed.

We'd been eating and talking and drinking, and I must have

fallen asleep. Clearly, Pat had put me to bed. I didn't sleep in a bra, or panties for that matter.

I shed the underwear. I managed to slip back into bed without waking Pat. I couldn't see him clearly.

Slowly it came back to me. My anger with Pat, believing he'd beaten up Ben and screwed up my life. That conclusion had seemed so right at the time.

I got a sour taste in my mouth recalling my idiot move of accepting the dinner invitation from that pervert Blaine. I shivered as the close call came back to me. I almost hadn't made it to safety. Some of the horrible ways it could have worked out buzzed around in my brain like an angry swarm of bees. I shivered. What if I hadn't seen him following, and he had followed me all the way home? What if Pat hadn't been here to scare him off?

Pat had been so understanding; he'd only worried about me. How could I have been such an idiot? Probably because I didn't know any better, because my previous boyfriends had taught me to expect the worst from them, rather than the best. Pat was different.

Was he a boyfriend? The way I'd treated him the last few days didn't make me very good girlfriend material.

The scar.

When he had shown me his scar and explained how it happened, how unfairly he and his brother had been treated, I'd felt awfully bad. He had been a hero that day, just as he was last night. Pat came from good stock, as Mom would have said.

I'd gotten drunk, really drunk. Now I remembered coming on to him, telling him how hot he was. It had always worked before, but not last night. What had I done wrong? Maybe I should have rubbed his crotch or undone his belt or something. He could have taken advantage of me——I had wanted it——but instead this dumb, broke carpenter had to be a gentleman.

It was the lawyer in the expensive suit, taking me to the expensive restaurant in his expensive car, who had been the sleazeball.

I had gotten everything backwards, but I could fix that.

I moved closer, careful not to wake him, not to touch him. Not yet. My nostrils caught the slight scent of spice and pine in his hair. It was Pat. I wasn't cold anymore, but my nipples were hard, and I was covered in goosebumps. The electric feel of being naked this close to him had me tingly.

I lifted my hand and slid it very lightly over his stomach. I moved my fingers down through the curls and found my prize. Not hard, but warm and soft.

"Hey," he said, waking up.

"Hey." I squeezed lightly. My prize was waking as well. I shifted myself and dove under the sheets to take him in my mouth.

"What are you doing?" he asked through the darkness.

"Saying," I said as I sucked the tip between my lips. "Thank you."

Then I took the whole length of him. My tongue played over him. I could fit him at this stage, but he was growing by the second. I released my lip lock on his cock to lick one hairy ball and then the other as my hand pulled and tugged.

He massaged my scalp as his breath hitched.

I licked around the tip several times, sucking briefly and licking again.

He had already grown too large for me to take all of him in my mouth again.

I licked his length from the crown down to the root and back again, his soft moan telling me how it felt.

He reached for my breast.

I released my hand from his cock and swatted him away. It was my turn to be in charge.

"No," I mumbled, taking a mouthful of cock as deep as I could.

He tried again to reach for me, but I shifted myself farther away. He gave up and went back to massaging my scalp with his fingertips, moving with the sway of my head.

I smacked my lips as I came off of him and ran my tongue in slow circles around the crown of his throbbing cock. I stroked him with both hands, back and forth, his pulsing thickness alive in my fingers. I ran my tongue down his length again, stopping at his balls. I lifted one and took it gently in my hand, rolling it around with my tongue while continuing to stroke him with my other hand.

My drenched pussy clenched as I yearned for his touch, but denied myself. I released his ball, and with two hands on his shaft, my mouth took his tip and I started to pump up and down.

I grasped tighter with my hands, moving in harmony with my mouth in and out, twisting with my hands on each stroke.

He was losing control. His muscles had tensed, and he gasped for air.

As I was furiously pumping his cock, licking and sucking, I almost lost my mind anticipating how this was going to feel inside me. I held him deeply in my mouth and hummed as my tongue caressed him.

His grip on my hair tightened.

With a thumb and forefinger, I took a vise grip hold on the root and slowly pulled him from my mouth, blowing air on his tip as it emerged from my lips. I let go of my prize and moved up to straddle him. Once atop him, I rested my hands on his shoulders and ran my saturated folds over his length, finally getting friction where I needed it.

He moved to caress my breasts, thumbing my hardened nipples, sending short little shocks through me as he pinched them in rhythm with me sliding myself over his length and back.

I maneuvered my sensitive clit over the tip of his cock, back and forth, sending shivers of excitement through me.

He pulled me down closer to kiss my breasts and run his tongue around my nipples, blowing cool air on the tender flesh. I continued to work myself into a frenzy, rubbing against him as he lavished his attention on one breast then the other.

In an instant, he flipped us over.

He ground his shaft over my clit as he nipped at my neck and shoulder. He surprised me again as he moved down between my legs.

I tried to clamp my legs together, but it was no use, he was determined and too strong. I didn't know what to expect. I was scared. I hadn't showered. What if I disgusted him? Neither Mike nor Trent had ever shown any interest in going down on me. I was afraid I wasn't clean enough. I speared my fingers in his hair and tried to push his head away.

His tongue delved the length of my folds, parting my inner lips, reaching my clit, and circling the engorged bud. His stubble scratched against my thighs as he moved.

I wasn't prepared for the sensations as he started his oral sorcery on my defenseless clit. I hadn't understood how good this could be. Now instead of pushing him away, I pulled at his hair for even more.

He pulled away slightly.

I urged him back, but was surprised as a finger entered me and found the sensitive spot he had showed me before. I moaned and my back arched up involuntarily as he massaged my G-spot.

As quickly as it had appeared, he withdrew his finger, and his tongue resumed torturing me. He moved the finger up to my mouth.

Once again my aroma filled my nostrils.

He pressed the fingertip on my lips, and I took it in, licking and sucking the wetness off. This seemed to be his thing, and it was hot as hell. It took my desire to a higher level.

Gripping his hair, I rocked my hips into him and spread my thighs wider to give him more access. As the sensations became unbearable, my panting and yelping became short and shallow. With little notice, my toes curled and the brilliant fire overtook me. Spasms of built-up tension rocked me, and I couldn't contain the screams that escaped my lips. I was afraid I might hurt him as my convulsing thighs gripped his head. Slowly, the relaxation came, and I released my death grip on him.

As my legs fell away, he moved up and kissed me gently, laying his heavy member on my abdomen. The taste was me, mingled with an aftertaste of him.

He rolled over and fumbled at the nightstand. The sound of the foil packet being torn open revealed what he had found.

I waited expectantly as he sheathed himself.

Without a word he rolled me over.

I pulled my knees up under me and poked my butt up, my face planted against the pillow, my pussy pounding with anticipation. He positioned himself behind me and forced my legs apart. In a moment he was pushing inside me, filling me to the limit.

"My God, you're wet," he said as he slowly pushed in. "You're so fucking tight, so fucking good," he hissed as he thrust into me.

I was drowning in a sea of desire. I wanted him to feel good, great, even better than great. The orgasms he'd given me had been so unbelievable, I wanted to repay him in any way I could. I matched his rhythm, rocking back against him as he speared me deeply. His balls swung forward against my clit with each powerful thrust. I reached back between my legs to tickle them as they moved.

He slowed his pace and pushed my legs together, removing my hand and putting his knees outside of mine.

I thought his incredible tongue work had emptied my pleasure reservoir, but I was wrong. He was so far inside me, and filled me so completely, that each thrust moved me to a higher plane. As the tension built again, I approached the cliff.

His firm grip on my hips pulled me against him with each slap of flesh against flesh as he pounded into me. My toes curled, and he moved a hand to my breast and pinched my nipple. Like a rubber band that had been pulled too far, I snapped, and he sent me once again over the cliff into a sea of rapture.

I screamed into the pillow as my inner flesh tightened around him with my convulsions. After several more hard thrusts, he stiffened, groaned, and lifted up, pulling my hips tightly against him, finding his release with a final trembling push.

We fell forward, and he moved his chest off to the side to spare me his full weight. His cock continued to throb inside me, thrilling me.

After a few minutes of cuddling, stroking my hair, and kissing me, my man went to the bathroom to dispose of the condom. He returned to bed, and I draped my arm over his chest, my head on the pillow of his shoulder, my breasts pressed up against his warmth, our hearts beating as one. I fell asleep with my man.

∼

P*AT*

THE BIG PICKUP HAD A BENCH SEAT, AND LIZ HAD SNUGGLED UP TO me in the middle for the ride to drop her off at her car this morning. The warmth of her next to me made the whole drive worthwhile.

I made it back to the Covington Industries building in plenty of time to catch Uncle Garth before his morning meeting. He was just the man to help me.

My phone rang as I exited the elevator on the top floor. It was Bob Hanson.

"*Good news, Mr. Covington. We've located Monica Paisley,*" he said.

I walked out of the elevator and straight toward Bill's office. "Bob, can you hold just a sec?"

I closed the door behind me and put my phone on speaker. "Bob, you're on speaker, and I have William Covington with me as well."

"*Great, saves me a few calls,*" Hanson said. "*I have good news. We've located Monica Paisley and have her under surveillance.*"

"What kind of surveillance?" Bill asked.

"We've placed GPS locators on both of her vehicles, and we've also managed to secure a service that will keep us continually apprised of her cell phone location."

"Bob?" Bill asked. "Is this good enough, in your estimation, to allow Emma to return safely to San Francisco?"

"Mr. Covington, that's your call to make. All I can say is we'll be able to monitor her movements quite well and could notify you if she were to leave here and go to the Bay Area. Your brother and sister-in-law would have some notice, and once she's up there, we can also let you know if she gets at all close to them."

Bill and I added Steven to the call. After we finished ribbing him about breaking his leg, it took him only a few minutes to understand Hanson's progress and make his decision. Emma would be heading back to San Francisco tonight.

UNCLE GARTH AND I TOOK SEPARATE CARS WHEN WE LEFT Covington HQ, so when I arrived at the office building downtown, I waited outside for him. I took the time to compose a little message to Liz.

> ME: my lucky coin came up heads you are going to have a good day

Her response came quickly.

> LIZ: I could use it

Uncle Garth arrived, and we went inside for our appointment.

The elevator doors opened on the sixth floor. "Mr. Covington and Mr. Durham to see Mr. Willey," Uncle Garth informed the receptionist.

Two minutes later we were outside his office, and Blaine Willey's assistant, Sophie, took him the message that Mr. Covington and Mr. Durham from Covington Industries had arrived.

I felt sorry for Sophie, having to work for such a jerk.

Uncle Garth sent a text message and put his phone away.

Willey came out and offered his hand to Uncle Garth. "Mr. Covington, so nice to meet you."

"I am Durham. This is Mr. Covington," Uncle Garth corrected him, pointing over to me.

I was in a suit instead of my Patterson carpenter attire, but recognition crossed Blaine's face a few seconds later. He offered me his hand.

I ignored it.

After an awkward moment of silence, he motioned us in, and we took seats across from him. It was an interior office without a view——obviously not a partner's office. His desk was clean, too clean for my taste. More often than not I found a clean desk belonged to someone without enough to do.

"So you're a Covington. You must be Steven Covington's brother." It came out more a question than a statement.

"He's my younger brother, yes."

An odd smile crossed Willey's face, as if he'd won a prize or something.

"You know Steven?" I asked.

I was being more polite to him than I felt.

His smirk grew. "Never met him. I know of him is all." He chuckled. "He worked for a firm down the street for a while."

Whatever the joke was, I had missed it.

Willey appraised me with a bit of a smirk. "I'm sorry, I had no idea you were a Covington when we met the other evening." He clasped his hands in front of him. "Well, how can I assist Covington Industries today?" he asked.

Uncle Garth leaned forward. "Mr. Willey, I am afraid that I

made the appointment under a bit of a pretense. We are not looking for any help for our company today."

Willey's brow creased. "I don't understand."

Uncle Garth lowered his voice. "We came here to assist you."

This seemed to completely bewilder the lawyer.

"It came to my attention this morning," Uncle Garth continued, "that you have been stalking young Patrick's girlfriend, a Miss Elizabeth Turner."

"Now stop right there," Willey began.

Uncle Garth halted him with a raised finger. "If Miss Turner were to refer this to the police, it could turn into quite an embarrassment for you."

"It was late——"

"Blaine," Uncle Garth interjected. "May I call you Blaine? I would hazard a guess that if charges were filed against you, regardless of the outcome, it might interfere with your aspirations to become a partner in this firm. So, my——our——advice to you would be to stay away from Miss Turner, and to lose her number."

Willey's face grew redder by the second. "I was just seeing that she got home safely."

"Patrick, you looked up the wording of the statute this morning, did you not?" my uncle said.

My turn had come to make him squirm. "The Cliff Notes version is that one who willfully and maliciously harasses another person and puts that person in reasonable fear for his or her safety is guilty of stalking."

"And she does fear for her safety?" Uncle Garth asked.

I nodded. "Absolutely."

Willey appeared on the verge of a stroke. "I did no such thing——"

A knock on the door interrupted him, and his assistant poked her head inside the office. "Sorry to interrupt, sir, but I have the district attorney on the line, and he is quite insistent."

Willey reached for the phone on his desk.

"Not for you, sir," Sophie continued. "For Mr. Durham."

"I will take it right here, Sophie. Thank you," Uncle Garth responded as he got up to lift the receiver on Willey's phone.

"Line two, sir."

Uncle Garth answered the phone with a smile to our host. "Brian, thank you for calling back so quickly. Can you hold just one moment? Thanks." He put his hand over the mouthpiece. "Do we have an understanding, Mr. Willey?" he asked.

Willey shrunk in his chair and nodded.

Uncle Garth continued on the phone. "Brian, we have an opening in our Saturday foursome at the club if you would like to join us... Splendid. Tee time is eight-fifteen... See you then." Uncle Garth hung up and sat back down.

Willey's face had drained of blood. He obviously didn't have the district attorney on speed dial like Uncle Garth did, and he was realizing right now how out of his depth he was. He looked both scared and angry at the same time.

Only a fool would try to mess with us after a warning from Uncle Garth, and I doubted he was a fool. Fear would win out over anger.

We excused ourselves from his office and thanked Sophie on the way out.

The elevator doors closed, and Uncle Garth laughed. "That was fun. Went rather well, I think."

"How'd you get the district attorney to call just then?" I asked.

He laughed. "It is amazing what a bottle of Macallan twenty-five can get you when you ask."

Uncle Garth's connections always amazed me. "What did that cost us?"

"Us?" Uncle Garth grinned. "Nothing. I told payroll to deduct it from your check."

I didn't argue. It would be well over a thousand dollars, but worth it to keep this dirtbag away from Liz.

And Uncle Garth was right. That was fun.

CHAPTER 24

Liz

Louise and Tina were huddled in the corner when I walked into The Ironhorse for my shift.

Louise waved me over. "I was just telling Tina, Mrs. Vandersmoot called me last night to let me know the restaurant sold."

"Do we know who?" I asked.

"She gave me a name, but I missed it. Apparently he's sending a new manager over today."

I took it as a good sign that Louise-the-worrier was happy about this turn of events. "And this guy is supposed to check us out?"

"No, not at all. She said they'd had people in already as customers, and they loved the operation, so they signed the paperwork last night."

A chill ran through me. I didn't like change. I didn't see how this could be good. Having Ben harp on us was bad enough. The last thing we needed was another new guy second-guessing everything we did.

Ben walked in the front door and waved to us. Jennie followed closely behind.

"Does he know?" Tina asked.

"No idea," Louise answered.

A little before opening time, Louise let a man in a suit in through the front door and showed him to the back. He carried a vase of roses in one arm and a box and some folders in the other.

"Anthony is his name. He's in with Mr. Perham now," she told us when she returned.

Ben came out of his office a few minutes later with a scowl on his face and made a hasty exit.

I worried this might turn out to be the start of a very bad day. I put my head down and got busy as Anthony appeared and called Louise into the office.

She emerged momentarily to grab a chair from the break room.

We had just opened the doors for the day when Louise came out and told me Anthony wanted to see me next.

I cringed and steeled myself for what was to come.

Louise whispered to me as we walked together. "Mr. Perham is gone for good. And Anthony seems quite nice."

That sounded good.

"I also put in a good word for you," she said. "I think you'll like him."

I took a breath, smoothed my apron, and opened the door.

"You must be Elizabeth Turner." He offered his hand. "I'm Anthony Soldano. Nice to meet you. Please have a seat."

I shook his hand before sitting. I couldn't remember Ben ever shaking hands with any of us. Or offering any of us a place to sit. He'd never had a chair in the office for anyone other than himself.

Anthony explained that he was the manager sent by the new owners, whose names he didn't mention. He had been in the restaurant business for over twenty years, as a waiter himself for most of that time. He said this was his first real experience as manager, and to please forgive him if he didn't know everything he should. He was here to help us, because we and the cooks were the important people, dealing with the guests and the food.

He was a complete change from Ben Perham.

I noticed he had already made himself at home, with pictures of his wife and children on the credenza.

I blushed when he told me he'd heard that Louise and I were the best waitresses in the restaurant. Although I did happen to agree with him.

"So, based on that, I want you to talk with Louise, and the two of you can tell me what shifts you'd like. I plan to work the other girls around that."

My heart raced. "Really?" This was great. I could go back to working my dinner shifts again.

He nodded. "Absolutely." He checked his notebook. "Would you please ask Tina to come see me next? Thank you."

He handed me some roses on the way out.

A boss that gives flowers? I could get used to this. I left the office floating on a cloud and sent Tina in next. The women all got roses, and he'd brought chocolate for the men.

I was so focused on my good fortune that lunch went by in a flash.

We finished the shift without a hitch, and even poor Jennie looked happy today.

I clocked out with roses in hand and a smile to match my mood.

Later that evening, I arrived at Myrtle Street full of anticipation after a long dinner shift. Pat's truck was outside, but I didn't see him. A vase of roses sat on the table.

How sweet.

He opened the back door a minute later and held up a small egg basket. "Eggs for breakfast."

Tosca followed him in and came over to greet me. She always started by sniffing my crotch. I still needed to break her of that.

"Good stuff, Tosca?" he asked.

"Pervert," I scolded him.

"Come over here, and I'll show you how much better I can do it."

I stifled a laugh and shook my head. He might be a pervert, but he was my pervert, and I liked him that way.

"The flowers?" I asked.

"To celebrate you being back on the dinner shift. I called Stacey," he said. "But she said you'd explain."

He put down the eggs and pulled me into a long kiss, the kind I had been waiting for all day. His tongue sought mine with delicate strokes amid the taste of apple and the smell of pine.

He cupped my ass and pulled me close as I reciprocated by rubbing myself against the growing bulge of his cock. His hand found its way under my shirt to tease the underside of my breast as he liked to do.

I laced my fingers through his hair, holding him to me as the heat within me built.

We broke the kiss when Tosca barked at the front door.

Pat went to check. There was nobody there.

He ushered me over to the couch and sat me down before going to the refrigerator and extracting a bottle of champagne. The cork bounced off the ceiling with a loud pop, and Tosca scampered after it. He poured the champagne into two plastic glasses.

"You'll never guess what happened today," I said as he brought the glasses over.

I admired once again how down to Earth he was compared to that snob Blaine. Just thinking of Blaine gave me a chill.

"I can tell by your smile that whatever it was, it was mighty good."

"The best," I said with a giggle.

He handed me my cup. "To the best, because that's what you are."

I took a sip. "You have got to stop doing that." I gurgled a laugh.

"Never. One thing you need to know about me: I never give a compliment that's undeserved."

My cheeks warmed. I must've been redder than a traffic light.

He took a sip of his champagne. "So tell me, what are we celebrating?"

I held up my glass, which held only about an inch of champagne. "You call this celebrating?"

"I call it drinking responsibly. I don't want you passing out on me again."

"Okay, so I go in to work today, and I find out our restaurant has been sold."

"No shit."

I laughed. "The new owners sent in a manager of their own, and Ben was instantly out on his ass."

Pat chuckled. "He deserved it."

"And the new guy, Anthony, seems really nice. But the best part is that I got my old shifts back, plus another dinner."

He took the glass out of my hand and pulled me up off the couch into a tight embrace and a voracious kiss. "Didn't I tell you you were going to get good news?"

I nodded and snuggled my face into his chest, hugging him tightly. "You have no idea how worried I was, with less money coming in and that wage garnishment thing. I wasn't going to be able to afford Stacey's tuition."

He kissed the top my head. "Buttercup, I told you it was all going to work out. You just need to have faith. Next thing you know, you'll get the scholarship you're hoping for. I'm telling you, things are going your way."

"I hope so."

He pulled that coin of his out of his pocket again and flipped it. "Heads says you'll get lucky on that too."

"I doubt it," I said.

The coin came up heads. He poured us both another glass of the bubbly.

I wasn't superstitious enough to believe him, but it made me feel good nonetheless. Everything he did made me feel good. I sat back in the couch and cuddled against his warmth, feeling protected from all the bad things in life.

"You won't leave me, will you?"

He pulled me tight and kissed me. "Never, Buttercup." He tousled my hair. "You couldn't get rid of me if you tried."

Finally, a man that won't leave me.

His effect on me was confusing. He could elicit uncontrollable excitement one minute and complete relaxation the next.

He was two-hundred-percent masculine, never discussing an emotion, but always doing little things to show me how he felt and how utterly protective of me he was. His touch was gentle and reassuring, except when I was being naughty and he shifted to forcefully playful.

Tonight I wanted naughty and playful, and I knew how to get it.

～

P*AT*

HER CRAP BOSS WAS OUT OF HER LIFE, AND HE HAD OBVIOUSLY been even worse to work for than I'd imagined.

Life was good. Best of all, she was happy, which made me happy.

My Liz was so perfect for me. She was laid back, real, compassionate to a fault, and sexy as hell. By comparison, all the other girls had been like Barbie, plastic caricatures of women. They were all different, but all the same. They'd all tried to be what they thought I wanted. They were too insecure to be themselves.

This morning I was up making scrambled eggs with a fresh batch from Mr. Busy's harem. Fresh was definitely best.

Liz had slept in this morning. Our sessions last night had worn her out, and she had worn me out. It was so fucking hot the way she rode me, giving me access to her perfect breasts, topped by tight, hard little nipples that were so responsive to my touch and my mouth. My cock came alive just thinking about it.

She came out of the bedroom in one of my T-shirts and teased me by bouncing over in my direction, her pokey nipples straining against the thin fabric. Her breasts bounced with each exaggerated step, just the way I liked it. She patted me on the ass as she examined the pan and leaned in to kiss my ear.

"Good morning."

She walked over to the dishwasher and leaned over to pull the silverware out. The shirt rode up. She looked back at me, still bent over. She was bottomless. She smiled. My girl was teasing me.

I turned up the heat to hurry the eggs. She was going to get exactly what she wanted right after breakfast.

CHAPTER 25

(THREE WEEKS LATER)

LIZ

GOING IN TO WORK HAD BEEN A PLEASURE SINCE ANTHONY HAD replaced Ben three weeks ago, and yesterday had been the best yet. Anthony had told me the wage garnishment order arrived, but he couldn't honor it because it had the old company's name on it. I was so happy I could have kissed him, but I restrained myself. He tore up the paper in front of me.

"I hear it can take the courts more than six months to get one of these things fixed," he'd told me.

So, I had a grace period to figure out what to do.

Pat had left extra early this morning, and he'd said he wouldn't be back until dinner.

Things had gone so well the last few weeks. I was spending a lot of nights over at his house, and although most of my stuff was still at my place, it felt good to be sort of living with him. Although it was farther away, his place worked out much better than mine, where the walls were paper thin. I had tried everything short of tape over my mouth, but Pat drove me so crazy that I just couldn't stay quiet, no matter how hard I tried. And, we had abandoned the condoms, which made it that much better.

I had the best time teasing him in the morning, walking around in one of his T-shirts, braless. My boobs jiggling and my nipples poking out, were an elixir he couldn't resist. We had christened all the furniture in the place, but one of his favorites had become taking me from behind, bent over the back of the couch. He filled me so completely, and the feral look in those amber eyes whenever I suggested it told me I was driving him into animal mode, and that's the way I liked my man.

I smiled to myself. I was warm and tingly between my legs just thinking about it.

Driving back from the lunch shift, I needed an idea for dinner. I settled on my five-alarm chili.

I parked in the driveway next to Stacey's car.

Candy jumped down from her perch on the windowsill as I opened the front door. She ran over, demanding to be picked up, but today she was going to take second priority to the envelope that had come in the mail.

It was a simple, white, foreboding envelope lying on the front table. The return address was Financial Aid Office, University of California Davis. I trembled as I tore it open. I hoped for good news, but I rationalized that if it was bad news, I wouldn't be any worse off than I was last week.

I pulled the letter out, closed my eyes, unfolded it in front of me, and then opened my eyes again.

I couldn't believe what I was reading. I jumped up and squealed with joy.

This was the best.

I had been hoping for a partial tuition scholarship, but the letter was for much more than that. It was full tuition, a books allowance, and a housing allowance. Fucking unbelievable. I had to blink back tears.

Stacey emerged from her room, bleary-eyed. "What's the problem out here? Can't a girl take a nap?"

"You won't believe what just came in the mail," I told her.

"Publisher's Clearinghouse?"

"No, better than that."

"I worked graveyard last night, and I have to go in for the swing shift tonight, so I don't have the energy to play twenty questions."

"I got the scholarship from Davis. The whole fucking enchilada."

Her eyebrows shot up. "Let me see." She raced over.

I handed her the letter.

As she read down the lines, her eyes got progressively wider. "This is great. I thought you only expected to get a partial."

"That's what they told me when I applied. Actually, it sounded like a long shot to get anything."

"So what are you waiting for? Pull out the ice cream. This calls for a celebration."

I stopped to pick up the persistent cat rubbing against my feet and held her as I extracted the chocolate fudge brownie ice cream from the freezer——the only way to celebrate.

First my boss, and now this. Things were seriously looking up.

I needed to celebrate with Pat when he got home, and I knew just what to do.

CHAPTER 26

LIZ

I USED MY KEY TO OPEN THE DOOR TO PAT'S HOUSE. HE WASN'T home yet.

Tosca came in through the doggy door to greet me, sniffing my crotch. Again.

I turned the oven up to 170 and put the food in to stay warm while I waited for Pat. Chili could wait a day; tonight was special. I went out back, with Tosca following me to Mr. Busy's henhouse. I located three fresh eggs and brought them back inside.

Pat still wasn't home, so I waited. He didn't have a television, so I couldn't watch *The Bachelor* or *Judge Judy*. Who doesn't have a TV these days? My Pat.

I went to the bedroom to change into the clothes I had brought in my paper bag.

It was the sexiest outfit I could put together. The shortest miniskirt I had left over from high school, with my Victoria's Secret bra and panties, and a deep V-neck top. I grabbed my purse and worked on my makeup——fire-engine red lipstick, mascara, and plenty of eye shadow. I even added a little perfume, then a little more. I strapped on my highest heels, and I was ready to party. I checked myself in the mirror and decided to ditch the bra.

Now I'm ready.

~

PAT

I HAD EXPECTED TO WRAP UP THE POPOVICH DEAL TODAY, BUT IT didn't work out. They wanted to have another meeting tomorrow ——in Newport Beach of all places. It was a crappy way to end the day.

But I noticed Liz's car in the driveway as I pulled up to Myrtle Street. When I opened the door, she was waiting on the couch. She got up and trotted over to me, her tits bouncing suggestively.

The sight of her braless with that short skirt jerked my cock to life, instantly straining against my jeans.

I barely had time to put my coat down before she launched herself into my arms. The warmth of her lips on mine and those wonderful tits squeezed up against me were heaven after the day I'd had. As our tongues met, my nostrils were filled with the unfamiliar scent of perfume. Tonight was special, it seemed. She wasn't usually a perfume girl.

The warmth of her in my arms grew even more exciting as I grabbed her ass and pulled her to me, only to find my hand gripping lace instead of cotton. My cock throbbed and demanded to be let loose as our tongues dueled hungrily, but only for a moment. I caught my breath as she broke the kiss.

She walked to the fridge, denying me any more. Her hips swayed in the miniskirt, and she wobbled slightly on her five-inch heels. She opened the refrigerator and bent over to look inside, giving me a show. What little skirt there was rode up and tortured me. She pulled a bottle of champagne out of the fridge.

My woman was a tease tonight. She opened the oven, pulled out bags of food from Tropics Burgers, and carried them to the table.

"What's the occasion?" I asked, trying unsuccessfully to avoid staring at her chest. My cock strained against my zipper.

She sat as I unloaded the bags. "I got a letter today," she said.

Her quick glance at my crotch told me she knew exactly what she was doing to me. She smiled, she was enjoying this too.

I pulled out the burgers and fries and set them on the plates. "From?"

She was all smiles and giggles. "The financial aid office at UC Davis. I got the scholarship," she chirped.

The way her tits bounced when she giggled was distracting as hell.

"That's terrific."

"I got the whole thing."

She bounced up and down in her chair, tits and all, driving me insane. She had no idea what she was doing to me.

"Tuition, books, and a housing allowance too."

"I told you, have faith and the magic coin will help you." I unwrapped my burger and took a bite to distract me from the show she was putting on.

"I don't believe it. I never in a million years expected to get the whole package. When I put in my paperwork and talked to them, it seemed like I would be lucky to get partial tuition at best. And now this. It's just like a dream come true. When I first opened it, I was prepared for the worst, you know?"

She started in on her hamburger.

We ate our burgers and fries as she told me all she knew about the veterinary program at Davis. She was a walking encyclopedia of knowledge. She'd memorized all the class names and descriptions in the curriculum. She had the whole thing planned out in her mind.

I hadn't told her about Boston yet. I had hoped to get her to transfer her ambition to the vet school at Tufts in Boston when I asked her to move with me, but after tonight it seemed that might be harder than I'd anticipated. I was going to have my work cut out for me. But that was a problem for another day.

I built a fire while she did the dishes and pulled dessert out of the fridge.

She brought our plates of chocolaty goodness over to the couch. "From DessertMagic," she said. "I hope you like it."

"Like it? I love it. You know how I feel about chocolate. It's the next best thing to you."

The compliment earned me a glowing smile and a fervent kiss as she sat down with me.

"You say the nicest things."

"You know me, no compliment is undeserved." I loaded up my spoon with some of the decadent chocolate mousse and brought it to her lips.

She opened her mouth, and I managed to get most of it in, but I purposely missed and got some on her cheek.

I kissed and licked it off to giggles from my girl.

She fed me a spoonful and deposited some on my nose, giving me the same treatment.

I put my spoon down and lifted her top over her head, taking in the sight of those marvelous breasts, which had been calling to me all night. I guided her to lie with her head in my lap, on my aching cock. I deposited the next spoonful on her left breast and painted it slowly around her nipple. Her eyelids fluttered as I shifted her so I could reach, and bent over to lick it off.

It took all my willpower to go slowly, when what I wanted was to devour not just the chocolate, but all of her. Each lick brought little murmurs of pleasure from my willing partner. I licked every inch of her breast, paying special attention to her nipple before I brought another spoonful to the other breast. I gave it the same treatment as my girl made delightful little noises at each stroke of my tongue.

I was lost. She was so soft, warm, and enticing. She was like a drug to my system, spreading throughout my entire being, intoxicating me, eliminating all my will, until all I wanted to do was breathe her in.

"Don't I get a turn?" she complained as I held her shoulder down and dribbled some on her belly button. She laughed breathlessly, music to my ears.

I shook my head. "I'm not done yet."

Liz

HE SAID HE WASN'T DONE YET, BUT I NEEDED A TURN.

I forced him to let me up, and I straddled him.

His mouth came instantly to my breasts, and the licking and sucking continued.

I rubbed myself over the hardness of his cock, still held captive by his jeans, as I gave him access to my breasts. I kneaded his hair and rubbed my soaked crotch on him harder.

I broke away and knelt on the floor in front him, yanking at his belt and then his pants, and finally hooking my fingers in his boxer briefs and unleashing the monster as his cock sprang loose. I told him to lie down——which he did without complaint for once—— and I got a spoonful of mousse, which I applied liberally to his throbbing shaft.

"Hold still," I told him.

His cock was bobbing around, making me miss with the chocolate.

"I can't. It's cold."

"Baby," I chided him.

I grabbed the tip with one hand while I smoothed the creamy chocolate over him with the spoon and started to lick. I worked my way slowly up his length, watching his expression as he tried to control his excitement.

His moans grew louder as I cleaned off the base of his cock and grasped him with my hand, stroking lightly as I continued to lick upward toward the end of him. His breath hitched and his cock twitched with every lick. I needed to do this more often. He was about to come unraveled.

I had finished and taken the crown of his cock into my mouth to finish him off when he jerked me up, rose off the couch, and hurled me over his shoulder.

Pat carried me into the other room, pulled down the covers, and I ended up flat on my back on the bed as he pulled my skirt and panties off.

He wasn't done with me yet. He spread my legs, lowered himself between my thighs, and began his tongue magic on me, sending shockwaves through my body, overloading my nerve endings.

Pat had the most amazing tongue. He bewitched me with it when we kissed, and he tortured me with it when he went down on me. I had been afraid the first time he introduced me to this, but it was now one of my favorite things. He circled my clit and sucked and flicked at the engorged nub, showing me no mercy. My legs trembled, and my breathing accelerated as he added a finger inside me, followed by a second. He fondled a breast with his other hand, thumbing my nipple.

I couldn't control myself. I clawed at his hair, but I couldn't reach any more of him.

"You need to come up here," I gasped. I could hardly breathe, I needed him inside me so badly.

He didn't relent. He pulled out his fingers and gave them to me to suck.

I pulled harder on his hair. Every nerve in my body burned, my breasts were swollen, and my core yearned for him.

"Come here, please, please," I pleaded. "I need you inside me."

He pulled his face up for a moment and replaced his tongue with his finger, playing a beautiful melody on my clit.

"The naughty girl can't have what she doesn't ask for," he said hoarsely, scraping his stubble against my thighs.

"Fuck me, Pat. Fuck me hard."

He had been teaching me the fun of talking dirty. I was a slow learner.

He moved up between my legs and kissed me hungrily, giving me another taste of me——me and chocolate.

I encircled him with my legs, pulling him in as he positioned that marvelous cock and entered my heat. I pulled him in close with my heels as he stretched me and filled me.

"Fuck me harder. Harder."

He did. The waves of pleasure quickly crashed over both of us, drowning us in ecstasy as I came quickly and hard, convulsing around him and screaming as he pounded into me harder and deeper. He stiffened, trembled, and groaned as he lost it as well, filling me with warm wetness.

He finally relaxed down on top of me, spent and satisfied as I stroked my hands over his broad back and through his hair. The throbbing of his cock slowly diminished as we caught our breath.

All my cares melted away in my man's arms.

My man.

CHAPTER 27

PAT

I HAD STOPPED PURSUING NEW DEALS WHILE I WAS SPENDING PART
time pretending to be Pat Patterson, but I needed to finish the
Popovich transaction, and I hoped today would be the day.

Getting to Newport Beach in the morning rush hour was a
bitch. But there wasn't anybody else Victor Popovich would nego-
tiate with, and this was just one of those days I had to suck it up.
The BMW was comfortable, but this morning I hated that Bill was
too much of a tightwad to get a company helicopter for trips like
this.

The negotiator in me knew that their choice of time and location was designed to take advantage of my frustration after the
long, stop-and-go drive.

But I kept my cool, and by the session after lunch, it was clear
that they were no longer concerned about the structure, timing, or
contingencies of the deal; it was just a matter of price. As was
common with many cultures, Victor Popovich had to convince

himself that he'd gotten the best deal possible and nobody could have done better.

But I guessed it was more than that. As the youngest son of one of the wealthiest oligarchs in Russia, he needed a win that would impress Papa at the next family gathering. He needed bragging rights.

We had already reached the price limit that Bill, Uncle Garth, and I had agreed to, and I couldn't go any higher, but I was having trouble convincing him. It just wasn't impressive enough.

If I walked away now, his pride might not let him reengage, and the deal would fail. It was structured as mostly Covington stock, so I decided to throw something of my own into the pot.

"Victor, we can't go any higher, but let me suggest one final concession."

He perked up at the mention of another concession from me.

"If at six months time you want to liquidate your Covington stock, I will personally buy it back from you at a twenty-five percent premium over the price when we close the deal."

He tried to seem dismissive, but his eyes betrayed him. This was the one-of-a-kind extra concession he could brag about.

My phone vibrated in my pocket, but I ignored it. It vibrated again. I had told Bill I would give him an update after lunch, and I was late. He needed to be more patient. Russians considered it a sign of weakness to interrupt a meeting to take a call.

We signed the papers a half hour later.

"One more thing, Victor," I said when we were alone. "You owe me a favor someday."

He slapped me on the back. "I like you, Patrick. You think like a Russian. Some day we meet for drinks and we trade favors." He laughed, always the negotiator.

I could see that if the day ever came, I was going to have a serious hangover the next morning.

I checked my phone on the way downstairs to my car. It was a voicemail from Bill. Monica Paisley was causing a problem again. He said Constance was going to send protection for Liz.

I had been afraid that bitch would surface in our lives again. The video Winston and crew had dug up had gotten Paisley booked for the arson of Emma's car, but she had quickly made bail, and a trial was months away.

My heart raced as soon as I heard that. Bill would only suggest something like that if he thought she was in danger.

Fucking Bill should have gotten us a helicopter.

I reached the car at a dead run and hit dial-back on the phone as I floored the German road-rocket. The tires clawed for traction on the pavement.

~

LIZ

I WAS IN THE KITCHEN AT PAT'S, CUTTING CELERY FOR TONIGHT'S chili, when the doorbell rang. I checked through the window.

A tall, strapping man with a military-style buzz cut and dressed in a coat and tie stood back from the door.

"Elizabeth Turner?" he asked when he saw me.

I didn't like the fact that he knew my name. Then I recognized him from that first time I'd waited on Pat at The Ironhorse. He was buzz cut guy, one of Pat's friends. I opened the door.

"Miss Turner, my name is Winston Evers."

"You're Pat's friend, right?"

"Yes, ma'am. I was sent to protect you."

"Protect me?" I took a breath. "Who sent you?" I asked.

"Mrs. Covington," he answered as he dialed his phone. "I'm from Hanson Investigations and Security. I'm getting her on the phone, if you'd like to verify that," he added.

I took the phone from him. "Hello?" I said.

"Liz, this is Lauren Covington. We met at the charity polo match a while back. Winston is there to keep you safe. I don't have time to explain right now, but you're in danger."

The somewhat familiar voice had relaxed me, right up until the *"you're in danger"* part.

"How do I know you're Lauren Covington?"

"Does watching a well-hung black horse in a barn ring a bell?"

The memory of the polo barn forced a giggle out of me. "Yeah, just a little."

"I need you to do whatever Winston says. He's ex-FBI. He's there to keep you safe, and you can trust him."

I couldn't control my breathing. "Safe from what?" I demanded.

"Just trust me for the moment. Let him do his job. I have to go." She hung up.

"Thank you, ma'am," Winston said politely as I returned his phone in a daze.

He stepped inside and immediately started exploring around the house.

I went back to chopping my celery——slowly, to avoid cutting myself. I was so distracted. I watched as he went from room to room, checking doors and the views out the windows.

"Ma'am, when do you expect Mr. Covington back?"

"Who?"

This poor guy Mrs. Covington had sent was obviously clueless, thinking a Covington lived in this hovel. He must be all muscles and no brains.

"Mr. Patrick, ma'am." He unbuttoned his coat, and the butt of a gun became briefly visible in a shoulder holster. An armed and clueless guy was not a good combination.

"Pat said late tonight. He has a job down south somewhere. And you call me ma'am one more time…" I waved my eight-inch chef's knife. "And you'll be singing soprano."

That lightened him up. He chuckled. "Yes, Miss Elizabeth."

He pulled out his phone and dialed. "Constance, I'm at the Myrtle Street house, and I have Miss Turner secured. This location is way too exposed for my taste. I suggest we bring her to the condo for the time being... Roger that." He hung up.

"Miss," he said, "I'm going to need you to come with me to Mr. Covington's condo. You'll be safer there."

I couldn't believe what I was hearing. "Now?"

"Yes, miss."

"No," I told him. Telling me to leave because he didn't like the scenery outside? Really? "No way."

"Miss, I have to tell you, the threat is both real and serious."

I went back to cutting the stalks and ignored him. Nobody was going to just yank me out of the house without any explanation.

"And if anything were to happen to you, Mr... Patrick, would break me in two and kick the pieces all the way to Texas."

That sounded like he knew my Pat all right.

I put my hands on my hips. Ex-FBI or not, I was not taking orders from some muscle-bound idiot.

"I'm not leaving until I finish getting this chili ready."

He wasn't happy about it, but he relented. "Yes, miss. Can I help?"

"You can chop the onion over there."

Even a grown man couldn't chop one of these onions without becoming teary-eyed. The big guy took my kidding well.

We finished the preparation, and I turned on the crock pot before agreeing to leave with him. I decided there was no reason not to trust Mrs. Covington.

He said everything would be explained to me when we got there, and he insisted I leave my car and ride with him. The big black SUV he drove looked like it had come straight out of a presidential motorcade, blacked out windows and all.

"Where are we going again?" I asked.

"The condo on Wilshire," he said as if he expected it to mean something to me.

When we turned in to the large circular entrance, a huge glass tower loomed over us. Except for central downtown, most of LA's housing consisted of small houses and low-rise apartment buildings, but this monster was a huge black monolith, towering over the neighborhood. A doorman greeted Winston by name as we approached.

The place actually had a doorman like in the movies.

"Oliver, this is Miss Turner. You can add her to the approved list."

"A pleasure to meet you, Miss Turner," the jovial old man replied as we crossed the marble-and-chrome lobby to the elevators.

Nothing cheap about this building.

I waited for Winston to select a floor. He pushed twenty-two, the top.

Where else would a Covington live?

A few moments later, we exited the elevator. "What is this place?" I asked as he turned his key in the lock.

"One of the Covington condos."

He opened the door into a huge great room with an entire glass wall facing out toward the city. You could probably see Long Beach from here on a clear day. The floor was oak, and the walls were painted a light gray with dark leather furniture and a gargantuan big-screen on the wall. A marble-framed fireplace graced the far wall. All quite modern. The attached kitchen area was open and spacious. What I wouldn't give for a kitchen like this.

A woman with short cropped hair that I didn't recognize got up from studying pictures and papers on the table. "Elizabeth, I'm Constance Collier."

I couldn't place her. "I'm sorry, have we met?"

"No, ma'am, but Patrick has had wonderful things to say about you."

"So you work at the same security firm as Pat?"

A concerned look flashed briefly across her face. "Sort of, ma'am. We're from Hanson Investigations and Security."

"Can we lose the ma'am? Please call me Liz, and just tell me what the hell is going on."

"In just a moment, Liz," Constance said. "Winston, you need to pick up Mrs. Covington at LAX at six," she instructed my over-sized bodyguard.

He checked his watch and nodded.

I perused the photos on the table while they were talking. They looked like blow-ups in several magnifications of video frames showing a man and a woman near a burning car and then getting into another car with front-end damage. This fit with what Pat had told me about his sister-in-law's car being burned after he'd picked her up that night at the Wendy's. But this was a Covington condo. Had one of his brothers married into the Covington clan?

The woman's face was clear enough, but the man was wearing a hoodie, and there weren't any shots of his face.

Constance took Winston aside and had a short, whispered conference with him.

He nodded several times, then took off his coat and opened the fridge. He pulled out a Coke and promptly dropped it. He exchanged it for another can.

And they trust this guy with a gun?

"What's the story with Mister Butterfingers?" I asked Constance in a low voice.

"He doesn't talk much," she whispered. "But he's smart as a whip. Ph.D in computer science. He and his brother hacked NASA a while back and turned off the lights on the International Space Station for half an hour."

"If you say so."

"He had to quit the Bureau because of it."

Winston sat down by the window and started typing furiously on a laptop.

"You know about the stalking incident a few weeks ago involving Patrick's sister-in-law?"

"Yeah, some crazy Monica lady was after her, but I thought you had found video or something that would land her in jail."

"These are from video feeds across the street from the Wendy's. Winston was able to hack the systems and download the images for us."

Now I was impressed. Maybe muscle man wasn't as dumb as he seemed.

"These pictures are from that night, but things have just escalated. This afternoon, we believe she set fire to his sister Katherine's house."

"My God. Is she okay?"

"Yes, luckily she's out of town today, at a conference in Las Vegas. She's fine——at least as fine as you can be when someone just burned down your house."

"So what does this have to do with me?"

"I'm afraid the fire means Miss Paisley's target list has expanded to the entire family, and perhaps people associated with the family, such as yourself."

A chill went through me just thinking about somebody insane enough to light a house on fire, and a car too. Looking at the pictures gave me the creeps. These two were off-the-charts, batshit crazy.

I sat down in front of the pictures and rearranged them a little, studying some of the close-ups.

"There is something familiar about this guy," I told her, putting my finger on the man in the picture. It bugged me. I couldn't place exactly what it was.

"All we can get out of these is the gang tattoo on his wrist: M8." She pointed out a blow-up of his arm as he opened the car door. "But that hasn't gotten us anywhere yet."

Constance's phone rang. "Yes, sir, the house is a total loss." She went into another room to continue the call.

∽

*P*AT

BILL ANSWERED INSTANTLY. "*PATRICK, YOU GOT THE MESSAGE?*"

"Yeah, go on."

"*It's Monica, we think. She burned Katie's house down.*"

My lunch congealed in my stomach. This was much more serious than I'd gotten from his voicemail.

"Is she okay?" My heart raced.

"*She's fine. At a conference in Las Vegas this week.*"

"Did they catch her?"

"*Not so lucky. Constance does have video from a neighbor's security camera that shows a woman setting the fire, but we can't get a positive ID from it. It matches her MO though, so she's getting more dangerous. Lauren and I made the decision to have Constance and Winston provide protection for Liz.*"

"Thanks. I'm on the way back from Newport Beach now. I'll give Constance a call. Then I'm going to find that bitch and kill her."

Constance answered right away, confirming that Katie's house was a complete loss. She filled me in on the fire and Winston's decision that the Myrtle Street house was not a defensible position if Monica came around.

She hesitated. "*Sir, she's with us here at your condo.*"

Silence. I was totally fucked now. I should have told her last night, or last week, or the week before.

"*Sir, do you want to talk to her?*"

My stomach was in a knot. What could I say? I'm sorry I lied to you? I'm sorry I put you in danger?

Constance interrupted my pity party. "*Sir, we haven't told her yet.*"

This was not a conversation for the phone. "I'll talk to her when I get there," I said.

Constance confirmed that we didn't know for sure where Monica was now. Her phone and car still showed her in San Diego, but Constance was worried she had ditched the phone and car. Liz was safe, and until Emma arrived this evening for her grand jury testimony tomorrow on the car torching, she was the only one other than me in the area. And I could take care of myself. Bill and Lauren were out in Boston visiting my brother Liam.

Liz was safe. That's what mattered. I could slow down now and relax. I moved over into the slow lane and decided to take it easy. I needed time to think. I had to figure out how I was going to tell her my last name was really Covington. How was I going to explain that I'd kept it from her this whole time? I ran through it in my mind and even tried it out loud, speaking to the steering wheel.

It sucked.

I was fucked. My leg was jittery. This was worse than the time I had peered over the edge of the Golden Gate Bridge.

I should've told her last week when we were at the beach, just the two of us. I should've broken this to her in my own time, on my own schedule. I'd considered having her pack a bag and whisking her away for a weekend in New York or New Orleans.

I tried another version, telling her it had been best for both of us. That sucked even worse. And it was a lie. I'd been selfish this whole time, trying to protect myself. I hadn't stopped to think about how this would affect her. How the longer I kept the charade up, the worse it would seem to her in the end.

My lunch threatened to come up. *Try to put yourself in her shoes*, I thought. I had to find a way to explain it to her that would show her it had really been a good thing. But I got nowhere with that. I'd created Pat Patterson. He was the man she fell in love with, not Patrick Covington.

That first time at The Ironhorse when she told me she'd only go out with a professional man———would it have worked if I'd told her then? Would that have made a difference?

I squinted into the sun for a moment and shook my head. I needed to focus, not second-guess myself. If I could do a deal with the mad Russian, I could solve anything.

My phone beeped with another call coming in. It was Steven.

"*Patrick, I'm worried about Emma. She's not answering her phone.*"

That set my stomach churning even worse. "I thought she was coming down later tonight."

"*No, that changed this morning.*"

"I'm going to conference you in with Constance," I told him. A few moments later I had all three of us on the call. "Steven, repeat what you told me."

"*Emma got a call this morning setting up a meeting with a lawyer at four o'clock this afternoon in LA. So she changed to an earlier flight.*"

"*You should have told us,*" Constance interrupted.

The clock on my dash showed a few minutes after four. I whipped around the Honda in front of me as I punched the accelerator.

Steven continued, "*We didn't think it was a problem because you said Monica was in San Diego.*" He sounded scared. "*Her phone is going straight to voicemail.*"

"*We'll go get her,*" Constance said. "*Who is she meeting and where?*"

"*I didn't take the call. All I have from her calendar is BW slash DP at PB,*" Steven said.

None of us knew what Emma's shorthand meant.

I dodged right and passed a minivan. Emma wasn't safe on her own.

CHAPTER 28

Liz

I CONTINUED TO SIFT THROUGH THE BLOWN-UP PHOTOS ON THE
table.

Constance emerged from the bedroom, waving a piece of
paper. "Winston, we have new data."

She placed it on the table. The note read *BW/DP PB 4:00.*

"The sister-in-law is already in town," she explained. "She has
a meeting with a lawyer. This is all we have on it, and she isn't
answering her phone."

The realization came to me slowly. I turned the picture of the
wrist tattoo upside down, and I had it.

"That's not M8," I said, turning the upside-down photo to face
them. "It's BW. I've seen that ink before. BW is Blaine Willey. He
works at Dershowitz and Pine, DP. Blaine Willey is the lawyer
she's meeting with."

"That's amazing, Elizabeth. My God, why didn't we think of
that?" Constance exclaimed.

I couldn't help but smile. I had solved something that the muscle-bound Ph.D and his girlfriend couldn't.

"We still need to figure out where," Constance said.

I had a vision of the multiple Forbes plaques on the wall and Blaine's snide mug as he'd told me he only ever ate at three restaurants because they served his preferred variety of wine.

"PB is Le Papillon Bleu, his favorite restaurant. You can't reach her because they have a no cell phone policy."

Constance gave me a quick hug. "You're a godsend, Liz. We would never have figured that one out."

I felt sorry that Mrs. Covington had to endure a meeting with boring Blaine.

Constance dialed her phone and gave my revelations to whoever was on the other end.

Winston ran to the door and left.

I wandered over to the fridge. I had solved the puzzle. Nice. *Coke or Dr. Pepper?* I chose Coke. I popped it open and got an immediate shower all over my shirt.

"Shit."

The fucking computer genius had dropped it.

I found a dish towel and cleaned up the floor, but my top was soaked and my bra was showing through. My outfit for tonight was ruined.

Constance was nice enough not to laugh. "I'm sure you can find a clean shirt in the dresser." She pointed to the bedroom door on the left. "Willey," she said. "There's something about that name." She shuffled her papers. "God dammit, Willey is Paisley's maiden name." She pulled a paper out of the stack. "Blaine Willey is one of her brothers." Constance redialed her phone while I went to find a shirt.

The bedroom was spacious, with a desk and separate sitting area.

The Covingtons sure have nice digs.

The first drawer I tried held folded men's underwear. The

second was more interesting, until I realized what it was——an assortment of women's panties and bras all in different sizes. A trophy drawer. The man had a fucking trophy drawer. A whisper of angst soured my stomach. I quickly closed it. I knew there were several men in the Covington family, and I hoped to God this wasn't William Covington's place. Poor Lauren, if it was.

The next drawer had what I needed. I took out a blue oxford dress shirt and changed into it. It was too big for me, but it was dry. I was checking myself in the mirror when I noticed the hat.

On the desk was Pat's Patterson Construction hat. He had been wearing it when he left this morning, and I knew it was his because of the distinctive mustard stain on the bill from our date at Tropics Burgers. I sat down at the desk and picked up a framed picture of Pat with two couples. I recognized three of the four as the Covingtons I had met at the polo match. A letter lying on the desk was addressed to Patrick Covington.

The picture of Pat with the other Covingtons. His hat on the desk. Patrick Covington?

The letter was signed William Covington, and it set a start date of September first for Patrick Covington to take over the Boston office and...

I tried to stop reading but I couldn't.

...become a full-time employee and director of Covington Industries. It thanked him. *The family really needs you*, it concluded in bold letters.

This can't be true.

The letter was dated two months ago, before Pat and I had met. My shoulders fell, and my blood ran cold.

He had planned to move this whole time and not told me.

The family really needs you——the one thing he couldn't turn down. The humiliation threatened to crush me.

I stomped out into the great room and spun Constance around. "Want to tell me the truth for a change? Whose place is this?"

The blood drained from her face. "Your Pat is..." she hesitated.

"Patrick Covington. It's his sister-in-law Emma that's in danger and his sister Katherine whose house burned down today."

I felt faint. I grabbed the chair and sat down.

"This is Patrick's condo," she added.

This was too much to process. I took a few deep breaths to steel myself, and I picked up my purse to leave.

"It's not safe to leave yet, Liz," Constance called as I opened the door.

I didn't care. I pushed the elevator call button. I pushed it again.

She came running after me. "I'll drive you wherever you want to go, but I can't let you go out by yourself, not yet."

She drove me to pick up my car at Myrtle Street. Her phone rang, but she didn't answer it. "He wanted to tell——"

I cut her off. "I don't want to hear it."

We drove in silence the rest of the way. My legs trembled, refusing to stay still.

I got in my car and started the engine.

Fucking liar.

~

*P*AT

MY PHONE RANG AGAIN. IT WAS CONSTANCE. "*WE HAVE AN address for her now.*"

She read it to me as I put it into my navigator. She told me it was Liz who had recognized the tattoo in one of the pictures we had. It belonged to Blaine Willey, that fucking scrawny-ass lawyer. My blood turned cold when Constance explained that Willey was Monica's brother.

I wasn't far away, but the freeway was clogged. I crossed three lanes, getting honked at and almost hit by a minivan, as I rushed off the exit. I hoped to make better time on the surface streets.

I turned left at the main drag the restaurant was on. The traffic was heavy, but a little bit of darting in and out of lanes helped me make good progress. I rushed through a yellow light, now only a couple of blocks away. I moved into the right lane, and as I got closer, I could see the restaurant ahead on the right, a block and a half away.

Emma. I saw Emma.

Someone was dragging her into a gray sedan.

I hit the brakes as a delivery truck pulled away from the curb, blocking my view. He stopped before the intersection as the light turned red.

I couldn't see past him, and I was blocked from moving around him. When the light turned green again, I got around him, but I couldn't see the gray sedan anymore.

My phone rang. Constance reported that Emma's phone had gone active again and was traveling northbound two blocks from the restaurant. This road had a concrete median divider with occasional trees. The low ground clearance of my BMW limited me to the three lanes in our direction. But there was no way I could get past the trucks ahead of me unless I got off this boulevard. I took the next left, and a quick right onto the parallel street. It didn't have a median and had less traffic and no lights. I was liberal in my interpretation of the stop signs, as Constance told me I was gaining on them. Finally I was ahead of them by at least half a block.

I ignored the next stop sign and took a quick right to intercept them. I got to the intersection as the light in my direction turned yellow. The gray sedan was first in line on the far side of the cross street. I cranked the wheel hard right at the last second and slammed into the front corner of the sedan on the driver's side.

The airbag exploded in my face as we collided with a crunch of metal and glass.

I beat down the airbag and rushed out of the car, flinging off my broken sunglasses.

Behind the baseball cap and sunglasses I recognized Monica fucking Paisley as the driver, sitting dazed at the steering wheel. In the backseat were Emma and that asshole Willey.

He started out the back door. A gun in his hand preceded him.

I kicked the door closed on his arm and slammed my weight into it. The gun clattered to the ground, accompanied by an awful scream from inside the car. I might have broken his arm, but I didn't care. I pulled open the door, yanked him out, and slammed him to the pavement.

Monica escaped the car on the other side and began running down the street.

I pinned Willey down and told Emma to get out of the car. She was safe now, and this asshole wasn't going anywhere. The cops could catch up with Monica.

I tasted coppery blood in my mouth.

Emma climbed slowly out her side of the car. She gave Willey a swift kick in the side as she reached me.

"Asshole," was all she said.

∼

LIZ

I DROVE HOME THROUGH THE TEARS. MY LEGS WOULDN'T STOP shaking.

Pat had been lying to me since the first day we met. Never once had he told me the truth. What was the truth anyway? He had a trophy drawer full of women's underwear. I was not going to be just another panty in his drawer or notch on his bedpost.

In hindsight, it was so fucking obvious. I was the poor little valley girl he needed to add to his collection. He probably had a list of types he hadn't laid yet, or maybe he was filling out the alphabet and needed an L or an E. No wonder he'd been so taken by my black lace panties with the pink crotch. The fucker didn't have that particular kind in his collection yet.

He probably sniffed them before going to bed, or something equally perverted. Maybe he put them on at night. No, that was definitely not it. That was one thing he wasn't guilty of.

Funny word, *guilty*. At least this time I wasn't going to be guilty of being a doormat, letting him blame me and leave me.

Pat had said he would never leave me. He'd said I couldn't get rid of him if I tried.

Liar, liar pants on fire.

How could I have believed that?

I blinked back tears as I saw that haunting face again from long ago.

My father's face from that day.

The day he left us.

The day he told me he loved me and then drove off.

I was ten.

He never came back.

He never called.

He never wrote.

We never heard from him again.

Ever.

My dad had lied to me. He'd said he loved me right before he left. He'd taught me my most important lesson: they all left sooner or later. The same had happened to Stacey with Timmy's dad.

Mom had told us a year after he left that Dad had gone to England and died in a car accident. She never remarried, and after a while, we all merely pretended he'd never existed. But he had. He'd said he loved me, and I had believed him. Then he'd left and was gone. Forever. The first, but not the last.

Trent and Mike had each lied to me and left. And both had left me brokenhearted. Step two followed on the heels of step one just as night followed day. I'd given them each a chance, and I'd gotten burned. Life kept teaching me the same lesson again and again because I was too fucking stupid to learn.

Until now.

Now I know better.

I pulled into our driveway and stopped the engine. It took a few minutes to calm down. I located a tissue, blew my nose, and dried my eyes enough to be able to go inside without looking like the heartbroken fool I was.

I opened the front door to find a new envelope lying on the front table. I held my mouth, trying to keep from puking. It was the god-awful bright yellow with big red letters that never brought good news. They probably wanted to tell me they were going to garnish my wages at The *new* Ironhorse, another reminder of how Trent had fucked me and then fucked me over. A perfect ending to my miserable fucking day.

Fuck 'em. Fuck 'em all.

I dropped the envelope in my purse. I was already late for my dinner shift. I called Louise. I couldn't bear to talk to Anthony or anyone else. I told her I wasn't feeling well, which was no lie, so I wouldn't be in.

She pushed, but I didn't tell her any more.

My stomach had recovered from the yellow-envelope shock, so I lifted the chocolate fudge brownie ice cream out of the freezer.

We hadn't finished it. That was about to change.

I left Pat a voicemail saying I didn't care anymore, I was done, and moving on. Have a good life and all that dear John horseshit.

I meant it——not the part wishing him well exactly, but the *we're done* part for sure.

I dialed my Auntie Joyce.

I would not be the victim this time.

~

*P*AT

I KEPT MY FOOT ON WILLEY'S BAD ARM AND THREATENED TO PUT my full weight on it if he moved a muscle. I felt jittery from the adrenaline.

The wimpy lawyer lay there, crying and mumbling incoherently in his thousand-dollar suit. He was proof that the clothes don't make the man.

The police arrived quickly. I had obviously created the kind of scene that got a lot of people dialing 911.

I held Emma in my arms. She was shaking violently.

"You're bleeding, Patrick," she said as she pointed to my face.

I felt the bridge of my nose——my fingers came away bloody. The airbag had broken my sunglasses, and they'd cut my nose and eyebrow. I could deal with this later. Emma was the priority.

I continued to hold her as she slowly calmed down. "You're safe now. It's over. Don't worry, I've got you."

"But I was so scared," she said over and over.

Thankfully, it didn't take the police very long to get the story straight and understand who the bad guys were. Emma wouldn't let go of me.

"Let's get you back to the condo and call Steven," I told her.

She nodded, and I ushered her into Winston's car. He had arrived a little after the accident, and mine would need a tow. I noticed a voicemail on my phone from Liz that I needed to listen to as soon as I got Emma safe.

Once inside the condo with Constance and an armed Winston, Emma settled down. The two glasses of wine probably helped too.

Winston broke out the first aid kit and tended to my face.

Emma and I called Steven and Bill, with Constance on the line to fill them in on the developments and put Steven's mind at ease. Emma was safe now.

Emma was calm enough now to report on the aborted meeting at the restaurant with the dirtbag lawyer.

This and the details Liz had put together gave us a clearer picture of what had been happening. It had been Monica and her brother, Blaine Willey, in the car that night following Emma. And the two of them had torched Emma's car.

Since that night had not turned out the way they wanted, they'd hatched this plan to get Emma to meet Blaine alone, so they could nab her.

Blaine had called Emma, claiming Uncle Garth had hired him to coach her prior to her grand jury testimony. The ruse had sounded legitimate enough to convince her to meet with him.

Luckily, Liz had picked up on the wrist tattoo and identified Willey. Otherwise they would have pulled it off——a scary thought.

Now that we knew who the mystery man was, it took Winston no time at all to find footage of the two of them driving Monica's pink-striped Mustang out of the parking lot earlier on the stalking day, along with footage of them bringing the banged-up car back late at night, and a clear face shot of Blaine getting out of the Mustang in the same hoodie and driving away in his Ferrari. We had them both now.

By ten o'clock that night, we had a commitment from Uncle Garth's friend the district attorney that Blaine Willey, attorney at law, was going to be charged with felony arson, along with his sister. The DA wouldn't commit to anything on the attempted kidnapping charge until he could review the police report.

Now that Emma was safe, I excused myself to call Liz. Constance told me she had escorted her back to get her car at Myrtle Street, and she said calling Liz *unhappy* would be a severe understatement. I prepped myself to explain the Patterson imper-sonation as I pulled up her voicemail.

It was worse than I expected. She said she was breaking it off. It had been nice, and she wished me the best——that kind of crap.

I didn't hear it all as my mind went blank. Her message tore my heart in two. I had fucked this up big time.

I asked Winston to get Tosca from the Myrtle Street house. I needed to stay here with Emma until this got resolved, and in her current mood, I couldn't expect Liz to care for Tosca.

I tried to call Liz but got no answer. I left her a message and tried calling again a few more times. Still no answer.

ME: Emma is safe thanks to you

ME: I bet you dream about me again tonight

I hoped maybe my standard evening text would get a response, even a sarcastic one. It didn't.

I should have told her.

The doorbell rang. I opened the door to find Katie, but she wasn't alone. And I recognized the low-life that had his arm around her. It was Nick Knowlton, the same fucker that had broken my stepbrother Liam's nose in high school. He'd been bad news then, and his cold eyes told me he was probably worse now.

Katie was dressed in full motorcycle leathers, and Nick wore a leather jacket. Riding a bike with this guy? Was she nuts?

I braced myself and stood in the doorway, hoping he'd make a move and I could pay him back for Liam, but Katie just shoved her way by me, and Nick turned away after telling her to remember their appointment tomorrow morning.

"What appointment?" I demanded after I closed the door.

"Nick is taking me over to see what's left of my house."

"No, he's not," I told her. "You're staying here with me until this whole thing is over."

Constance went into the other room, and Winston busied himself in the kitchen.

Emma sat on the couch with another glass of wine, seeming determined to stay out of this family squabble.

Katie stomped her foot. Her high heels didn't fit with the over-long leather pants she wore, but I kept that to myself.

"Stop trying to tell me what to do," she said.

"You're staying here, and that's final." I went back to my bedroom to try calling Liz again in private.

Still no answer.

Then I heard the front door slam.

I came out of my room. "Where'd she go?" I asked Winston.

He just pointed to the door.

"Come back here!" I yelled as I lunged for the door.

When I got to the hallway, Katie had already entered the elevator.

I sent Winston after her, but he came back empty-handed.

"She left with Nick," he reported.

"Well, go after them."

Winston came over and fixed me with a stern gaze. "Calm down, Patrick. I know Nick. She's safe with him. Protecting you guys here and finding Paisley has to be the priority. And besides, where would I go to find her?"

He had a point. I was probably overreacting. I needed to calm down and focus on Emma and Monica, and of course Liz. Monica couldn't know any more about where Katie was now than we did.

CHAPTER 29

Liz

I HAD BARELY SLEPT LAST NIGHT, THINKING ABOUT HOW STUPID I'D been. I had broken my rule and brought it on myself, and now I had to escape the problem.

"But why are you leaving, Auntie Liz?" Timmy asked again.

This was the worst part. Saying goodbye, at least for now, to Timmy. I sniffled. He was making this extremely hard.

"Because I have to go back to school now that your mommy is finishing up her degree."

"But you can go to school here."

Stacey intervened to help me. "No, Tim, she has to go to school up north. Just like you have to catch the bus right now." She pulled him and his backpack toward the door.

I wiped my nose and got back to packing my things. The school registrar's office had given me a code to register for classes for the summer quarter when I'd thought I might take an online course. Now I planned to take a full load plus some. With the scholarship, I could afford to start now instead of waiting until next year. Things were coming together. I could leave LA behind and get on with the next stage of my life.

Pat was my past, and Davis Veterinary School was my future. I would need some income on the side, but not too much. I wasn't worried. I was a good worker. Who wouldn't want to hire me?

Stacey returned from seeing Timmy to the bus. "I still think you're making a mistake," she said.

"We've been through this," I told her.

She'd kept after me for hours last night.

"You've said a million times that you wanted to date a rich professional type, and here comes one, and you throw him away."

It wasn't fair when she used my own words against me. "But I never said *lying* professional, now did I? And he's not a professional like a lawyer or a dentist or whatever. All he does is go out to bars and collect women. I don't even think he has a job."

She crossed her arms. "You don't know that for sure."

I started another cup of coffee. "Didn't you hear me about the trophy drawer?"

"You don't know about that for sure either."

"What kind of guy has a drawer full of different sizes of women's underwear? And bras? And did I tell you about the ripped ones? He just wanted to add a pair of mine to his fucking collection."

That stopped my sister, but only momentarily. "I'm just saying, you need to get off your high horse and talk to the guy. What's so hard about that?"

Hard? She had no idea how hard it was to realize what a doormat I'd been since I met Pat Patterson in his big pickup named after his high-school girlfriend. He'd lied to me every single day.

I poured my coffee into a travel mug for the trip and added a Splenda packet. I gritted my teeth.

"What's the use? He would just lie about it anyway. I'm done. Can't you understand that?"

"From what I saw, he's a good guy, and he cares about you. Just calm down, take a breath, and work it out with him."

"Cares for me? He didn't care enough to be honest. So now he's the good man, and this is all my fault?" I threw up my hands. "I forced him to lie? I'm sorry, I am not having this discussion any more. I didn't do anything wrong. And anyway, he's going to leave, so it doesn't matter."

"You don't know that for sure either."

"He's taking a job with the family company in Boston come September. I saw the letter. And you can add that to the list of lies. Remember his little saying? FCF? It's embossed on his fucking wallet, for God's sake. Family comes first means he has to take the job with the family company, and where does that leave us with me going to Davis? Huh?"

"So that's really what this is about, isn't it?"

"Look, he's leaving in September. I'm just moving up the clock so we don't waste any more time together that we'll regret later."

"Right," Stacey said sarcastically.

"Right. The black and white on paper is the one truth. He's leaving."

Stacey finally gave up.

I continued packing. I didn't have a lot of stuff, but since I wasn't coming back, I needed to fit it all into my little shitmobile with the animals and hope it didn't break down on the way. When I got to my nightstand drawer with the cards, I stopped, and warmth overtook me. I sat, and the tears welled up again.

There in the drawer were a dozen Christmas cards from Santa, neatly packed in a plastic bag. Each Christmas these cards came to Stacey and me with twenty new twenty-dollar bills folded inside and an inscription that read *Merry Christmas, Love Santa*. The return address was always *The North Pole*, but the postmark was always Sacramento.

We didn't know anyone in Sacramento and had always suspected they came from Auntie Joyce. We called every year to thank her for her cards, although she always claimed they must be from Santa and told us we should believe in the miracle of Christmas. I wiped my eyes and put the bag in my purse.

Auntie Joyce lived in Winters, not far from Davis, and she'd told me I could crash there until I found a place of my own. So her house was my destination for today. It was four hundred boring freeway miles away.

I stuffed as much as I could in the trunk, the backseat, and passenger seat. I left enough space on top for the dogs and the cats. I tied a string on each cat's collar so I could control them somewhat when I had to get out of the car to pee and gas up. I dreaded the thought of one of them getting loose at a stop.

"Promise me you'll call him," Stacey said as I loaded the last cat.

I climbed in, closed the door before a critter could get loose, and cracked the window.

"Soon as I get there," I lied.

The message I'd left Pat was the last communication I planned on having with him. It was the only way to keep my sanity and stay safe.

"Please don't tell him where I went," I added.

She shook her head. "Chicken," she called as I backed out of the driveway. We waved to each other as I drove off.

I would miss her and Timmy, but I wasn't a chicken. I was being mature. Best for me to leave it all behind before I got myself in any deeper and he hurt me even more.

I had left a voicemail for Anthony telling him I had a family emergency up north and needed to leave town. I hated to lie to him ——he had been so good to me. But I had no choice. It was an emergency, my emergency. I had to leave.

"Good riddance, Pat fucking Covington. You are not going to make a fool out of me," I said to my car full of pets as I merged onto the freeway heading north. "You can't leave me, because I'm leaving you, you fucking bastard. This is one girl you can't add to your list of conquests."

It felt good to say it out loud. Missy thought I was talking to her and reached around the headrest to lick my ear. This was going to be an awfully long drive.

~

*P*AT

"HER MESSAGE SAID SHE WAS MOVING ON. THANKS FOR THE GOOD times and goodbye, that sort of thing," I told Emma the next morning over breakfast at the condo.

Tosca joined us, lying at my feet, waiting for something to drop.

I hadn't slept at all last night, worrying about Liz, wondering what she was thinking, and second-guessing all the things I'd done and not done. The dull ache in my chest ate away at me. I had tried to call her, but she wouldn't pick up, and now my calls went straight to voicemail.

"And she won't take my calls," I continued.

Emma put her toast down. "Give her a day or two, Patrick. She's a smart girl. She'll come around after she gets over the shock. You realize this wouldn't have happened——"

"I know. You don't need to rub it in. I already got the lecture at a hundred decibels from Katie this morning."

My sister had reminded me and then reminded me another three times how she'd warned me that my fake-name approach was the wrong way to go. I had surrendered my pride and admitted she'd been right. Again. It was so painful having little miss I-don't-do-relationships giving me relationship advice.

Emma added jam to her toast. "Just saying."

"I give. Just mark me down as too stupid to take advice."

I was the problem-solver; I could fix anything. I didn't know how to fix this yet, but I could get there. I had to.

"Don't forget stubborn," she added.

I tore the corner off my toast and dropped it for Tosca. I left Emma finishing her breakfast and went back to my room.

I stared at the job offer letter from Bill. I had accepted it before I'd even met Liz, not that I had a choice. Liam was leaving the company to go to medical school in the fall, and Bill needed me to take over for him and run the Boston office. As a Covington, family came first, and this wasn't really an offer. It was an obligation, one that, for the sake of my family, I couldn't shirk.

Liz had just learned Pat Patterson was a fabrication. When I told her about Boston and asked her to move away with me and leave her family, it would now be that much harder to swallow. There had to be a way to soften it. I just didn't have the answer yet.

First things first, I needed to explain that Pat Patterson had just been a way to get to know her without my name messing things up the way it had so often in the past. I could kick myself for not finding a time to tell her before now.

I disregarded Emma's advice and called Liz again. No answer. Kicking the desk didn't fix the problem, but it made me feel better.

"Patrick, stop throwing a fit and come out here," Emma called through the door.

"Talk to me about her," she said when I returned.

I settled into the chair. "She's smart, which goes without saying because she got accepted into the UC Davis Veterinary program. She's probably the most compassionate person I've ever met. When I first bumped into her, she had stopped on the side of the road to help Tosca here."

I patted Tosca's head. "She'd been hit by a car that didn't stop. She wasn't Liz's dog, and Liz had no idea who the owner was, but she was determined to take care of her. Which, of course, makes perfect sense because her goal in life is to become a veterinarian. In addition, she wants to buy a ranch and set up a retirement home for horses that are too old to be ridden anymore."

Emma stirred her coffee and waited for me to continue.

"She has a zest for life. She makes me laugh at myself, and she enjoys simple things. She's great with her nephew, and I can tell she would be a great mom herself."

It should have seemed strange to be talking about Liz as a mother, but it didn't.

"Did I tell you she even tried to scare me off by pretending her nephew was her son?"

Emma laughed and shook her head. "No, but that sounds like a really good boyfriend test. And I'm guessing you passed."

"Of course. I'm great with kids."

"I didn't mean you weren't. I meant you passed because it didn't scare you off like it would most guys."

"Yeah. Tim is a great kid."

"So, what else?"

I got up to refresh my coffee. "She's been dealt a pretty shitty hand in life. Her Dad died when she was young." I returned to the table. "Her Mom died recently, and she stepped up to take care of her sister and nephew. She quit college so she could put her sister through nursing school. Stacey, that's the sister, is just about to finish now. She's responsible, and she puts family first, just like we do."

Emma smiled and nodded. "What else did you learn about her yesterday and today?"

"Well, she's observant and clever. Constance said she's the one that put together the upside-down tattoo thing to identify that piece of shit Willey as the second person in the car that night they were chasing you."

Emma cringed. "Yeah, and I'm incredibly grateful for that, but what else have you learned?"

I wasn't catching on to what she was after here. I shrugged.

Emma gave me another half minute of silence before telling me what was on her mind. "I'd say Katie only had it half right. She was right that it was stupid to start a relationship with a lie the way you did, but you were right about the other half."

I was dying to know what I was right about after enduring all these lectures on how unbelievably fucking stupid I was.

"You found out she doesn't care about the name or the money. Otherwise she'd be here this morning, overjoyed to find out you're a Covington. Instead, she's off somewhere wishing your name had really been Patterson all along and you were dead broke."

I smiled. Emma had nailed it. Tiffany or any one of the other gold-diggers I'd been with would have been upset for five minutes, but right back in my lap after that. Nothing would have overridden the greed, or the lust for recognition.

I had missed it while I was busy feeling sorry for myself—— the silver lining on my fucking storm clouds. Liz was exactly what I'd been looking for, a woman who cared for me as me, not because of my name or money.

Except that she didn't care for me at all right now.

"You know, Patrick, when she's ready, you need to tell her just what you told me about her. She won't be able to resist you. It's obvious how head-over-heels in love with her you are when you talk about her. It's so much better than just saying I love you, although you need to keep saying that too."

My smile disappeared. I had fucked up. Me, the fuck-up king.

"Not you too?" Emma shook her head and raised her voice. "You didn't tell her you loved her?" she demanded. "You Covington boys are the biggest idiots. You're just like my Steven."

I shook my head. "Guilty."

"Lauren told me Bill was the same. You boys really have a genetic deficiency going on here. How can you be so clueless about women? It's not just about getting into her pants. You have to get into her mind as well. Since high school, guys have been telling us how much they care for us, right before they unhook our bras, so saying it once or twice doesn't mean much. You have to say it and then repeat it, and not just when you're pulling her clothes off."

"But I showed her every day. You have no idea all the things I did for her."

"That's a start, but she needs to hear it too, and often. What did you do for her? Tell me."

"She had a pervert of a boss, so I got him fired, for one."

Emma laughed. "That's a good one. What did she say to that?"

I hesitated. "I didn't tell her I was behind it."

Emma's face scrunched up. "Humble is nice, but pretty stupid right now, don't you think? So, you don't tell her you love her, and you don't tell her the things you're doing to show her you love her. I'd say you're batting a solid zero here. I'm with Katie. You're dumber than a fucking rock."

I had no excuses to offer. I got up to do the dishes. I had to escape this for now and focus on how to fix things when Liz was ready to talk.

I love you: three little words that shouldn't be that hard to say a dozen times. Maybe two dozen to go with two dozen red roses. It sounded like a plan.

I had endured lectures from both Katie and Emma, but I was better off for the experience, which is something I would not have guessed yesterday.

Boy, am I the fuck-up king.

CHAPTER 30

LIZ

GOING UPHILL ON THE LONG I-5 STRETCH LEADING OUT OF LA, I had to stay in the right lane, being passed by big-rig trucks. The horses in my little car's engine had long ago retired and been replaced by out-of-breath hamsters.

The wind made it hard to keep my little shitmobile in the lane. The steering wheel only suggested a direction for the car to go, and it didn't stop me from occasionally running over the dots on the lane dividers. Checking the rear-view mirror, I couldn't locate either of the cats anymore, but one of them was bawling its fool head off.

I pulled into a gas station after the downhill into the valley, realizing I should have filled up before loading the car and also regretting my second cup of coffee. I unbuckled the seatbelt and checked behind me for the cats. I was greeted with a face full of doggy tongue from Missy. No cats in sight. They seemed to have burrowed into my pile of junk somewhere to escape the dogs.

I exited the car quickly, filled the tank, and emptied my bladder. When I opened the door to get back in, Tasha shot out the door. I managed to grab her by the string and her tail before she got away, and I yanked her back into the car. I got the door closed with only a few scratches on my arm for my trouble.

Whose bright idea was it to have the cats loose in the car?

Once in the central valley, it was much hotter than LA. My air conditioner went from sort of working, to not working at all. I cracked the window to get a little fresh air. LA was bearable, but the summer heat in Davis would cook me without working air conditioning. By mid-summer, driving in the Sacramento Valley with the window open would be about as comfortable as pointing a hair dryer at my face.

Just another thing I need to spend money to fix.

The cotton fields of the lower San Joaquin Valley gave way slowly to the almond orchards of the mid-valley as I droned on, battling to keep my four-wheeled menagerie from wandering out of its lane. Families passed me with the children pointing at my car, no doubt laughing at the girl with the dogs lying on top of three feet of clothes in the backseat, their tongues flapping in the breeze.

There was a loud pop, and my car lurched to the right.

I nearly went off the road and down the embankment toward the California Aqueduct alongside the freeway. I managed to keep the car on the pavement, just barely. A horrible *rap-rap-rap* sound came from under the front as I pulled over onto the narrow shoulder, halfway to nowhere. I could just imagine the headlines: *Los Angeles water supply restored after Aqueduct shutdown to recover the bodies of a woman and pets after traffic accident.*

The wind of a passing truck whipped grit in my face as I opened the door and climbed out. I managed to close the door without any escapees running out onto the freeway. I fished a hair band out of my jeans pocket and pulled my hair back into a ponytail. The cars and big rigs whizzing past a few feet away almost blew me over.

I moved around to the front of the car, and my stomach rioted at the sight. My right front tire was mostly shredded.

Now I was stuck on the side of the interstate with a flat tire and the spare in the trunk under half of my belongings. I tried to settle my rolling stomach. I had never changed a tire before, and I was going to get to learn in this heat in the middle of nowhere, with a steady stream of rapidly passing vehicles.

I used the car key to pop the trunk and started to unpack my belongings onto the dirt, praising my decision to at least put some of my clothes in paper shopping bags.

The sun beat down on my back. I had almost reached the bottom of the trunk when a Highway Patrol car with flashing lights pulled up behind me. The officer exited his cruiser and, after briefly surveying my situation, offered to help.

Together we were able to extract the spare from under the floor of the trunk. It was so small it looked like it had come off a shopping cart, but the officer assured me that was normal. Things were looking up. I had never known for sure if I even had a spare.

Just as he was finishing tightening the lug nuts, a series of trucks rolled by a little off the pavement, almost grazing my car.

The wind from the trucks knocked over two of my paper bags of clothes, and now my entire supply of clean panties and a few shirts were blowing across the roadway, getting run over by the constant stream of traffic on the interstate. I wasn't stupid enough to try to retrieve any of them. I was going to have to make do with the one pair of underwear I had on.

The officer pointed out the obvious: I should have put the clothes back in the trunk after taking the tire out. At least he didn't give me a ticket for littering.

After an hour, I had finally squeezed my remaining belongings back into the trunk. It was easier now that some of them had blown away. The price of being a dumbshit today was no clean undies to my name.

Wet dog tongues greeted me as I climbed back into the driver's seat. I still hadn't seen the cats since Tasha's escape attempt, and I hoped they hadn't been crushed under the piles of junk and the weight of the dogs.

Before he drove off, the officer had pointed out the notice on the spare tire that advised keeping my speed down to fifty, and he said to get a real tire put on right away. So now everyone and everything was passing me, with a share of honks and middle fingers coming my way. Constantly having trucks just a few feet from my bumper, urging me to go faster before they passed me, was not improving my mood.

By the time I got to Stockton, a new odor told me that at least one of the cats was alive somewhere in the back, and relieving itself. I gritted my teeth and opened the window a tad more.

Whose bright idea was it to feed the cats this morning?

～

*P*AT

I WAS MEETING PHIL AT OUR USUAL STARBUCKS. I STILL DIDN'T have a plan for going to get my woman. I had decided to listen to Emma and give Liz a day or two.

I took a table near the window after I collected my usual mocha. Jamie behind the register had given up on putting her number on my cup.

A familiar voice surprised me from the doorway. "There he is, and at our table no less."

It was tall Gladys, holding the door open so short Gladys could push her walker inside.

I had inadvertently taken their usual window table. I got up to move for them.

"Nonsense, young man, you sit right back down, and we'll join you," short Gladys called.

Tall Gladys was already nearing the register. She could motor along behind the walker faster than many people walked. I'd always suspected she only used the walker to keep short Gladys company.

Short Gladys made steady progress in my direction as I rearranged the chairs to accommodate them.

"I'd be honored to join the two of you this morning," I told her.

Short Gladys took her seat and waited for tall Gladys to return from the register.

"I'll get your coffees and be right back," I told them.

When I returned, they were dividing up their change on the table. I'd brought extra sugar packets with me. They'd explained once before that they only used real sugar, none of those artificial chemical sweeteners for them.

"Now, you must tell us what's troubling you, Patrick," tall Gladys said.

The comment took me completely by surprise.

"Give me your hand," short Gladys said.

I offered her my hand, and she examined my palm.

"We saw you through the window, and we can tell you're not your usual self this morning," tall Gladys told me.

"It's a woman," short Gladys exclaimed, tracing a line on my palm.

I pulled my hand back. "I'm fine this morning, but my sister-in-law did have some trouble a few days back."

"Did you see that?" tall Gladys said, pointing at my face.

"Sure did," short Gladys answered. "That's a sure sign. Patrick, you're fibbing. We can tell."

"I told you, I'm fine."

"There it was again," short Gladys said.

"Clear as day," tall Gladys echoed. "You're fibbing again."

Phil appeared behind tall Gladys. I hadn't noticed him entering the shop.

"Got room for one more at this table?" he asked us.

The twins kindly agreed, and Phil ordered as I rounded up another chair.

"His name is Phillip. Nice man," tall Gladys told her friend.

"I know that," short Gladys answered.

Phil came back to the table and joined us.

"We were just asking Patrick what's bothering him," tall Gladys told Phil.

"I know it's a woman," short Gladys added.

"Got that right," Phil told them.

I gave him the evil eye, with no obvious effect.

"Her name's Liz," he added.

I stepped on his foot under the table, but got no reaction.

"Nice name," tall Gladys said. "See that? There it is again," she said pointing at my face. "We were right. He was fibbing."

"Clear as day," short Gladys said. "Is she pretty?" she asked Phil, ignoring me.

"You bet."

"But is she nice?" tall Gladys asked him.

"The best, at least from what I hear. But Patrick won't let me near her, afraid I'll steal her away from him."

I had to chuckle. "That'll be the day."

"So what's the problem?" short Gladys asked.

"She left," Phil said.

I grimaced. This was not a conversation I wanted to have with the Gladys twins.

"So what are you doing here?" tall Gladys asked me.

"He's too stupid to figure out how to get her back," Phil answered for me.

"Thanks for the vote of confidence," I said.

"You should be chasing after her," short Gladys said. "Women like that."

"It's pretty simple," tall Gladys offered. "You just give her what she wants most."

"That's what I said," Phil told them, punching me in the shoulder.

I flipped the hat off his head. It hit the floor. "It's not that simple."

Phil picked up his hat. "You hear what I have to put up with? The guy negotiates million-dollar deals on a daily basis, and all of a sudden this is too complicated."

"Easy for you to say," I replied.

Phil had struck a nerve. He was right. I was stuck without a solution for my problem.

The Gladys twins kept badgering Phil for details on Liz, but I wasn't paying attention. They could laugh all they wanted at my expense. Tall Gladys had told me the solution, and Phil was right. I'd been too stupid to see it.

After a few more minutes of ribbing from my tablemates, I checked my watch and excused myself. Phil told me he wanted his truck back, as the Corvette hadn't worked out the way he had hoped. So I made a plan to trade rides with him tomorrow after work. He stayed to joke around with the Gladys twins.

I needed to get Liz what she'd always wanted. It wasn't any more complicated than that.

"Flowers are always a good start," tall Gladys called as I left.

I am going to fix this.

Liz

AS I DROVE ON, FRAGMENTED MEMORIES OF PAT CAME BACK TO haunt me. I would remember the enjoyable times, and warmth would fill me. Then I would almost puke as the vision widened out and I saw that terrible hat——the Patterson Construction hat that now only reminded me how gullible I'd been.

How I had not even asked simple questions? How I had taken for granted what I thought I knew about him and been so wrong?

But I was only half the problem. No, I wasn't even that much of the problem——maybe a tenth of the problem. It all started with his lies. Everything came back to that. Why should I have had to question what he told me or what he didn't? It was his fault, completely his fault for being a lying sack of shit to start with.

I shivered. I had to stop this. I had to move forward to the next phase of my life, one without Pat fucking Patterson or whoever he was. He couldn't leave me and ruin my life. I had fixed that. Now it was time for me to forget him and move on.

The trip had taken longer than I'd thought with the flat tire and the construction delays in Stockton, not to mention being limited to 50 miles an hour. The dogs were either sleeping or passed out from the fumes right up until I turned into Auntie Joyce's driveway. I had cracked the window to get enough fresh air to survive the cat poop smell, and now that we'd arrived, they both wanted to stuff their noses outside.

Auntie Joyce stood back as I managed to find the cats and get all the animals into the house without losing one. She greeted me with a long hug and helped me tackle the unloading of my junk.

Dinner was a simple meatloaf with thankfully no questions about my circumstances and why I needed to show up on her doorstep with absolutely no notice. She wanted to hear about Stacey's progress through her program and how Timmy was doing in school.

My aunt didn't have a television in her house. She simply sat down in her reading chair after we did the dishes. She picked up a book from a stack of romance novels and started to read. She offered me one.

I declined. Those were for people who believed in happy endings. The dogs needed to be walked, and the cat poop in the back of my car needed to be cleaned up.

When I opened the car door, I almost lost my dinner and cursed the cats again. I should have taken away their food this morning.

When I finally got ready for bed, I was dead tired. I had brought my special pillowcase and pulled it on over the pillow. Stacey had put my favorite quote on it as a Christmas present: *Some friends have to walk on four legs so they can carry around such big hearts*. I always knew my four-legged friends loved me, no matter what.

Which was more than I could say for some two-legged ones.

Bone tired, I sank into my pillow.

The next chapter of my life starts now.

P*AT*

THE TWO DAYS EMMA HAD SUGGESTED I WAIT BEFORE CONTACTING Liz had passed. No word from her. My calls and texts still weren't being answered.

I took Gladys' advice and visited the florist. I arrived at Liz's house with a dozen blooms for each day I had missed her.

Neither of the cars was in the driveway or on the street when I arrived, and my knock at the door went unanswered.

When Stacey's car rolled up, Tim got out first.

"Uncle Pat," he called as he ran up to me.

I lifted him up into a big hug. "Hey there, big guy."

Apprehension filled Stacey's face as she closed the car door. "She's not here," she said as she walked up and put her key in the door. "Timmy, why don't you go inside for a while?"

"But I wanna stay out here with Uncle Pat," he complained.

I gave him the stare and pointed inside.

"Yeah, I know. Men do what they have to," he mumbled.

I tousled his hair as he went. "Good man, Tim."

He rewarded me with a smile as he took his backpack inside, and Stacey closed the door.

"You have a fine kid," I told her.

"Shush, don't let him hear you say that. He's now my little *man*, thanks to you. And nice flowers."

I shuffled my feet, unsure how to start. "I need to talk to her."

Stacey's brow furrowed. "I'm sorry, Pat. Didn't she call you?"

"No, and she won't answer my calls either."

She invited me in to talk. She offered a beer, but neither of us was in the mood.

We sat on the couch. One of the pillows was embroidered with: *Some friends have to walk on four legs so they can carry around such big hearts.*

"That's Liz's favorite saying," Stacey told me.

Liz certainly loved her animals. That saying was so typically her.

"She's going to make a terrific vet some day," I said.

Stacey nodded.

"When do you expect her back?" I asked.

She cast her eyes downward. "Pat, she's not coming back. She left two days ago to go back to school up north."

That was a gut punch.

"She promised me she'd call you when she got there to explain."

My stomach dropped. Things were clearly worse than I'd expected. I needed to talk to her, but more importantly, I needed to understand where her mind was.

"Stacey, she means the world to me. The Patterson thing just got out of hand. I didn't want my name to come between us."

Stacey reached out to me. "You need to let her go, Pat. She made up her mind to go back to school, and I don't see how that can be changed now. It has been her dream forever, and she just can't do a long-distance relationship. You're going to have to let her go."

That was one thing I was *not* going to do.

I thanked Stacey and left the flowers with her, mad at myself for not chasing Liz down as soon as I'd gotten Emma to the condo a few days ago. My heart felt like it had been ripped out and thrown into a bottomless pit.

I could have prevented this if I'd acted sooner. I knew I would need time to convince Liz to go with me to Boston, including getting her accepted into a veterinary program out there, but I didn't doubt I could do it. Nothing was out of reach for me if I approached it properly.

Now that Liz was set on going back to Davis, it was going to be a lot harder. She had committed herself, and it was going to be a bitch getting that turned around.

I pounded the steering wheel in frustration as I drove. All I got for my effort was a terrified look from the lady in the car next to me at the stoplight.

A full bottle of Blue Label awaited me back at the condo. It wouldn't stay full for long.

I've fucked this up royally, but letting her go is not an option. I can't live like this.

CHAPTER 31

LIZ

WITHIN A FEW DAYS I HAD GOTTEN MY OLD JOB BACK AS AN assistant at the veterinary practice run by Dr. Scalise. It wouldn't pay much, but experience with the animals was what I yearned for, after all. Dr. Scalise had written a recommendation for me that was probably key to my acceptance at the vet school. I'd helped out a lot in the office with the small animals before I left.

Now he needed help going out and getting dirty at the local farms and ranches on the large-animal side of his practice. Mostly we would be dealing with horses and cows, with a fair number of sheep, goats, and pigs mixed in.

I was going to get my DVM degree, start my ranch, heal people's animals, have a gazillion dogs, and be happy. Alone. Without a man to ruin my life. Dogs were so much easier.

Leaving had been the right thing to do. Taking charge of the situation was better than being a victim of it. I had prevented another heartbreak. I hadn't given Pat the chance to leave me.

Checkmate. I win.

I had won after all. I was in charge of my life.

This evening I was headed back to Auntie Joyce's house smelling worse than when I'd first arrived. Catching and holding on to a pig in his muddy enclosure is smelly work, and a lot harder than I'd imagined. It took me a dozen tries and ten minutes to catch the slippery sucker. This was probably why the senior assistants chose to work in the office.

After a long, hot shower, I was ready to rejoin the human race. I dumped my purse out on the bed, looking for my bottle of Tylenol to relieve the aches and pains from an afternoon of pig wrestling. That despicable yellow envelope tumbled out, along with that silly paper umbrella Pat had given me.

Hawaii, my ass.

I threw the umbrella on the dresser and picked up the envelope. I tore it open. I was going to take a Tylenol anyway, so I decided to get it over with and read the latest bad news courtesy of my asshole ex-boyfriend.

The letter was a complete surprise. *Dear Miss Elizabeth Turner*, it started. *The above described debt*, blah, blah, blah *has been satisfied.*

SATISFIED?

I didn't expect them to be satisfied until they'd drained every last drop of blood from my body. I blinked several times, refocused, and started again at the top. It said the debt had been paid off. They must have finally caught up to Trent, or he'd found some other gullible girl to help him pay for things. I danced out into the kitchen. Things were going my way.

I shared the good news with my aunt over macaroni and cheese. She found my hog experience hilarious as I recounted my day. This job was going to give her washing machine a real workout, if today was any indication.

As usual, she settled into her reading chair after dinner with a romance novel. Today's choice had a half-dressed guy on the cover. I pulled out the Animal Reproductive Physiology textbook I'd gotten at the UC Davis bookstore and settled into the couch.

She wasn't the only one reading about sex tonight. I reached the first set of diagrams.

Why do they call it doggy style, anyway?

Because it's also cat style, frog style, horse style, and elephant style, among others, according to my book.

I closed the book and crossed my legs. This was not helping. I got up and returned with the Microbiology textbook instead. I opened the thick book and started to read. I got all of three pages in before his face appeared again. I couldn't get Pat out of my head in the evening or out of my dreams at night.

I closed my eyes. Time heals all wounds, I'd been told, and with time, I could forget Pat.

"Do you want to talk about him?" my aunt asked, breaking me out of my trance.

"Who?"

"Why, the man, of course," she said.

I hadn't mentioned a thing about Pat since arriving.

"Lizzy dear, you didn't rush up here just to see me. It's plain as day that you're running away from something. I don't think you've become a criminal, so it has to be a man."

The old lady was more astute than I'd given her credit for.

"I'm here because Stacey is finishing her nursing program, and the scholarship I got will let me start back on my degree. That's all."

"If you say so. But I'm here when you want to talk about it."

I went back to my book, but it was no use. I couldn't get Pat out of my head. I turned the page, and he was there again.

For ten minutes, I tried to study. I wanted to get a head start on my classes. It had been a while since I'd done the full-time student thing, and I'd expected it to be hard. But this was beyond hard; it was impossible. I went over the same paragraph three times before I really got all the words. I gave up.

"Okay. His name is Pat," I announced.

I had kept it bottled up inside, and it hadn't gotten any better, so I might as well try talking through it with my aunt. Maybe that would put it behind me.

"Tell me about him. How did you two meet?"

I tried to start at the beginning. "I met him when I stopped to help a dog that had been hit by a car."

"He hit a dog?"

"No, he stopped to help me catch the dog, and he took the dog with him because I was on my way to work and couldn't take her with me."

"That's nice."

It was. "Yeah, and then he came by the restaurant and pretended to be my boyfriend to keep me safe from my creepy boss that was hitting on me, and he drove me home."

The memory of the kiss distracted me momentarily. It had been my first kiss with Pat, and I would never be able to forget it.

"Protective, that's nice," my aunt said, pulling me back to reality.

"Yeah, and he kept coming by even though I told him I couldn't date him."

"Persistent, huh?"

"Very. And that weekend, he showed up at an event I was catering, and when my car wouldn't start, he took me on this dinner date at Santa Monica Pier before driving me home."

"That sounds romantic."

I couldn't lie. "It was."

Recalling our kiss at the top of the Ferris wheel brought back feelings I needed to squash, feelings I needed to forget, to move beyond.

"And he wasn't scared off when I implied that Timmy was my son. He had us over to his house to teach Timmy to swim, and he was just great with him."

I wasn't about to recount the embarrassing conversation about petting his cock.

"Isn't it a good thing that he likes children?"

"Yes, it is, but then he threatened to beat up my boss, and I got my shifts cut back, so my money problems got worse because of him. Because he couldn't control himself."

"Is this the same boss you said was a creep?"

"Uh-huh."

"Well, in my day, before all this women's-lib nonsense, a man that would fight for you was a good thing. I guess that's all changed now, and not for the better, if you ask me."

"No. That's still a good thing." I decided to leave out the whole episode where I went on a stupid date with Blaine because I was mad at Pat.

"So far this Pat fellow sounds pretty dreamy to me. So what happened?"

"It's sort of complicated."

"I'm listening."

"His sister-in-law was being chased by a crazy woman that slashed her tires and burned up her car, and then the same lady burned down his sister's house."

"My God, that's terrible."

"Well, we caught the crazy lady and her brother."

"You said *we*."

"Well, I hope he caught them. I just helped by identifying the crazy lady's brother."

"So you were heroes together then?"

"Sort of. Yeah, I guess that's right. Well anyway, I found out he wasn't who I thought he was. Instead of being in construction, he's a member of a really rich family. I didn't even know his real name."

"I see."

"He'd been lying to me about who he was the whole time."

"And what else?" she asked, leaning forward.

"What else what?"

She put her hot chocolate down. "What else had he been lying about? Is he already married?"

"No."

"In the mafia? Escaped from prison? What?"

"No. Nothing like that, but he is supposed to take a job with his family's company in Boston in the fall, and he didn't tell me about it."

"So what did he say about all this?"

It was a simple enough question, but my answer sounded silly. "Nothing. I didn't confront him. I left."

She took a sip of her hot chocolate. "Oh dear, now I see your problem."

Finally, somebody agreed with me. Stacey thought I was wrong, and I was sick of fighting with her about it.

"Lizzy, you poor thing. You found a man that chased you even when you pushed him away, likes children, stood up and fought for you, and is rich to boot. You got scared and left on an impulse without even talking with him, and now you regret it. I can see why you're so unhappy."

She had totally not heard me. "I'm not unhappy."

She raised a finger. "You can lie to yourself all you want, young lady, but don't you try that on me. If this is you being happy, I'd hate to see you sad."

She picked up her book to go back to reading. "Good talk."

She didn't understand this either. I tried reading my textbook some more without any success.

"Really good talk," she added a few minutes later.

The conversation kept rattling around in my head as I tried to read. I headed to my room a half hour later.

I'm not scared; I'm moving forward. I don't regret it. I'm staying safe.

～

PAT

MY FIRST CALL WAS TO TONY AT THE IRONHORSE. HE SAID HE didn't have a forwarding address for Liz. Her check was auto-deposited. But he would ask discreetly. One of the staff might be able to give me a lead.

Emma had gone back home to Steven, so I was surprised when a key turned in my front door lock.

Juanita emerged from the hallway with her cleaning supplies. She went back into the hallway and returned with a paper bag, which she brought over with a cheerful smile.

"Yesterday when we clean Mister Bill's unit, his wife, she tell me you not happy. So my daughter, Maria, she make you cookies." She produced a Tupperware container from the bag and opened it. "She hope you like chocolate chip."

My face flushed. Her thoughtfulness was touching.

"Absolutely. You tell Maria thank you very much from me."

Juanita nodded vigorously and hummed to herself, going about her cleaning.

I munched my way through three scrumptious chocolaty cookies. Chocolate was truly the food of the gods. My next call was Bob Hanson. He and his sources could find anything and anybody, pretty much. I didn't think Liz was hiding, but I wasn't getting an answer other than "up north" out of Stacey.

I filled him in on the general situation as far as I knew it. Liz had left and was planning on going back to school at UC Davis, so she wouldn't be too far from there.

I gave him her cell number, the details I could remember of her car, and what I knew about her family.

He told me that unless she was serious about hiding off the grid, he could locate her pretty quickly.

I finished a few more cookies while I waited to hear back from him. I figured I needed a location before I could go any further with my plans.

Juanita approached with concern etched on her face. She had been listening. "Mr. Patrick, the *señorita*, she leave?"

Her worry was touching. "Yes, but I'll find her."

"I change my mind. She no good for you, Mr. Patrick. She leave you, she *loco en la cabeza*. You find another."

"I don't want another."

I didn't want anybody else. Juanita meant well, but I wasn't going to debate this with her.

"This *chica*, she no want you, she *loco*."

"She's not loco, just mad," I told Juanita. It was definitely not good that in Juanita-speak Liz had descended from *señorita* to *chica*.

Juanita shook her head and went back to working in the kitchen. The humming had ceased.

"The *chica*, she *loco*," she mumbled again as she cleaned the stove.

Thankfully, it didn't take her long to finish in the kitchen and move on to the guest bedroom, so I didn't have to listen to any more mumbling.

Bob Hanson called back. "Patrick, I have some information for you. A few days ago a CHP officer helped a motorist with a flat tire on I-5. The license plate is a match for your girl's car. And we have her using her credit card at various places the last few days in Davis and Dixon, so she has stopped traveling and is staying near there, west of Sacramento.

That was enough to nail it for me. I went to my room and packed a bag. I was heading to Davis to get my woman. The drive would take all day, and hopefully Hanson would make more progress during that time. I packed my laptop and put the rest of the chocolate chip cookies and two Dr. Peppers from the fridge in my backpack.

I grabbed the bag of dry dog food and Tosca on the way out.

The BMW was still out of commission, so I climbed into the truck and joined the throngs on the 405 north, with Tosca riding shotgun.

I called Judy, Bill's assistant, and asked her to book me a hotel in Davis.

"Just make sure it's dog friendly," I told her.

I also had her book me a rental car. I wanted to blend in as much as possible. Then the hard part: I had her connect me to Bill.

"Bill, I'm quitting the company, and I can't take the job in Boston," I told him bluntly.

I felt terrible letting him down like this, but I had no choice. Liz had to be my top priority.

Silence.

"*Patrick, I really need you. The family needs you. Liam starts school in the fall. We have to have someone we can trust out there.*"

"I'm sorry. I just can't. I'm going after Liz."

He didn't say anything for the longest time.

"*Good luck then. Let me know if I can help,*" he finally offered, and I was sure he meant it.

I made a pit stop in the Central Valley for three quarter pounders, a chocolate shake, and gas. This truck got shitty mileage. Back on the road, I gave the dog her burger and dialed up Phil.

"Phil, I can't meet this afternoon after all. I want to keep Maggie a little longer."

"*Any longer and you'll have to fucking buy her from me.*"

Why not? "Fuck it then. I'll trade you straight up. You keep the 'Vette, and I keep the truck."

"*You shittin' me?*" he asked.

"We'll trade pinks later when I get back. I need the truck."

"*It's the girl, isn't it? She's really got you all fucked up.*"

He was right that Liz had gotten to me, but not the way he thought. "No, bud, you got it ass backwards. Everything was fucked up until I met her."

He didn't respond right away. *"Then put some of those fucking Stanford MBA deal-making skills of yours to work and go fix it."*

My friend understood.

"That's the plan," I told him.

Shortly after that, Tony called with my first concrete information. He had learned from one of The Ironhorse waitresses that Liz was staying with her aunt near Davis. He didn't have her name, but I passed the info on to Hanson.

The drive was boring as hell, and I was glad I hadn't chosen long-haul truck driver as a profession. I wasn't cut out for the monotony of these endless freeways. I hadn't slept hardly at all the last few nights, busy worrying about Liz. The occasional phone calls were all I had to keep me awake.

I pulled off at a Starbucks before I reached Stockton for a double extra-shot mocha to help me stay alert. By the time I reached the outskirts of Sacramento, Hanson's boys had learned that Liz's aunt's name was Joyce Faulkner, and they had an address for her in Winters, fifteen miles west of Davis.

Uncle Garth called to tell me that they had caught Monica, and as expected, the DA was adding attempted kidnapping to the felony arson Monica and Blaine would be charged with. He said there was still nothing firm to tie Monica to the fire at Katie's house, but he was working it with the Hanson people.

He must have heard from Bill that I was going after Liz. He gave me one of his pithy sayings before he hung up:

"John Wayne said it best: When the going gets tough, the tough get going."

It was dark when I reached the La Quinta Judy had booked for me. Davis was a small college town with modest accommodations, but this would do just fine. I needed to be close. It was too late to pick up the rental car, so Tosca and I settled into the motel.

A quick walk down the street to the local grocery store and liquor store and I had my rations for tonight: a pint of rocky road and a fresh bottle of Blue Label.

I dug into the ice cream, pulled out my pad of paper, and opened my laptop to start my search. I had a mission and a plan. Nothing could stop me now. I knew what I would be dreaming about tonight: success.

I hit the sack near midnight after a glass of belly-warming scotch. Followed by another larger one.

Liz, I hope you're still dreaming about me at night. I'm counting on it.

CHAPTER 32

Liz

My aunt was leaving for the store when I got back from work.

I pulled off my shoe, limped to the kitchen, and found a Ziploc baggie. I filled it with ice cubes and a little water. The cold relieved some of the pain. Today we'd been giving injections to horses, and one of them didn't take well to the needle. Tennis shoes were not the right footwear for working around skittish, thousand-pound animals with steel shoes.

Sturdy work boots were now on my list of things to buy with my first paycheck.

The side of my foot was black and blue, but it was hurting less than it had earlier. Dr. Scalise had examined me and proclaimed that it was no big deal——my foot wasn't broken. Easy for him to say. He wore steel-toed boots. Still, I trusted the doctor enough to skip going in for an X-ray, which Stacey would have insisted on if she were here. Such was the life of a large-animal vet. Working with horses, cows, and the like was one part medicine and two parts wrestling.

It always amazed me how puny humans like us could get horses nearly ten times our size to do what we asked without kicking us into the next township, or stomping us. The poor horse hadn't meant to hurt me. My foot had just been in the wrong place at the wrong time. I had learned a lesson about being careful that I wouldn't forget.

Auntie Joyce returned from shopping with a small bag of groceries and announced that tonight's dinner was going to be her special tuna casserole. She nearly fainted when she saw the color of my foot.

I explained the accident. We agreed about my poor choice of shoes and agreed to disagree about my sanity. I had charted my course, and I was sticking to it. But she did change my mind about waiting for my paycheck to get boots. It moved up to my list for tomorrow.

After dinner, my aunt plopped herself down in her usual chair and opened up the romance novel she hadn't finished yesterday. The title was something about Vikings, and the cover featured a shirtless, muscled hunk with long hair. Of course she could believe in happily-ever-after endings if she believed muscled Scandinavian hunks ran around shirtless in the frigid, snowy north.

I went to my room, opened my backpack, and pulled out my Microbiology book. As I did, the baggie with those Christmas cards I'd brought fell out. Mom had merely smiled and insisted that if the envelope said they came from Santa, that must be true. But the cards had come even after Mom died, so she couldn't have been their source. That had settled it. It had to be Auntie Joyce.

I decided now was as good a time as any to have a chat with my aunt.

She looked up from her book as I approached, smiling, as was her nature.

"Auntie Joyce, I just want to tell you again how thankful

Stacey and I have been over the years for these wonderful Christmas cards."

Momentary confusion wrote itself on her face until she recognized the cards in my little bag. "That's so nice of you to say, Lizzy, but those aren't from me."

I was prepared for the denial. I pulled out one of the envelopes. "We know better than that. They're all postmarked from Sacramento. Of course they're from you."

She smiled, but did not acknowledge the obviousness of my observation. "No need to thank me. It's important for family to take care of one another. It's just what we do."

She wore older, somewhat threadbare clothes, and nothing in the little house was new. Her car was older than mine, and even the romance novels were from the library. The cards had truly been gifts from the heart if she'd parted with that much money on her limited budget.

Her reminder about the importance of family brought back an image of Pat's wallet and the *FCF* embossed on it. Family really should come first. That's why I knew it had been right for me to leave. I needed to make it easy for Pat to do the right thing and follow through on his commitment to his family.

Family should come first for all of us.

∼

PAT

I HAD SHOWN UP FOR OUR FIRST MEETING DRIVING MY RATTY OLD pickup, with Tosca in the backseat. But the dismay evident on her face disappeared as soon as I handed her my business card: *VP of Acquisitions, Covington Industries.*

Tracie Barnett's heels echoed in the open space of the large, empty house. She was dressed in a light blue business suit with a single-strand pearl necklace, the perfect image of a successful real estate lady. She had been the first to answer my early morning calls and was also willing to devote herself full time to my search, putting all her other clients on hold for a few days.

Sunshine came through the windows onto the warm oak floors. A skylight and tall ceilings lent the space an airy openness. The kitchen opened into the family room with an unobstructed view out the back through tall windows. A pair of ducks paddled in the small pond to the left, and the picnic table under a large oak tree next to the pond looked like an idyllic spot for a picnic lunch. The pool off to the right of the shaded patio would provide a welcome respite on a hot summer day.

Although the kitchen appliances were a bit dated, the layout was good and large enough, and the dark color of the cool granite countertops offset the light-colored cabinets. The bedrooms were also spacious enough, with a large walk-in closet attached to the master. There was a dedicated office, and a room that would be perfect as a gym. This house had good, solid bones.

We went outside and toured the back of the property before returning to the house.

"Tracie, I think this is the one," I told her. "What do you think we need to offer to get a quick close on this house?"

Tracie responded immediately. "In today's market, we should get a pretty fast answer to a full-price offer on something that has this many days on market."

"And what do you think qualifies as fast?"

"We normally would give them forty-eight hours to respond, and twenty four would be fast."

"That's way too long. I want to write the offer with a response due six hours from now and closing in two days," I told her.

Her jaw dropped. "But, but, there's just no way to get all the inspections done and financing in place in two days."

"We're not doing inspections. I've seen enough. No inspections, no contingencies, no financing. All cash in two days. Only title insurance, nothing else. And write it for fifty thousand over asking."

Tracie quickly regained her composure with a smile and nodded. I was obviously her kind of customer——lots and lots of money and absolutely no brains. She opened her Kate Spade bag, brought out the forms, set them on the table, and started writing.

"One other thing, Mr. Covington."

"Pat," I corrected her again.

"If you really want to make an impression with the seller, I would make the deposit more than the three percent that's standard in California."

"Make it ten percent. No, twenty percent."

She laughed. "I meant five or six, but twenty will definitely get their attention."

I truly was her kind of customer.

Ten minutes later, she had a written offer ready for me to sign.

I signed, initialed all the pages, gave her the deposit check, and we were ready to go. My stomach churned as she replaced the key in the lock box, and I stayed out front as she drove off to get the offer to the selling agent. I was more nervous doing this small transaction than I had been in most of my larger corporate deals. This one was personal.

I let Tosca out of the truck again, and we went around back to wander the property that was soon to be mine. Ours.

A warm calm filled me as I started to visualize the future.
Our future.

WITH SOME TIME ON MY HANDS, I PICKED UP THE RENTAL CAR, a nice, nondescript sedan. At the end of the day, I navigated to the address Hanson had gotten me earlier. I parked a block and a half away on the wide street and began to rehearse my speech again

——out loud. Not that I was going to use it today, but I couldn't help myself.

My mouth was dry. I was on the fourth or fifth iteration, and it wasn't getting any better. It sounded more lame every time.

Why did women have to be so difficult? I loved Liz, I screwed up, I was sorry——it should be as simple as that.

But it isn't, is it?

Around six I began questioning whether I had the right place. Then her little blue car drove up and parked in front of the small tan house I'd been watching.

I sat up tall.

My Liz got out. She stopped to brush dust off of her clothes. She had mud on the knees of her jeans and her boots. My heart ached with how beautiful she was. She walked to the front door and was gone.

I squelched the urge to follow her and knock on the door. I needed to get her in an environment where she couldn't run away or close the door without hearing me out. This was too important to screw up.

I turned the sedan around and returned to my lonely motel room. My leg started to tremble nervously again. I needed a plan to get her alone. I still needed to work that out.

You are mine, Liz. You just don't recognize it yet.

Liz

THE AROMA OF TOMATOES, BASIL, AND OREGANO GREETED ME AS I opened the door. Something Italian was clearly on the menu for tonight. I took off my muddy new boots just inside the door and wandered into the kitchen. Meatballs were grilling in a skillet, and a pan bubbled with a fragrant tomato sauce.

"Spaghetti and meatballs," Auntie Joyce announced joyfully as I dipped a spoon in to taste the sauce.

"Absolutely delicious," I pronounced before heading to my bedroom to change.

The assistants in the office got to wear lab coats, which kept the dog and cat hair off of them. But out in the field with Dr. Scalise and the farm animals was a dirtier environment than I'd imagined. The upside was working outside in the fresh air and sunshine, and meeting the down-to-earth ranchers and farmers. It also meant avoiding the neurotic housewives who brought in their darling dachshunds with bad breath.

Dinner was filling and scrumptious. Auntie Joyce could work wonders with the simplest ingredients. That was something I had yet to master.

My aunt cut into a meatball. "Have you heard from him yet?"

I feigned ignorance. "Him who?"

"Why, the one you've been pining for, of course."

"I'm not pining in the least," I lied.

I knew I needed to move forward somehow, but my thoughts kept dragging me back to Pat.

Somehow she could read my thoughts. "Whatever you say, dear," she said, without making it sound as sarcastic as it was.

My mood vacillated with my memories. One moment I would remember seeing the letter sending him to Boston, and hearing Constance as she explained that the sumptuous penthouse condo was Pat's and his name wasn't Patterson after all. I would be jittery with anger and sure of my path. I had to move forward without him. I couldn't let him destroy me. I just couldn't. There wasn't enough Super Glue in the world to put my heart back together again if I allowed that.

Other times I would see a man and a woman holding hands, or a man petting a dog, or just a hamburger. Any of these and more brought back memories of good times with Pat——no, way better than good. For a short time, he had healed my heart and showed me what it could be like on the sunny side of reality, where life was carefree, laughter flowed freely, and simple things made me smile. Where a simple touch could brighten my day.

Then the cycle would start again. I would see my father's face, and Pat's face——it was so confusing. I couldn't risk the pain again.

Thankfully, Auntie Joyce changed the subject to ask me about my day with Dr. Scalise.

After dinner was cleaned up and the dishwasher loaded, she picked up a new novel and settled into her reading chair.

I went back to my room and decided to do battle with the dresser and put the rest of my things away.

I lost the battle.

The top left drawer opened, but the others wouldn't cooperate. I gave up and returned to the couch with my Microbiology book for another go at studying.

"Is there some trick to opening the drawers on the dresser?" I asked my aunt as I sat down.

She looked over her glasses at me. "No trick. The top left opens; the others don't."

I thought about it for a moment. "I could get it fixed for you."

"Absolutely not. I like it just the way it is. It reminds me of what's important." She went back to her book without explaining further.

It seemed it was up to me to pull it out of her. "How does a dresser that doesn't work, remind you of anything important?"

She put her book down with a smile and took a sip from her ever-present hot chocolate. "My father, your grandfather, made it as a wedding present for my mother. It's handmade, with love. He was so in love with my mother, and in such a hurry to finish it, that he didn't take time to let the wood acclimate. So it swelled up later, and the drawers got stuck. He offered to fix it for her, but she refused."

She took another sip of her hot chocolate. "I asked her about it once. She said it was a reminder that even good people with the best intentions can make mistakes."

She took another sip before continuing. "I like it because I think it teaches me two lessons. One, that even good people make honest mistakes, and two, that it's also important how we respond to those mistakes. She thought his intentions were more important than the mistakes. And that's the way I want to remember the two of them, so I like it just the way it is." She went back to her novel.

I opened my Microbiology book after removing the cat from my lap. The other cat lay on the back of the couch, purring near my ear and making it even harder to concentrate. The words swam in front of me as I mulled my aunt's explanation of the dresser.

CHAPTER 33

LIZ

"WHAT'S NEXT ON THE SCHEDULE?" DR. SCALISE ASKED AS HE slid behind the wheel the next afternoon.

I opened his old leather appointment book, which sat on the seat, and gave him the next address.

"ETF, the patient is a ten-year-old quarter horse named Doc," I told him, reading his shorthand.

"ETF——equine tooth float," he told me. "Horses need dentistry too. A horse's teeth grow about an eighth of an inch a year. They grind them off as they chew their food. The problem is, a horse's upper jaw is wider than its lower, so the surfaces of the teeth don't end up flat."

One of the great things about working for Dr. Scalise was how much he enjoyed teaching as we went about the day.

"So, horses have a tendency to get sharp edges on their teeth, which can make them real uncomfortable when they're chewing," he continued. "A horse that can't chew is not going to stay healthy for long. Our job is to rasp the teeth flat, which is what we call floating."

Getting a horse to take a rasp in his mouth didn't sound like an easy proposition to me. We turned to the right at the intersection, and Dr. Scalise explained my part in the procedure. He would sedate the horse, and I would need to hold his head up. That was no easy chore, as a horse naturally hung his head low under sedation.

I'd had to hold a horse's head up for five minutes the day before yesterday, and it had been a challenge. The horse had gotten a deep cut and couldn't go without stitches. Getting a stitching needle anywhere near the face of a horse that hadn't been heavily sedated was only for people with a death wish.

We reached the address and turned into the drive. The sign read *Four Legs Retirement Ranch*.

"This used to be the Armstrong place. They moved down to Arizona six months ago. I guess it finally sold," Dr. Scalise told me as we parked on the gravel drive. "You locate our patient," he said pointing to the barn. "And put him in the cross ties while I get my equipment."

I stopped for a moment. My insides were warmed by what I saw on the front of the barn. I liked these people already. A large plaque next to the door read: *Some friends have to walk on four legs so they can carry around such big hearts*. They had chosen my favorite quote.

I went down the aisle inside the barn, checking for our patient. The smell of pine shavings permeated the air. There were at least twenty stalls, all empty so far. The barn was extremely upscale, with rubber matting on the aisle floor instead of dirt or concrete. I found the horse midway down. He was a good-looking bay quarter horse gelding.

The name tag on the feed door said *Doc*, matching our appointment book. The tag listed his owner as Elizabeth, the lucky girl. The last name was covered over with blue tape. The stall had a thick layer of clean, fresh shavings and opened to a long paddock outside.

I breathed in a lung-full of the fresh pine aroma. They took good care of their horses here. I slid open the door and put the halter on Doc. He nuzzled me as I led him out into the aisle, paying particular attention to my pocket, which held horse cookies for when we were done.

Dr. Scalise came in with his supplies and set them down. He disinfected the horse's neck and gave him an intravenous injection of tranquilizer.

I undid the cross ties, which weren't safe now that we'd sedated the horse, and reattached the lead rope.

It didn't take very long for Doc's eyelids to become droopy and his head to start hanging down. And suppressing a giggle, I noticed his head wasn't the only thing now hanging down. A male horse's first response to the sedative was to drop his dong, a sure-fire indication that it was working.

The doctor's phone rang, and he answered and listened intently for a few moments.

"Liz, just stay here with him until he comes out of it and then you can put him back in the stall. I'll be back as soon as I can to pick you up. Got a colic emergency I need to tend to."

I nodded. There was nothing for me to do now but wait. The horse's head was already heading for the floor, and sedated horses couldn't be forced to go anywhere. They just locked up their legs and became wobbly, four-legged statues.

I scratched his withers and talked softly to him.

A dog wandered into the barn and started toward me, its tail wagging expectantly. The friendly yellow lab reached me and sniffed at my leg, followed by my crotch, demanding to be petted.

"Hi." The voice came from the entrance.

I stiffened and looked up to see someone at the doorway. I couldn't make out the face against the back-lighting of the bright sunshine, but I knew the voice.

Pat.

I didn't say anything in response. My chest tightened. I wanted to hide, but I was trapped, like a fly on fly-paper. I had to stay with the horse, which was getting drowsier by the minute. There was no escape.

I reached down and gave in to the dog. It was Tosca, the Labrador that had introduced us those many weeks ago.

Dr. Scalise had driven off with my lifeline. My phone was in the truck. The phone didn't take well to getting stepped on by live-stock, and I hadn't enjoyed cleaning it off the time it fell into the pig slop, so I had established the habit of leaving it in the truck.

How had Pat found me out here alone in this barn in the middle of nowhere?

He walked toward me. "Nice horse you have there."

He wore his usual jeans and work shirt, with the fake Patterson Construction cap. So much of him was fake.

"You wouldn't know a nice horse if it kicked you in the ass. And he's not mine. He belongs to some girl."

"Lucky girl," he said continuing toward me. "And if it kicked me, I'd know it wasn't nice."

"What are you doing here? I told you it was over, and I meant it." I tried to make it sound as final as I could, even though his sudden appearance was making me question that.

I couldn't deny the pull he still had on me as he approached. I had to be strong.

"We have to talk," he said with his hands in his pockets.

"We just did. I said all I have to say. And if you need a refresher, just pull up the voicemail," I responded. "It's over. It's full-on, in-the-rear-view-mirror past."

He was silent as his cat-like eyes bored into me.

I broke eye contact and checked Doc. My hand was shaking.

Pat moved up to rub the horse's drooping forehead. "Then I'll talk to your horse here, and you can just listen."

This man made a mule look cooperative. I crossed my arms and waited for the lying to begin. What choice did I have?

"Liz, I have to apologize for not telling you my name earlier. I'm not sure how it got so out of hand."

I knew. "I'll tell you how it got out of hand," I spat. "You lied to me every single time we were together, you asshole."

I hoped swearing at him would get him to leave me alone.

It didn't work. "I agree it wasn't right. I screwed up. And it wasn't because of you; it was because of me. I was being selfish. I was trying to protect myself. My family name has always screwed up my relationships with women."

I rolled my eyes.

"I meant to tell you sooner, but I didn't get the chance. I apologize for that. But everything else I told you——my feelings and everything else——was the truth, each and every day. Everything we did and felt for each other, that's all real."

He thought I was stupid enough to believe that? What fucking feelings? He had never really shared his feelings with me, other than fucking me.

"What about lying about what you did for a living? And where you lived?"

He inched closer. "I told you that wasn't my house up front. I told you I was staying in it for Phil, and that was the truth. As for being a carpenter, I never told you that. You just assumed I was, and I didn't correct you. I told you I had my fingers in a lot of pies, and I do. I do a lot of different things."

He was trying to confuse me. Now I couldn't recall a time that he'd actually had said he was a carpenter.

"Omissions are just as bad as lies," I stammered.

It wasn't fair that he hadn't told me the truth.

He closed the distance some more. "Look, I'm human. I screwed up. Let's start over." He offered me his hand to shake. "Hi, my name's Patrick Covington."

I chose firmness over rudeness. I took his hand and shook, pulling mine back quickly.

"Let me remedy that now by filling in some of the things I've neglected to tell you." He took one of my hands in his.

I didn't pull back; for some reason I couldn't. The warmth of his touch brought unwanted feelings to the surface and welded my hand to his.

"All that matters to me is you. One of the things I didn't tell you," he continued, "is that I took care of your boss *for you*. I did that for you."

He was manipulating my feelings, and my brain was off kilter. He was trying to mix me up.

"You must be off your meds, cowboy. You beat him up, and as cute as the gesture was, it almost cost me my job. That's not doing me a favor."

He squeezed my hand gently and fixed me with those amber eyes. "No. I told you I *didn't* beat him up, and that was the truth. But what I didn't tell you was that I fired him."

"What?"

"I bought The Ironhorse," he said very slowly. "And I had Tony fire him."

I gasped. My legs became wobbly. Now my world was spinning out of control. My heart thudded against my ribcage. I couldn't believe he'd done that for me. He bought the restaurant just to fire Ben? Anthony was Tony? Anthony worked for him? I had worked for him?

"How could you not tell me that?"

"I did it for you." His gaze fixed me in place as he held my hand. "But I couldn't tell you. How could Pat Patterson have afforded to do that?" He shifted his weight.

"Also, about your little car-loan problem with that douchebag ex of yours, Trent… I bought that debt from the collection company and had them tell you it had been paid off."

Somehow, it just didn't make sense. So much of what I knew for a fact he was telling me was wrong.

"And I also didn't tell you that I arranged for your Davis scholarship."

I pulled my hand back. "No?"

"Yeah, pretty stupid, because it let you leave me, which is the last thing I wanted."

He was right. The scholarship is what had given me the freedom to leave LA so quickly.

"I don't understand. Why?"

"Because I love you, Elizabeth Turner, with all my heart."

What the hell?

That shook me to my core. My heart raced. He says that now? I searched his eyes and saw only warmth and sincerity, not the deviousness I expected.

He moved closer. "Liz, I quit Covington. This is my new home, here with you."

Now he was talking gibberish.

"Give me a break." I knew he still had to go to Boston. The printed page didn't lie.

"I think Winston Churchill said it best," he told me. "There is nothing better for the inside of a man or a woman, than close contact with the outside of a horse."

It was a touching sentiment for someone who had never ridden before.

"This is my new home, here with you and the horses," he said.

I couldn't process this. How could I believe him?

"What about Boston?" I managed to squeak out.

His eyebrows shot up. He hadn't expected me to know about Boston.

"I'm not taking the job in Boston. I quit Covington. Like I told you, my life is here now. Here with you and your horse." He went over to the name tag on Doc's stall and pulled off the blue painter's tape that had covered the owner's last name. It read *Elizabeth Turner*.

"You got me a horse? I can barely afford to feed myself, much less take care of a horse."

"Elizabeth, I'm giving you more than just a horse. I'm giving you this whole ranch."

He took my hand again. "You're the best thing that has ever happened to me. You're smart——no, make that brilliant."

I felt an unwanted blush rising in my cheeks.

"You're compassionate, unselfish, and the way you've put your own life on hold to take care of Stacey and Tim is just… Well, it's exactly the way I would want the mother of my children to be."

He pulled a box out of his pocket.

Oh my God, was this happening? My heart threatened to explode out of my chest.

He held a jewelry box. I felt faint.

"I'm giving you my last name as well——that is, if you'll have me, Elizabeth Joyce Turner. Will you marry me? Will you become my wife?" he asked with loving eyes.

My legs trembled. I was speechless as tears welled in my eyes. This was like the impossible ending to one of my aunt's stupid novels.

I dropped the lead rope and jumped into his arms. The jewelry box, which he hadn't opened yet, fell to the floor as I pulled him in for the kiss I was too stupid to realize I'd been longing for.

I needed to smell and taste my man, be held by him, crushed in his embrace.

He obliged with fierce insistence, claiming my lips with a kiss that left me breathless.

I ached to be held like this, my breasts pressed to his chest, my hands in his hair, and his in mine. The heat that radiated from him warmed me and soothed me. The touch I had denied myself healed my soul.

It was a good thing the horse had been well sedated. The little jewelry box fell between his front feet, and would have gotten crushed if he had spooked.

"Is that a yes?" Pat asked as we broke the kiss.

Tears ran down my cheeks. "I must be doing it wrong if you can't tell... Of course it's a yes."

I couldn't believe what was happening. A Covington could have a supermodel, an actress, a singer, anything he wanted. But he had chosen me.

I couldn't catch my breath. "This ranch? It's yours?"

He laughed. "Of course not, Buttercup. It's ours. You said you wanted to set up a retirement ranch." He extended his arm. "I give you the Four Legs Retirement Ranch: fifty prime acres, and I figure enough room for at least a hundred horses."

This was unbelievable. I'd told him my dream of setting up a retirement ranch for horses someday. But I always figured someday was a decade or two or three in the future——if I could possibly earn enough money and move far enough out into the sticks to afford some land.

He picked up the jewelry box and opened it, presenting me with the most gorgeous diamond I'd ever seen. It was so big, it looked like its weight would throw off my walk.

"You like it?" he asked.

I blinked back tears. "It's a little bit big, don't you think?"

He pulled the ring from its velvet embrace. "Only the best for Mrs. Covington."

"What if I want to keep my name? I'm kind of attached to it after all these years."

He positioned the ring to slide it on my finger, but paused. "That's the only nonnegotiable item," he said.

"Hmmm, let me think."

His brow furrowed as I paused.

"Well, of course I'll take your name, even if it is harder to spell."

He slid the ring on my finger.

I held it up, admiring it and the love it represented.

The horse, *my* horse, was still under as I hugged my man and tried to stop the tears of happiness, taking in all that had just happened.

Pat had saved me from Ben, and from my mistake with Trent's loan, and had made vet school possible——all without taking credit for it. He'd done those things just because he wanted to help me. How had I found such a wonderful man?

My man.

CHAPTER 34

PAT

I HAD FINALLY CLOSED THE SINGLE MOST IMPORTANT DEAL OF MY
life, and now I could hardly wait for the rest of my life to start.

But we had to wait for Doc's tranquilizer to wear off before I
could show her our new home.

"I still don't understand how you managed this," I told Pat,
shaking my head. I mean getting me here, without the doctor
around."

"Simple enough. Dr. Scalise is a romantic. When I explained
that I wanted to propose to you, he was more than willing to help
arrange this. The emergency call? That was me. There is no emergency. And I told him not to plan on coming back. I wasn't taking
no for an answer."

"Pretty sure of yourself there, cowboy."

"Just determined. I love you. You mean the world to me, Liz,
and I don't plan on living without you. One way or another, I was
going to convince you to be my wife."

She started to cry again and hugged me, burying her head

against my chest. Luckily these were tears of joy, and nothing could have made me happier.

We stood there clutching each other.

Eventually, the horse recovered from the sedation. Liz led him back into his stall and pulled a few horse cookies out of her pocket, which Doc eagerly crunched.

"How about I show you around our new home?" I suggested.

We slowly wandered the property, taking in the pastures, the shelters, the hay storage, and finally the pond. Tosca couldn't restrain herself, and she wandered into the water and back out, giving us a shower as she shook herself off.

Liz was giggling and smiling and happy, the way she deserved to be.

We went by the pool and into the house.

She danced from room to room as I showed her around. "This looks just like the stuff from the Myrtle Street house."

She hadn't let go of my hand. We were like teenagers as we traversed the property and toured the house, stopping for the occasional hug and kiss. I was the luckiest man alive today.

I nodded. "Yup, I told Judy to match it as closely as possible. I wanted to be reminded of our first days together." I smiled as I patted the back of the couch, one of my favorite places to have her.

She smirked. She knew exactly what I was referring to.

She rewarded me with a giant hug, the warmest smile, and love in her eyes. "You're turning into a softy."

"Only when it comes to you," I responded.

In the bedroom, Liz opened each of the drawers of the dresser.

"Looking for something?" I asked.

"Just checking to see if anybody else's underwear is in here," she said, shooting me a look.

I cringed. She must've seen more than the Boston letter the day she was in my bedroom at the condo. "Never any but yours. Those others were relics from a past life. I promise."

She sniffed, but seemed satisfied. After a moment, she offered me a smile.

"Tomorrow will you help me find a horse for me to ride?" I asked. "I didn't want to do it without your expert advice."

It had taken me almost all day to find exactly the right horse for my woman. Doc was a gentle, well-trained quarter horse from good cutting stock. The rancher that sold him to me even had me get on and ride around a bit to show me how gentle he was. It had been a blast.

"I can't. I have to work," she complained.

"No, you don't. I already cleared it with Dr. Scalise. Call it an engagement present."

The love mixed with lust in her eyes was a clear indication that it wouldn't be long before we tried out some of the furniture, and not just the bed. I had my eye on a section of wall to recreate our first night.

Judy had also nicely gone to the grocery store and stocked the fridge earlier today, so we started dinner.

She's mine, all mine.

EPILOGUE

LIZ

THE CAT'S PURRING WOKE ME. A FACE FULL OF FUR WAS NOT MY favorite way to start the day. I pushed Tasha off my pillow and off the bed. She was demanding breakfast, but that was just tough. I wasn't going to be trained that easily.

It had been three blissful months since that day Pat had found me in the barn.

I turned over to face him.

He was lying on his back, his breathing slow and steady. The peak in the sheets over his abdomen told me he had his normal morning wood. "Waking up in a tent," he called it.

I carefully slid under the sheets and licked the tip of his cock. It sprang up slightly, accompanied by a soft moan from my man. I grasped the shaft and started to give him the blowjob I'd promised him last night.

Blowjob was such an odd word, because there was a whole lot of licking and sucking going on, but no blowing. But who was I to complain? It turned him on incredibly when I talked dirty and used that word.

And there was nothing better than my man when he was turned on.

I continued my lip-and-hand action for only a short while before I straddled him and positioned his tip at my entrance. I slid down, little by little, taking in his length as he stretched me fully.

He fondled my breasts and sucked on my nipples. We began moving in unison as I rocked my hips and he glided in and out.

Before long, I came undone. As I approached the pinnacle of my climax, I rode him harder and moaned louder.

He moved his thumb to massage my clit, and I started yelping, still unable to control myself, and not really wanting to. There were no neighbors nearby to hear us. The waves of pleasure over-took me quickly, powerful spasms surging through me as my eyes shut tightly and the blood rushed in my ears. The earthquake that rolled through me clenched my walls around him as I screamed.

He moved his hands and massaged my breasts as I came down off of my high and could breathe again.

I rocked back and forth, urging him on. I pinched his nipples, kissed his neck, and nibbled his ear.

He took my hips and guided me as he thrust harder and deeper. He tensed up and called my name, grabbing my hips tightly, forcing me down on him, spearing me deeply, forcefully. Satisfac-tion wrote itself on his face with a final thrust.

I collapsed on his chest as his cock continued to throb inside of me. This was always the best part, the ultimate closeness between us as we fulfilled each other. I was totally relaxed, totally complete ——the perfect beginning to a new day.

As my breathing recovered, I focused on the clock. Slowly I realized how late it was. I had put up darker curtains yesterday, and we hadn't set an alarm. I climbed off of him and out of bed. "We better get a move on, cowboy, if we're going to make our flight."

He checked the clock and quickly rolled out of bed to start the shower.

Before we left for the airport, my old boss Tony called Pat.

I waited to hear the news.

"Absolutely. Let's get the cops involved," Pat said.

After that he mostly just said *uh-huh* and smiled at me as the conversation continued.

"I think that's a good call, Tony. She should do well. And thanks so much for all the help. You've been great." He hung up and gave me the short version while we finished getting ready.

Tony had discovered why my previous manager, Ben, had been fiddling with the registers so often. He had each of them programmed to funnel some of the receipts to a separate account during different parts of the day. Since he'd taken over, Tony had been concerned that the totals didn't match what he thought they should be, given the crowds coming in.

But it had taken him a while to figure out the scam. Ben had been stealing from the Vandersmoots——and from Pat, since he hadn't reset the registers before he got fired.

Pat wanted Tony to get the police involved, and Ben was going to get what he deserved. The pig.

Tony had decided he wanted to go back to being the head waiter at Cardinelli's, Pat's brother's restaurant——the place Pat had poached him from when he bought The Ironhorse. Tony said he missed the customer interaction and had discovered he didn't like being a manager after all. The great thing was, he had recommended Louise to take his place as manager of The Ironhorse, starting next week.

I couldn't have been happier for her. I knew she would do a great job.

Pat slung his backpack over his shoulder and wheeled our bags to the door.

~

WE HAD MADE THE FLIGHT JUST IN TIME, AND THANKFULLY IT HAD been a boring, but smooth, six hours.

As we started our lunch, Pat finally got off the phone with Vincent Benson, who had wanted some advice on a deal he was considering.

He was the son of Lloyd Benson, who was on the Covington Industries Board of Directors and seemed almost like a father figure to Bill and Pat. Pat had solved the problem of Covington Industries needing someone in Boston by recruiting Vincent to take his place. The Bensons and Covingtons had always been close, and Vincent was somebody Bill knew he could trust implicitly.

Pat had done what he always did——he'd found a solution to a problem that gave all the parties what they wanted. I wanted to go to vet school at Davis, Pat wanted to move to Davis to be with me, and Bill wanted somebody he could trust in the Boston office to take his stepbrother Liam's place.

This had also allowed Pat to set up a consulting practice specializing in deal negotiation, which he could run out of our ranch. He was much happier doing this consulting than running a business, he told me, even if it was the family business.

I finished chewing the onion ring I had dipped in special pineapple-mustard sauce and took a bite of my Tropics Burger. Some of the sauce oozed out onto my fingers.

Pat pulled a folded envelope out of his pocket. "This came yesterday. I forgot to give it to you."

I smiled as I opened it. It was from the Shasta County Sheriff's Office. Pat had tracked down Trent and started wage garnishments on him to pay back the truck loan he'd saddled me with. This was our first check: three hundred dollars and change. It served him right.

I held up the check. "This makes three douchebags getting what they deserve."

"Yeah, but Monica and your boyfriend Blaine haven't been sentenced yet."

It took a sip of my drink. "Should we fly down and watch?"

"Waste of time," he mumbled with food in his mouth.

He was right. They weren't worth the effort.

The sun was bright, and the fronds of the palm trees swayed in the warm breeze.

"I promised you I'd take you here, didn't I, Mrs. Covington?" Pat asked.

I loved it when he called me that. "Yes, you did," I said before filling my mouth with burger.

I thought back to that day. The wedding had been idyllic, just a small affair in the backyard of our ranch, by the pond. With the summer heat in Davis, we had gotten tents to keep people out of the sun and had set up a wooden dance floor on the grass.

A string quartet for the ceremony had been a perfect addition.

We kept it small, with just family and few friends. Pat had arranged a charter jet to bring everybody from LA for the afternoon and take them back in the evening; marrying a Covington certainly had its advantages.

Stacey had been my maid of honor. Timmy had grumbled about it, but he did a great job as the ring bearer.

Louise marked me off her list, told me Tina was her next project to get married off. I wished her luck and suggested Jennie was likely to go first.

He twirled the little paper umbrella in his drink to get my attention and took a sip. He had ordered a Blue Hawaii, and I was sticking with my usual Mai Tai. He raised his glass, and I clinked mine against it. "To adding Doctor to your name," he said.

I could drink to that. "You do know it's a four-year program?"

I was starting in a little over a week. A rather large donation to build the Covington Large Animal Barn at the veterinary school had expedited my start date, and I was about to begin the last leg of my journey toward my goal of adding DVM to the end of my name. There were certainly benefits to being married to a Covington, even if he did leave his dirty clothes all over the floor.

Pat's signature dimples appeared with his broad smile. "With your brains and work ethic, it's just a formality."

The undeniable love in his eyes warmed me even more than the rum in the drink.

I threw an onion ring at him and hit him right on the neck. It fell down his shirt.

"I told you to stop that." I couldn't keep from blushing. He never stopped complimenting me, and though I was trying to train him to do it less often, it wasn't working.

He fished the onion ring out of his shirt and licked it suggestively——his way of promising I would be punished later, and his tongue would be the weapon. What a weapon.

I was getting wet, and my cheeks heated up to a four-alarm fire. These little food fights could be sexy as hell, and the punishment for being naughty was even better. At times like this, I didn't know how I'd been lucky enough to find a man like Pat.

He took a bite of his Paniolo Burger, and I went back to mine.

I crossed my legs, trying to take my mind off of all the possible ways he could torture me with his tongue. I closed my eyes and enjoyed the warm trade winds on my skin for a moment. I concentrated on the rhythmic sound of the surf a few dozen yards away.

Our table was under an umbrella looking out toward Waikiki Beach at the Tropics Bar and Grill. Diamond Head beckoned on the other side of the bay. Pat had promised a hike inside the crater of the old volcano, if I was up for it. It sounded fun.

"Uncle Pat!"

I turned to see Timmy running our way, followed by Stacey trying to keep up.

Pat had brought us all out to the Hilton Hawaiian Village for a week of sun and surf before we had to start school——Timmy in LA and me at Davis. He had asked my aunt to join us as well, but she'd negotiated to have him send her to a romance readers convention instead. It was just her thing.

We had flown from Sacramento this morning. With the time

difference we arrived in time for lunch. Stacey and Timmy had arrived a little later from LAX. They had just taken their luggage up to the room.

Actually, calling it a room was a bit of an understatement. Pat had booked the Presidential Suite for us at the top of the Rainbow Tower, overlooking the beach. It was so far up, my ears popped in the elevator.

"Hey, bud." Pat tousled Timmy's hair. "Pull up a chair." Pat waved our waitress over as my sister pulled out her chair. "Stacey, there aren't enough words in the dictionary to describe how beautiful you look today."

She blushed scarlet as she sat. "Liz, can't you get him to stop that?"

"I've tried, but some dogs are just too old to train." I tossed another onion ring at my husband. He ducked, and I missed.

The waitress came over and took their lunch orders.

"I wanna go swimming," Timmy announced after she left.

Stacey glared at him.

Timmy got the hint a little late. "Please?" he added.

"Gotta wait an hour after lunch. That's the rule," his mother informed him.

Timmy pouted and fidgeted in his chair. "But I don't wanna wait."

Pat fixed him in place with a stern look. He didn't have to say a thing. He really had the touch with Stacey's little man.

Timmy calmed down. "I'm sorry, Mommy. Babies complain, but men just do what they have to."

Pat tousled my nephew's hair again. "That's right, Tim, and if you do well enough in the Super Pool today, we can try the ocean tomorrow."

Timmy brightened. "Deal." He stuffed an onion ring in his mouth.

"Hey, Tim, I've got a job for you." Pat pulled Timmy close and whispered in his ear while Timmy nodded and a smile grew on the boy's face. "Can you do that for me?" Pat handed him the room card key.

"Sure." Timmy got up and started off.

Stacey rose to follow him "Hold on, Timmy."

"Stace," Pat said, pointing back to her seat. "Trust me. He'll be okay."

She froze and grimaced. "But..."

"Plant your butt in that chair and let him grow up," Pat said.

"Bossy a little?" she shot back, glancing in Timmy's direction as she slowly sat.

"Trust me," Pat replied.

Pat was a good influence for Timmy. Whenever we saw him, Pat had made a point of giving him tasks that required increasing responsibility to perform on his own. Half the battle had been getting Stacey to let go.

"But where is he going?" she asked.

"Take a breath. He's fine," Pat told her.

She huffed and grabbed an onion ring.

I changed the subject to explain the news we'd heard this morning about my old boss and his thievery.

Stacey was aghast and agreed with us that he deserved prison or worse. There were times when she was in favor of the old punishments, like tying someone on top of an anthill. This time I agreed with her.

My phone dinged with a text. It was from Rodrigo, just checking in to tell us everything was running smoothly back at the ranch.

As the number of horses had grown, I'd hired Rodrigo to run the ranch operation and manage the workers we had. He'd made such a good impression that day at the polo grounds that I'd sought him out, and he'd been a great hire. He cared deeply about the animals, and we used so many Mrs. Pasture's horse cookies now, we bought them by the barrel.

As we ate, Stacey told us how much of an improvement her

new job was. She had changed from working at Memorial to working in a plastic surgeon's office. She checked her watch, concerned that Timmy had been gone for so long.

Pat reached across to touch her arm. "Don't get your knickers in a twist, Stacey. Have faith."

Reluctantly, she continued. "The hours are so much better. In post-op at Memorial, though, the patients didn't talk. These women come in, and every one of them thinks her nose is wrong, she has too many wrinkles, or her boobs are too small. I swear they're all neurotic. Dr. Thornbird listens to them so patiently. I just can't do it."

"Hollywood," I said.

She rolled her eyes. "Yeah, but bless them, they pay well, and no nights or weekends anymore. I spend most of my time helping with the laser treatments. The good part about that is I get to tell them to be quiet. No talking during the procedure, I warn them, or it won't work. That shuts them up every time."

Timmy returned with a piece of paper in hand. He put the paper down by Pat and attacked his burger.

"Tim, do you have something for your mom?" Pat asked.

Timmy put his food down and gave Stacey a kiss. "I love you, Mommy." He gave her the slip of paper.

Her eyes went wide when she opened it. "Why, thank you so much, Timmy."

He crossed his arms. "Tim," he corrected her. "I want to be Tim."

Stacey agreed to the name change with a giggle as she handed me the paper. It showed a one o'clock appointment for her at the Mandara Spa for a full afternoon session. Pat was determined to spoil us rotten. It also had an afternoon reservation for Timmy at Camp Penguin for kids on the resort.

After they finished eating, Stacey took Tim back to the room to get changed as Pat and I shared another Mai Tai.

"What about me?" I asked as I tapped his leg under the table.

He leaned over. "You get a personal massage session later," he whispered with a wink. "Do I get my wish this afternoon?"

I wasn't sure what that wish was. He had so many of them.

He twirled the paper umbrella in his drink with a devilish grin. "You don't remember?"

I was drawing a blank. There was something I was supposed to remember, and I was blowing it. The sun and surf were supposed to relax us and let us forget everything. It was working.

He continued playing with the umbrella. "Our first date?" He asked.

Now I remembered what it was. "You forgot that wasn't really a date."

He had wished to see me in a bikini on Waikiki Beach that first afternoon that we'd shared a meal at Tropics Burgers in LA.

I smiled. "Sure, if you buy me a surfing lesson. It's something I've always wanted to try but never had the courage to do in California."

Pat was going to get his wish all right. I had already gotten mine. I'd wished he was a doctor or a lawyer, but this was even better.

"No, we start with paddle boarding," he said.

I gave him my pouty face. "Surfing."

He pulled out his favorite coin. "Tell you what, I'll flip you for it. Heads we go surfing, tails paddle boarding."

I nodded, even though I desperately wanted to surf.

He flipped the coin. Heads.

"Surfing it is," he said. "We can get a couples lesson."

He put the coin down and pulled out his trusty old wallet, with FCF on one side and the family company logo on the other, to pay for lunch.

He treasured that wallet. I'd had it repaired by a leatherworker to give it a new lease on life. He gave me so much, and it was one of the few things I could give him that he didn't already have.

"I'll help you change," he said with a grin as he put some bills on the table.

That meant my man was going to give me my tongue torture *before* our surfing lesson.

We got up to leave, but I rushed back to the table. Pat had forgotten his coin. I retrieved it before the busboy got there. I turned it over in my hand. There was something odd about it. Both sides were heads.

A double-headed coin.

This explained everything. This was the essence of Pat: he'd fixed it so I always won.

I caught up to him and nonchalantly handed over the coin without a word.

My man.

∽

IF YOU ENJOYED THIS BOOK, PLEASE LEAVE A REVIEW.

THE FOLLOWING PAGES CONTAIN AN EXCERPT FROM BOOK 1 OF THE series: **The Billionaire's Trust**, an excerpt from Book 2 **The Youngest Billionaire**, and a Sneak Peek at Book 4 of the series: **Protecting The Billionaire**.

.

EXCEPT: THE BILLIONAIRE'S TRUST

CHAPTER 1

BILL

MONICA HAD COME BACK AGAIN TONIGHT, RUBBING HER TIT against my arm as she leaned in, intentionally for sure. Her weapon of choice tonight was a sexy red dress cut even lower than the last one, showing cleavage deep enough to create its own gravity well. She licked her lips again as she flirted with me at our bar before closing.

Two nights ago, she had pursued me at the restaurant, asking to speak to the owner to gripe about her scallopini and then flirting with me when I came over to hear her complaint. The dish was prepared just the way it should have been. It had been hard to listen to her words with her cleavage right over the plate. Was she a D or a maybe a Double-D? Who knows, but certainly more than a handful, and with nipples protruding through her tight black low-cut dress, it was difficult to keep my eyes up. Distracting as hell, to say the least.

In college, my fraternity brothers had kept up a running debate on whether more than a handful was wasted. Even though I had attended an all-boys Catholic high school, my vote always surprised them by being on the *more is wasted* side. They generally favored the *more is the better* side of the question, and she definitely had more.

Ever since I broke up with Jane, my mode of operation had been *C-E-D* Charm, Enjoy, and Discard. I wasn't into one-night stands. It took more than one night to truly enjoy a woman, to learn what pleasure she had to offer, and to show her the pleasures I could offer her. A week or two was good, but beyond that, it was time to move on. The last few weeks had not allowed the time to even get through *C*, much less to E with anyone. Too much work and too little play was making Bill grumpy … and horny.

She wore too much makeup for my taste, but she was certainly a willing candidate. Although my usual rule was to avoid entanglements with any of the guests at our restaurant, she looked like she would do her best to be an *E*-ticket ride, something to distract me and allow for some exercise. Taking things in hand, so to speak, had been okay for a few days, but it didn't get the job done over the long haul.

Getting to the question of her place or mine took but a millisecond with Monica. She managed to put her hand on my arm twice and my thigh three times on the short drive over. This girl was beyond eager.

I turned the key and held the door to my condo open for her.

Once again, Monica managed to lightly brush against my thigh as she passed. She sashayed over to the full-length window overlooking the city, her hips swaying seductively. No doubt that this woman knew I was watching her. What man could resist? She knew precisely what she was doing. "This is so beautiful. Look at that view."

I had become a little too immune to the skyline. "Sure is, and it looks even better when the wind clears out the smog layer."

"I don't see how it could get any better. You are so lucky to see the city like this."

I opened the wine fridge and took out two bottles. "White or red?" I held up one of each.

She hesitated. "Red, so it won't matter if I spill on my dress," she said with a giggle. A real genius, this one, but that wouldn't matter when her clothes came off.

I carried two glasses of the well-aged Cabernet and motioned to the couch.

As soon as I sat, she kicked off her heels and drained her glass with one hand while the other was on my thigh, inching up little by little. I was already getting hard by the time she finished her glass. Her left hand had found its way up to my crotch. "My, what do we have here?" she purred as she lightly licked at my ear and rubbed her tit against me.

I was getting harder by the second. This vixen liked to take charge, but little did she know that would change in a few minutes. I got up and sipped more of my wine as I led her toward the bedroom.

Such a waste. I had opened a superb Cabernet, and we had no time to enjoy it.

She put her glass down as we entered the bedroom. "Why don't you use the bathroom first, and I'll go second?"

"Just make yourself comfortable," I said as I rounded the corner into the master bath. I could hear her unzipping her dress as I slid out of my jacket and brushed my teeth. When I returned, she was removing her lacy red bra and hungrily looking me up and down, finally focusing on the bulge in my pants.

"Ooh, la la, am I going to have fun tonight." Clad in only a pair of panties that read *ALL YOU CAN EAT* in black lettering, she traced her finger across my chest as she passed me on the way to the bathroom, rubbing the tip of her tit against my arm as she passed. It didn't look it, but it felt real.

Looking forward to her return, I picked her dress up off the floor, folded it, and placed it on the chair along with the bra.

Then I saw it.

She had placed her phone oddly on edge, on the shelf up behind the chair and facing the bed. I picked it up. It was recording video, and she had pointed it straight at the bed.

The fucking bitch.

Of course. This had been way too easy. She had tried to set me up for a blackmail video. I killed the recording and turned off the phone, placing it right back where it had been. I clenched my jaw. After those panties, what a temptation she had become. I fished out my phone and started the audio recorder to protect myself, placing it face down on my dresser.

Two can play this game.

I composed myself just as she rounded the corner, returning from the bathroom.

I handed her lacy red bra back to her. "Put this back on. You're moving a little too fast."

Her perky smile slowly turned to a frown.

"Put it back on and let's do this right." I pointed to the kitchen. "Let me get the champagne."

A smile returned to her face. "Aren't you the charming one?"

I found a bottle of Moet, uncorked it, and returned from the kitchen with two glasses. I poured both glasses and handed her one. "To fame and fortune." I lifted my glass to hers.

"To fame and fortune," she said with a devilish smirk.

She was hoping for a quick fortune in her future. After a sip, I traced across her thigh with my free hand and stood. "Do you like caviar?"

She shivered at my touch. "Sure." Her eyes lit up.

I returned to the kitchen with a smirk of my own, grabbing a can of Beluga caviar from the fridge along with the cream cheese. I took her clutch from beside the couch as I got a box of water crackers and put six on a plate.

"What is taking so long? I'm getting lonely in here," she called from the bedroom.

"Doing caviar right takes a few minutes," I answered. I lightly spread cream cheese on each of the crackers and placed them around the tin of caviar on the plate. A small spoon in the caviar finished the preparation as I located her driver's license in the clutch. Katya Droznik from Pasadena, and she had turned thirty-one last month. I replaced the license in her clutch and carried the caviar toward the bedroom. "I think you'll like this. Fresh Beluga."

She was sitting up on the bed waiting with a refilled glass of champagne. "Took you long enough," she pouted, patting the bed beside her. She had put her bra back on.

"Like I said, some things can't be hurried." I set the plate down on the nightstand and took up my glass. "Hold still." I dabbed my finger in the glass and gently traced a circle of champagne over the swell of her left breast. "Don't move."

She trembled and giggled.

I sniffed the champagne circle, taking in her scent as she blushed and giggled some more. "You smell delectable, but you need to hold still." I repeated the procedure with the other breast, getting another shiver from her. I licked the champagne off her breasts to even more giggles. I took a cracker and dabbed caviar on top. "Do you like caviar?"

She smiled mischievously. "You bet, and I could think of some-thing better to lick it off of than a silly cracker."

This one was full of the devil. "Well, Monica," I said, raising my glass to hers for another toast. "To truth or consequences."

"Truth or consequences," she repeated with an amused look as we both sipped.

"Want the caviar, Monica?" I held the cracker up in front of her. "What's your last name?"

"It's sort of silly." Another giggle.

"Go ahead. Try me." Will she go with truth or consequences?

"Dempster, and don't laugh."

Consequences it is then. "Strike one." I pulled back the cracker and put it in my mouth, savoring the salty taste.

"What the hell?" she almost screamed. Her amused look had been replaced with a dumbfounded one.

"I can tell when a woman is lying to me." I spooned caviar on another cracker. "Next chance, Monica. Where do you live?" I held the cracker up and pulled it back as she grabbed for it. "Now, now, hold still. Where do you live?"

Indecision clouded her eyes as she pondered her answer. "Santa Monica," she said with a quiver.

"Strike two." She had chosen consequences again. I slid the second cracker into my mouth.

Her demeanor was moving steadily toward angry as she gulped down more champagne. "Why'd you bring in that damn caviar if you're not going to give me any?" She painted a pout on her face and slid her hand up my thigh.

I brushed her hand away. "You need to follow the rules, Monica."

"I don't like these rules. I want to play." Her hand reached for me again as I got off the bed.

I spooned caviar on the third cracker. "Monica?" This was going to be the killer question, the hardest for her. "How old are you?'

"You should be able to tell I'm not jail-bait," she spat out, the anger surfacing again.

"How old, Monica?"

"Twenty-seven, if you must know." She looked like a frightened little girl trying to put one over on the teacher.

This time, I put the cracker back on the plate and laid the plate down. My aching cock was going to have to wait another day. I stood and grabbed her phone from the shelf. "Strike three."

I walked over and dropped her phone in my aquarium.

She shot up off the bed. "You fucking asshole. That's a new phone," she screamed.

I threw her dress at her. "Get the hell out of my house, thirty-one-year-old Katya from Pasadena."

The shock instantly turned her white. She slipped the dress over her head and shimmied into it.

"You can zip it up outside. Get the hell out," I shouted, pointing to the door.

The expression on her face was priceless. She rushed to the aquarium.

"Those are Lionfish in there. Their sting is deadly."

The color drained from her face. She hesitated as she looked into the tank.

"Put your hand in there and sign your own death warrant." I was exaggerating. The sting hurt like hell and might kill a small child, but a grown woman would just be miserable for a few days. Very miserable.

She continued to gaze into the tank. I didn't think she could get any whiter, but she did. "You fucker. Who keeps fish like that?" For a second, it appeared she might tempt fate.

"The kind you don't mess with. Now get the hell out." I grabbed her wrap, opened the door, and threw it out into the hall. "Out!"

"Fuck you." She stopped trying to get her heels back on and scurried out the door as I swatted her on the ass. "Fucking asshole," she added as I slammed the door behind her.

"I may be an asshole, Katya, but I didn't fuck you."

CHAPTER 2

LAUREN

I WAS RUNNING LATE AGAIN. THE LINE AT STARBUCKS HAD BEEN longer than usual this morning and the Grande five-pump hazelnut half-caf soy latte, extra hot, with a dash of cinnamon for my boss was in one hand as I juggled my purse and the marketing presentation I had worked on last night in the other.

As I rounded the corner into Marketing, Marissa Bitz, my boss at Covington Industries, tapped her foot, waiting for me. She greeted me with her usual charm. "You're late again, Zumwalt." She was only about three inches shorter than me, but all of us towered over her in the flats she wore to work. Something about bad ankles that we didn't care to have explained to us.

Welcome to my world. The best pay in the city for somebody at my level, but the worst boss. She was a total bitch and lazy as hell, but it could have been worse. At least she didn't have BO, a pot belly, a receding hairline, and hit on me.

Thank God for small miracles.

Her Highness waited for me to deliver her coffee, looking out over the ugly horn-rimmed glasses that made her look even older than her forty years. "I'm sorry, Marissa. The new barista was a little slow today." We were told to call our boss by her first name. It was too easy for her last name to come out sounding like the bitch we all knew she was.

Marissa took a sip of the latte I handed her. Her face curled up into a sneer as she spat it into my trashcan. "This isn't right. How many times do I have to tell you five pumps, not four, and definitely not six?" Her face reddened as the wailing continued. "Take this back right now and get it right."

She shoved the Grande cup back at me, a small splash of coffee landing on my blouse as I grabbed for the cup before it hit the floor. Two weeks ago, I hadn't been fast enough, and I was the one who got blamed for the spill on the carpet outside my cubicle.

I bit my tongue briefly. "Right away, Marissa," is what came out of my mouth while my brain was thinking *get it yourself, bitch.* I had learned the hard way she did this about once a week to exert her power over us peons. The first time she did it, I protested that I had gotten it right, and Mt. Vesuvius had nothing on the Marissa eruption that ensued. I was not going down that road again today. Brandon needed me to keep this job.

Jimmy gave me a consoling look as I turned and headed back to the elevator on my assigned coffee run for the witch. Being the two newest in the office, he and I were assigned alternating weeks of coffee duty. Jimmy and I had learned the hard way that this hazing was just routine for her witchness. Harold had been the most recent marketing grunt to graduate out of coffee runs, and he had confided in me that it went easier for him when he learned to bring back a Venti on the return run instead of the original Grande.

I will not be trained so easily.

She had such rotten taste in coffee. I always dumped the 'bad' latte in the trash as I left the elevator and headed across the street for the second cup. I contemplated my revenge as the elevator passed the floors with a series of dings. I'll swat a fly or two and bring them to work to add to her coffee next time she sends me back like this, or maybe I'll add a worm. The door opened and I started out. I looked down at the cup, smirking to myself. Flies in her latte. That would serve the witch right.

I ran straight into him.

The lid was still on the coffee, so it didn't spill on his jacket or my blouse. But I lost my grip on the cup. I jumped back instinctively. The collision with the floor was too much for the plastic and cardboard contraption. It splashed, getting both of our shoes. I was so caught up in my revenge fantasy I hadn't been looking where I was going.

"I'm so sorry, Miss," he said.

"No, it was all my fault. I'm the one that wasn't looking," I responded without looking up. I was using the one napkin I had been carrying with the cup to blot the coffee off my shoes and ankles. Gus, the security guy from the front desk, rushed over with some paper towels.

The guy I bumped into handed me a handkerchief. "Here, use this." His voice was low and cool like a chocolate sundae.

I nearly melted when I stopped long enough to get a look at him. Not a guy, a man, Adonis in the flesh. A chiseled jawline, short stubble, kissable lips, the lower one a little pouty, a crop of slightly windswept light brown hair, and wide linebacker shoulders, all covered in a blazer with no tie and the top few buttons of his shirt open, showing just a hint of chest hair. I lost my breath and all rational thought fled. Warm blue eyes, like warm tropical water, smiled back at me. A smile to die for. A smile to make your pants fall down and dimples cute enough to cause instant paralysis.

He introduced himself as Bill.

I couldn't get my brain to mouth connection to work for shit with my few remaining functioning neurons. "Lauren," I mumbled. I trembled as I leaned over to concentrate on mopping up the witch's coffee before I made a bigger fool of myself. When I looked back up, the elevator door was closing.

He was gone.

Shit. I was a complete fucking dork. I didn't even get his whole name or what floor he worked on.

Gus and I finished the cleanup quickly. Bill had disappeared without retrieving his handkerchief. I walked across the street to Starbucks. How would I find out where Bill worked in the building? I would have to get his kerchief back to him—after I cleaned it, of course.

What a fucking klutz.

Could I possibly make a worse impression?

EXCERPT: THE YOUNGEST BILLIONAIRE

CHAPTER 1

STEVEN

I HELD MY EYES CLOSED AGAINST THE SOFT MORNING LIGHT filtering in. I let my ears acclimate to the breathing of the woman beside me. I was waking up in a tent this morning. I was hard. Some people wake up drowsy. Some people wake up energized. I wake up horny. My morning wood was as hard as ever. I rubbed my eyes and raised myself up to check the clock on the other nightstand.

She reached around behind her, grasped my cock, and started to stroke me. Lynn was her name, but she was actually Miss May in the airline's calendar. May was a beautiful month. She had long dirty-blonde hair with pale blue eyes, a kind smile, a cute little nose, and wonderful double-Ds over a narrow waist, nice hips, and a soft little ass. And boy, did she know how to use those hips.

If an ordinary picture was worth a thousand words, her picture in the calendar was worth a library. Good enough to be in a Victoria's Secret catalog, and it didn't do her justice. She felt even better in bed than she looked, and Lynn wasn't shy about trying some-thing new. Yes, May was a beautiful month, and now I only had to find Miss June to beat my brother.

Last night, I posted a picture of Miss May at dinner with me on the private family Instagram page. I was now two months ahead of Patrick. He'd challenged me to this contest because I had a little free time after graduating from law school before I started at Ernst and Schwartz. He was trying to do the July through December months before I finished January through June. It had taken me four flights before I hooked up with Miss May last night. Now, I was a lock to win.

I moved closer to her, reached abound, and cradled her breast. "What would you like to do today?" I whispered into her ear.

She purred. "I think this is a good start."

"I meant besides this. Would you like to go for a bike ride on the beach? Or, we could rent some surfboards. Have you ever been surfing?" I knew this was just a stopover for her. Her flight out was tomorrow. We had all day together and another night.

She thought for a moment. "Surfing sounds like fun, but I don't have a suit with me."

I kissed her neck. "We can get you one."

She paused her hand work. "Surfing then."

I pulled my hand away and got up. "Breakfast time."

A pout formed on her face. "Later. Come back here."

I walked out to the kitchen, not bothering with a robe. "Bacon and eggs, or waffles?" I yelled back.

She didn't know yet the treat I had planned for after breakfast. "How 'bout I lick your sausage?" she yelled back.

That's the spirit. Just not yet.

I started the coffee machine without responding.

She came into the kitchen wearing one of my tee shirts. Her nipples teased me from behind the thin fabric. "Bacon and eggs," she answered, giving up on inviting me back to bed just yet.

I pulled the food from the fridge and realized I shouldn't have given her that choice. The state of my hard-on made wearing an apron problematic, and I didn't want to chance a grease splatter by cooking bacon on the stove. I had tempted fate once before, and it had not been a good day. I wrapped the bacon in a paper towel. Microwaved bacon would suffice this morning. I didn't plan on dodging hot grease.

She fetched the orange juice.

I pointed out the cabinet with the glasses, and she pulled them down after patting my ass seductively as she passed behind me.

She located the silverware and the plates, while I got the whipped cream out of the fridge and the salt and pepper for the eggs.

My cock kept twitching at the sight of her bouncing breasts under the tight tee shirt. The length of it just barely covered her ass and teased me with the thought that she was pantie-less underneath. I kept hoping she would bend over. Just a little. When I had finished the scrambled eggs, I added the bacon and brought the steaming plate over to the table. "House rules, no clothes at breakfast," I told her.

She slipped the shirt off and sat on it with a grimace. "That's not fair. I don't get to see anything." The table was cherry, and she was right. She couldn't see much, while I had a great view of her chest. She didn't know it yet, but the whipped cream wasn't for breakfast.

We talked about her flight schedule next week while we ate.

I couldn't keep my eyes off her gorgeous tits. They bounced ever so slightly as she ate and talked. They beckoned me, and my dick stayed hard thinking about what I was going to do with the whipped cream after breakfast. I was an expert at pleasuring a woman. The key was in tailoring my actions and the movements of my hands, my fingers, my mouth, my tongue, and my cock to her responses. Reading her movements, her whimpers, her moans, her shudders, and her occasional words to read her responses to my actions was the key. Each woman had her own set of responses that guided me in what she wanted and what she needed to find her pleasure. There was no such thing as a woman who had trouble coming multiple times, just one that hadn't been shown how to yet.

That's where I fit in.

I had gotten her up to three in a row last night. Four was my goal this morning.

"That was good," she said innocently as she finished off her eggs.

I lifted the whipped cream can. "It's nothing compared to what comes next."

A mischievous grin spread across her face as lust filled her eyes.

A key sounded in the lock on the door.

Shit.

The door slammed opened, and Katie marched in. "You forgot," she screamed at me. Damned Katie still had a key to my place.

Lynn quickly grabbed the tee shirt and dashed to the bedroom.

I was trapped. I didn't have anything handy to wear. "What the hell are you doing here?" I demanded, scooting in closer to the table. "You can't just barge in here. And give me back that damned key."

"I'm your Saturday morning appointment, don't you remember, honey?" she yelled loud enough to make sure Lynn would hear it. "It's my turn now. Get rid of her so we can get it on, honey," she added loudly.

Katie had the worst timing and even worse manners.

She took Lynn's seat across from me. The anger in her eyes was unmistakable. My sister was seriously pissed at me, and Hurricane Katie was ramping up to a Level-Five storm.

It hit me. This was Saturday, and I had promised Katie I would help her with some cloak and dagger work at her firm. She wanted me to look over some contract papers. I was trapped in my seat with my hard-on under the table. But that problem was going down by the second with my angry sister sitting across from me. "Why didn't you just call?" I asked.

"Your phone was off, little brother, and this is a lot more important than Miss March or whoever. I need your help," she growled back with eyes dark as night.

"May," I corrected her.

Lynn reappeared, clothed, and shot both of us a disgusted glare as she scooted to the door and slammed it on her way out. She didn't bother with goodbye.

I scowled at Katie. "That was mean. She was a nice girl."

Katie giggled. The storm had lifted. She was seriously enjoying messing with me. "Since when do you go for nice girls? If I screwed up your date, that's just too bad. You skipped out on me last weekend, and this is really important. I need you, and you promised."

She turned toward the window. "Now go get dressed, little brother. We only have a few hours before Sam gets back to the office and I don't know when I'm going to get another chance."

I dressed quickly. Katie had a right to be pissed. I had lost track of the days. It was my fault for forgetting I had agreed to help her this morning. I had been a dick and blown her off last weekend, chasing Miss March. I owed it to her to help.

She said we needed to do it when the office was empty. It was super important to her for some reason she wouldn't explain, but she was family. Family always came first for us. I would do anything she needed, and she would do the same for me.

I grabbed my phone, turned it on, and joined Katie in the kitchen.

Katie smirked at me. She twisted the whipped cream can in her hands. "You don't take this on your eggs, so I'm guessing you had other plans for it." She put it back in the refrigerator.

I smiled back at her, but I didn't reward her with an answer. It was a good thing she hadn't arrived twenty minutes later.

Lynn was a nice girl. She didn't deserve how my sister had just treated her. I would have to send her flowers and explain that Katie was just being a bitchy sister.

CHAPTER 2

FOUR WEEKS LATER.

EMMA

"Just text me when you need to be rescued."

My heart fluttered.

That's all he said as he stood directly in my path and handed me his card. Piercing emerald green eyes appraised me, complete with full, thick eyelashes, the kind that should be illegal for guys to have. Tall, dark, and handsome didn't begin to describe this hunk. "Steven. Steven Carter, at your service." The words mesmerized me as I looked up to see them escape his kissable full lips that drew me like a magnet. I wasn't short, but he was well over six feet, with shoulders broad enough to make Atlas envious, along with a chiseled jawline to die for.

"From what?" I rasped, barely getting the words out. The dark-haired man blocking my way had me completely flustered. I had bumped into plenty of tall guys before, but right now, they all seemed like boys compared to this man. A real man. An eleven on the ten-point scale.

He nodded toward the dining area. "Your blind date, of course.

You'll want to put that into your phone before you get back to your table, Miss...?" He stood there waiting, demanding an answer.

I should have shouldered my way past him back to my table without a word, but I didn't have the willpower. I lied and used my favorite bar name. "Tiffany. Tiffany Case." All that awaited me at that table, after all, was boring Gordie.

In college, my girlfriends and I would use fake names when we went out so we wouldn't get stalked by any of the guys we met. I had tried a few Bond Girl names and settled on Tiffany Case. She was a redhead, like me, and not as obvious as Pussy Galore. When I used my real name, Emma Watson, people didn't believe me anyway because they had seen Harry Potter and I looked nothing like her.

He licked his lips. "Tiffany. Lovely name. It suits you." Satisfied, he turned back into the dining area.

I more than glanced at his ass as he strode away. A lot more. I had slipped up. I couldn't ignore the sudden heat he caused in me. Surprised by him, I had forgotten I was using Miranda Frost for my *SuperSingles* date tonight. I had to remember I was Miranda to Gordie and Tiffany to Steven. Steven. I liked that name. The card was white with a gilded edge. Steven Carter and a phone number, nothing else. He had caught me on my second trip to the restroom. I couldn't stomach more than a half hour at a time of my date tonight. I lingered in the hallway for a moment as I fingered the card. Suddenly, tonight wasn't totally wasted. I added the stranger as a contact before stashing my phone back in my purse, along with the card. I pasted on a smile and made my way back to the table, where Gordie was waiting anxiously to bore me to death on the topic of insurance.

"And the difference with whole life is..." I zoned out as he droned on, digging into my meal with the occasional nod.

Cardinelli's was an expensive place, and I was damned if I was going to leave without getting to finish my lasagna. I just had to tough out another half hour of how marvelous it was to sell insurance. Life, home, car, pet, mortuary, you name it, Gordie sold it. There was something to be said for getting into your work, but this was supposed to be a first date. I wasn't doing a second with Gordie. He had lied about his height. He was shorter than me, even without my heels on. They all lied about something.

From my seat, I could see my mysterious green-eyed rescuer over Gordie's shoulder, and he held up his phone with a questioning look. Gordie had no clue as I smiled at Steven. I took another bite of my lasagna. The quicker I got this date over with, the better.

My phone buzzed on the table with a text.

MEGAN: I'm home

"If you need to answer that, I understand," Gordie said as I glanced at the message. That was sweet of him.

"It's just my sister telling me she got home okay."

Gordie smiled and put down his wine glass. "So is she checking to see if you need to be rescued from your date?"

Busted.

"No, we're good." He had guessed our code all right. If I didn't answer right away, she would call with an emergency that would give me an excuse to leave the restaurant. "She's just checking in." I texted her back.

ME: OK

I put the phone down. "How's your carbonara?" That got Gordie settled down. I felt bad lying to him. He wasn't handsy, and he didn't seem like an axe murderer or anything. He just couldn't help that he was less exciting than cold oatmeal. I flipped my phone on silent and put it in my lap. Just one more thing to do.

At school, I had become an expert in texting under my desk without the teacher seeing, and now that was going to come in handy as I decided I felt more sorry for Gordie than anything else. I would amuse myself by texting the green-eyed hunk with the dark brown hair, even if he was sitting with that knock-dead gorgeous blonde.

ME: Not tonight thanks

He laughed with his date over Gordie's shoulder. And my phone vibrated in my hand. Good thing it wasn't on the table anymore. Gordie kept rambling on as I nodded.

STEVEN CARTER: So you go for the low IQ type

When I chanced a peek, Steven was looking directly at me. I smiled at him over my date's shoulder as I typed my response. Gordie smiled back.

ME: Why say that?

STEVEN CARTER: Any guy that spends all night talking about himself without finding out what

Finding out what? Steven was right about talking all night. Gordie got that prize. A few seconds later, the answer appeared.

STEVEN CARTER: a beautiful woman like you has to say

His text didn't make any sense.

STEVEN CARTER: must have the brains of a mollusk

I giggled. Now it made sense. Gordie smiled, happy that I found something he said amusing.

ME: It wouldn't be fair and maybe I can learn something
from him.

That was a stretch, more an outright lie. Maybe this is how
Indian snake charmers did it. They talked to the cobras about insurance until they fell asleep. I called the waiter over and asked for
some more iced tea.
Need more caffeine so that I won't doze off.

STEVEN CARTER: He's a moron nothing else worth learning

"Don't you like the lasagna?" Gordie asked. He had noticed
that I wasn't inhaling my food anymore.
I lied. "I was just letting it settle a bit. It's very good. There is
just so much, and I need some tea to wash it down." I couldn't eat
and text at the same time. I dropped my phone in my lap and
started back attacking my meal.
A few minutes later, Gordie was filling me in on the intricacies
of insuring homes against fire in the foothills when my phone
vibrated again.

STEVEN CARTER: Tuesdays and Thursdays are the only days
for a first date

I had chosen Tuesday evenings because my sister Megan made
it her mission to come over on Monday nights to 'help me' go
through the website candidates. She thought I needed help finding
a suitable date. She was right about my needing help, but guys like
Gordie were not the answer. There was a serious lack of candidates
at the museum where I worked. Most of them were ancient enough
to have sailed over on the *Mayflower*, except for Jonathon, and he
was gay. I had finally agreed to try the *SuperSingles* website, and
so far, the results had been pretty disappointing. Gordie was busy
quoting me automobile theft rate trends, so I had to entertain

myself texting with Steven. Gordie had been talking so much that he hadn't gotten very far on his meal yet.

ME: Why?

STEVEN CARTER: Monday is no good - they only talk about the weekend games they watched

He had a point there.

STEVEN CARTER: Friday is out because they know you don't have work - they might expect a late night treat

No argument from me. Megan and I had already ruled out weekend nights as not first date-appropriate.

STEVEN CARTER: Wednesday you will get some comment about wanting to hump you because it is hump day

I giggled because that had really happened to me once, and the guy actually thought it was funny. Gordie gave me a slightly puzzled look before he continued. He didn't think what he was saying was giggle-worthy. I guess loss ratios were not meant to be funny.

STEVEN CARTER: Most important I'm here Tuesday and Thursday mostly

So the guy was here two nights a week. That would rack up some serious points on your credit card. I recalled seeing him here before, more than once, but he was always with that blonde knockout who was sitting with him again tonight. Some girls have all the luck. They have the looks and get the good guys, and the rest of us are stuck with the Gordies of the world.

STEVEN CARTER: Better luck next time maybe number five is your lucky number

ME: What makes you think this is number four?

STEVEN CARTER: I can count

He was right. Gordie was my fourth *SuperSingles* date in as many weeks. I put my phone away and smiled at the implication. *He noticed me.*

Gordie caught my smile and thought it was meant for him as he started to try to sell me on buying whole life insurance for myself. A half-hour later, I passed on dessert and got out of the evening before I lost my sanity. Gordie was nice enough to pick up the check. He said it was deductible for him, but I thanked him sincerely nevertheless. Half of a big bill was still a lot for me. Gordie gave the valet his ticket as we said goodbye and I walked toward my car. Valet parking was an extravagance I didn't need.

Mama always said, "You have to kiss a lot of frogs before you find your prince," but at least I got out of this evening without having to kiss this frog. On the way to my car, I took my phone out of my purse to call Megan and tell her I was heading home. It was still on silent, so I had missed the last text.

STEVEN CARTER: Have a nice evening Tiffany

I turned to look back at the valet stand, and he waved to me, with his date standing at his side.
What does his date think of that?
I waved back and dialed Megan.
He had waved.

∾

321

STEVEN

I HAD MY BAR EXAM STUDY MATERIAL SPREAD OUT IN FRONT OF me in my little cubicle at the Ernst and Schwartz Santa Monica office. It was easier to focus here than if I went downtown, but right now, I had trouble focusing because of her.

Tiffany Case. There was something familiar about her name, but I couldn't place it. I pulled out my phone and reviewed the text conversation I'd had with Tiffany last Tuesday for the millionth time. She had said it wouldn't be fair to her dipshit date to cut it short. She had more fortitude than any woman I had ever met if she was willing to endure Dudley Dipstick all night just to be fair to him. *It wouldn't be fair.* The words stuck with me. *It wouldn't be fair?* Just who has moral standards like that?

I had noticed her several weeks ago when she first came into the restaurant. She was a striking redhead with one-in-a-million sapphire blue eyes, curves in all the right places, and a figure that would make Jessica Rabbit envious. She was the complete opposite of the 'I only eat lettuce and carrots' under-nourished Hollywood wannabes that abounded in the LA basin. I could barely take my eyes off her that first night, and she had come back each Tuesday afterward. So far. For some reason, this girl, who was all class, got stuck going out with a string of complete dipshits. She had an air of innocence about her. If she was picking these losers, she was in serious need of a self-esteem transplant and a real man to show her what she was worth.

Last Tuesday, we were seated only two tables away, and I could hear the numb-nuts trying to sell her insurance, of all things. Seated across from a gorgeous woman and all he could do was go on and on about his insurance business. Blah, blah, blah. My sister Katie almost had to restrain me from going over and dragging the guy out by his tweed blazer to save her from him.

Katie and I had a standing date to meet on Tuesday nights at

Cardinelli's in Westwood. My brother Bill and his partner, Marco Cardinelli, had turned it into the premier place for fine Italian dining on this end of town. That was before my father died and left Bill to take over the company business. Now Marco ran it single-handedly while Bill was just an investor. The menu was great, and it was located midway between Katie and me. Every once in a while, Marco would give us a new dish he was working on to taste test. Katie loved that part.

The family was going in too many directions since Dad had died. He was the glue that kept us together, so I tried to fill in as best I could after his death with these family dinners.

I had promised my dad before he died that I would become a great lawyer, something like Perry Mason, and help people in need. So far, that had amounted to three years of law school and now a first-year associate gig at E&S, as we called it. I still needed to pass the California Bar to be a real lawyer. So far, all they had me doing here was researching the most boring briefs and running papers down to the clerk's office. That and the occasional coffee run to keep me in my place. Being a first-year associate meant JD on my card instead of ESQ and a meager paycheck. For the firm, it meant billing me at the higher full associate rate to their clients and pocketing the difference. First-years were valuable that way.

Monica suddenly rounded the corner to my cube. "Want to catch lunch, Steve?" Monica Paisley was a partner at the firm and my boss for now. I was Steven to everybody else. She insisted on calling me Steve, her little power play.

"No, thanks. I still have some catching up on civil procedures to do." That was partly the truth. The other part was that I had no intention of spending any social time alone with Monica.

She waved goodbye. "Okay, rain check then."

"Sure."

Over my dead body.

To say that Monica had a reputation was putting it mildly. The rumor was that she had something on two of the senior partners.

My guess was photographic evidence of past affairs with her. She used this leverage to keep them from putting a stop to her trolling in the first-year pond.

In the two summers I had interned here at E&S, she had made boy toys out of three different first-years that I was aware of. One of them was flattered and thought she was kinky but fun. However, for the other two, it was something to be endured to avoid a bad recommendation. She was in her forties at least, with bleached blonde hair and boobs that were definitely fake, and she wore red high heels every single day, regardless of her outfit.

She had all the subtlety of a rhinoceros and was even less appealing. I considered getting a doctor's note with a nasty medical diagnosis that would keep her at bay when the time came. However, that was still on my to-do list. This was one time I was glad to have family money behind me. You didn't mess with a Covington because we had billions in resources and the connections to fight back. But if I used that leverage, it wouldn't stop her from exacting her revenge when it came time to write my recommendation, so it made more sense to just avoid her for the time being. Money couldn't buy me a way around the moral character recommendations I needed from a firm like E&S to get into the state bar. A fact she had reminded me of already by waving a gray envelope at me my first week here. The envelope was addressed to the Committee of Bar Examiners and contained two recommendations she had already typed up, one bad and one good. Which one she sent would depend, she had told me.

After Monica left, I couldn't get the words from last Tuesday night out of my head, nor could I stop seeing those eyes. *It wouldn't be fair?* Couldn't Tiffany see that it wasn't fair for her to have to deal with Dudley Do-No-Right Dipstick all night long when there were so many better men out there? Men who would listen to her, men who would ask her what she thought, what she was interested in, what she had done, and what she wanted out of life. A man like me.

At the end of the night, I was pleased to see that she was smart enough to have driven herself and be done with the douche bag.

I decided to risk texting her about tomorrow night.

ME: Got another date setup for Tuesday??

I waited, and when no response came, I finally got back to studying Civil Procedure. This was the section on the bar that killed the most careers, and I was not going to be one of its victims if I could help it.

Half an hour later, a response arrived.

TIFFANY: Not yet, but that is the plan. Will you be there?

ME: Sure, let me know when you need an out

I was careful to type 'when' not 'if' as I considered my next line.

ME: Is this guy any better than the last moron

I didn't get a response. Shit. I'd overplayed my hand. I probably shouldn't have sent it. Mad at myself for pushing too hard, I went back to my study materials. All I saw on every page was Tiffany's enchanting smile and those eyes. I had to turn this around somehow.

TIFFANY: I won't know until tomorrow.

The text came at the end of the day. She was still talking to me… well, not talking, but at least texting.

Tomorrow evening can't come soon enough.

EMMA

"THAT ONE. NO, UP ONE MORE." MY SISTER, MEGAN, WAS looking over my shoulder as I scrolled through the possibilities for the fifth Monday night in a row. "Now that guy is hot, and a CS degree too. He probably makes a ton." The guy she picked out for me on the *SuperSingle*s website wasn't half bad. However, he wasn't half good either.

Megan's experience with men had not translated into an ability to pick out winners. Hot to Megan meant clean-shaven. She had the mistaken idea that if a guy could learn to shave every day, you could teach him whatever else you needed to.

"He has possibilities," I mumbled.

Like none and less than none.

I popped another red M&M in my mouth and scrolled down farther. "He probably still lives with his mother." Computer guys often did.

"Emma, we've gotta get you laid, and computer geeks can be real steady too." That was Megan-speak for *I wasn't much of a catch myself, so I ought to set my sights a little lower*. Her thought was that if you went after the guy whom the other girls ignored, then he would be appreciative and a great guy who would cherish you and stick with you. So far, it hadn't worked out that way for her.

I huffed. "You can't trust a thing they post anyway. They're all liars, just to different degrees."

Braydon, Megan's latest catch, wasn't any better than her last three, and he once again disproved her theory. He was currently teaching Megan that a dorky guy could be an even bigger jerk than he was a dork.

At least she was getting some action, which is more than I could say for myself, but if dating a guy like Braydon was the price to get laid, count me out. Getting some had never been Megan's problem. Her self-esteem had always been low, and she was not very good at making a guy wait.

On the next page, I found a possibility and hit the *Like* button before Megan got a chance to veto him. Jason sounded nice. He had a math degree, he looked clean-cut, and although he wasn't moving the needle on the hotness meter, he seemed to be low on the dork scale. He had a job in financial services, if I believed his bio. He liked to bicycle and he had a dog.

"I like him," Megan said. "He has big hands. You know what that means." She laughed.

I ignored her. We went on for another half hour down the listings and I sent likes to another two guys before I got my first response. It was from Jason. With a little luck, a dinner was right around the corner.

"Tell him Cardinelli's tomorrow night," Megan insisted.

"Not again. It's kind of expensive."

"No shit Sis. If he can't afford the place, you don't want him anyway." That part made sense, I guess. "Look at it this way. You've got a fifty percent chance that he's a gentleman and he picks up the tab anyway and another fifty percent chance that you like him, so it's money well spent if you split the check. So you only have a one in four chance of having to pay for a wasted date."

"So far, your math isn't working. I had to pay twice already, and they were both a waste of time and good makeup." This didn't make any sense. I could find out if I liked the guy for a lot less at Round Table, but I didn't feel like arguing the point with my big sister. After fifteen minutes of back and forth with Jason, I had a date set for tomorrow night at Cardinelli's. I hadn't told Megan about the green-eyed hunk, Steven. She wouldn't have believed me anyway.

No way.

CHAPTER 3

STEVEN

I ARRIVED AT CARDINELLI'S BEFORE KATIE. A QUICK CHECK OF the dining room showed that I was ahead of Tiffany, so I moved to the bar with a view of the front entry and ordered a glass of Pinot Grigio. I waved over Katie when she walked in.

She climbed up on the stool across from me, her back to the entrance. "Bad day at the office, eh? Opting for a liquid dinner tonight?"

"Yes and no." She was partly right. "I just wanted to start slow is all."

She smirked. "Are we waiting for that redhead again?"

Was I that transparent?

"What redhead?" I said, feigning ignorance.

She waved the waitress over. "The one you drool over every time she comes in. The one you have had us skip a window table for so you could sit near her the last two weeks." She pointed her finger at me. "The one you corralled by the restrooms last week.

The one you were texting with all during dinner last week. Ring a bell, Steven?"

I shrugged my shoulders. My sister enjoyed being a pain in the ass.

"The one you left in the middle of our dessert for so you could follow her outside. Is it coming to you yet?"

I couldn't ever keep a straight face with Katie. "I do not drool."

"Yes, that one." She chuckled. "Now give it up, little brother. What's her name?"

There was no sense trying to hold out on Katie. Ever since she made me cough up the name of the boy who had left her a note in middle school, I could never keep a secret from her. "You were done with your dessert anyway," I protested. Tiffany appeared over Katie's shoulder. Just the sight of her warmed my blood and sent a jolt of electricity straight through me. She met up with some shrimp of a guy in the front. Tiffany deserved way better than him. Way better.

Katie noticed the change in my expression and turned around in time to see Tiffany. She punched me in the shoulder and whispered, "Yes, that one, little brother. Now, what's her name?"

"Tiffany. Her name is Tiffany Case." I kept my voice low as I watched the two of them enter the dining area.

Katie leaned forward. "Steven, you are so cute. You're like a little puppy dog, wagging his tail and drooling."

"I don't drool," I repeated.

"In all seriousness, Steven, listen to me." She grabbed my hand. "Be careful with her. Treat her like a real woman, not one of your normal bimbos. Got it?"

"What's that supposed to mean?"

"Steven, I know you. I can see it in your eyes."

"Katie, you're not the best source of dating advice."

"Shut up, you look just like Bill did when he met Lauren, so go slow and don't screw it up or you'll regret it."

The mention of Bill and Lauren stopped me cold. I had been out at Columbia when it had happened, but Patrick and Katie had filled me in. Bill went off the deep end when Lauren left him. It nearly destroyed my brother. If Patrick hadn't echoed what Katie had told me, I would have thought my sister was messing with me. My oldest brother, Bill, was as solid as the Rock of Gibraltar. Nothing fazed him. I couldn't ever have imagined a breakup with a girl causing a bit of heartburn. He always had an inexhaustible supply of willing women, and he went through them like Dixie Cups.

Katie woke me out of my reverie. "Steven, if this one is different from those calendar girls, then you need to treat her differently, okay?"

Different.

I motioned toward the dining area. "Will you help me then?"

She climbed down from her stool. "Within reason."

That was good enough for tonight.

EMMA

AS I APPROACHED THE RESTAURANT, MEGAN TEXTED TO WISH ME good luck, informing me that Braydon insisted on a movie night, so she wouldn't be able to give me a rescue call. She was allowing Braydon to run her life again. Without a call from Megan, I would just have to hope Jason wasn't any worse than Gordie had been. I put my phone back in my purse after reviewing Jason's photo so I could recognize him. We had agreed to meet by the ficus tree just inside the door.

A man in a khaki suit stood up as I walked in. My heart dropped to the floor.

Why do they all have to be liars?

You were supposed to post a recent picture of yourself, but Jason had a distorted view of *recent*. He was a lot older than his picture, with a significant paunch and a receding hairline. His profile also listed his height as average, but he was shorter than me. Jason's lies were the worst combination yet.

Jason led the way. All of my other dates had been gentlemen and offered to let me walk first. I guess in the new era of women's lib, I shouldn't have taken it as meaning anything.

At least Jason seemed to be less self-centered than Gordie last week, and he didn't drool like Bryce the week before, but he did talk quite loudly.

At his age, maybe he has a hearing problem.

He ordered a bottle of wine and bruschetta for an appetizer, announcing that dinner would be on him. That moved him up a notch in my estimation.

I started to tell him about myself. I told him how I had worked in an art gallery after school before landing my current museum job. There were way more art history grads than there were good jobs. The gallery job paid next to nothing, but it was a start, and what else could I do? Work at Jamba Juice then move up to Starbucks? We were both Santa Clara University alums, so at least we had that in common.

He had gotten a math degree and moved into financial counseling.

"Is that like being a stockbroker?" I asked.

He frowned. "It's quite a step up from being a stockbroker," he told me coldly.

I felt embarrassed that I had insulted him without meaning to.

"Stockbrokers are just used car salesmen with better suits."

I had to laugh at his description. I didn't know any stockbrokers, but I had met my share of slimy car salesmen. So far, it seemed this was going to be a pleasant evening after all, if I overlooked the outdated photo angle.

He smiled. I couldn't make out much from his eyes. There was no spark there. They were dull.

After glancing at the menu, which I had almost memorized, I ordered the Chicken Fettuccine Alfredo.

"You don't really want the Alfredo. It's much too rich. The lady will have the Ensalata Regina," Jason told the waiter.

The waiter raised a questioning eyebrow in my direction. I smiled politely, biting my tongue, determined to not make a scene. My stomach turned. The waiter withdrew and Jason moved several notches up the jerk scale. With his paunch, he should be the one getting the salad, not me. I thought it but I didn't say it. I couldn't decide which was worse, his implying that I needed to diet or his trying to keep the bill down because he was paying. Either way, it was insulting. I shivered. I adjusted my sweater closed a bit more.

As the meal wore on and he downed more wine, things got worse. Jason was trying to impress me with stories of the Hollywood big shots he consulted for.

As if I give a shit.

He was getting louder as he drank more, with his glances at my breasts becoming longer and more lecherous. If any of his clients heard a recording of this conversation, they would probably fire his ass in a nanosecond. Discretion was not a word in his vocabulary.

He was the oldest of three. His two younger brothers from his mother's second marriage were MMA fighters. He got the brains, he said, and they got the brawn.

Who got the charm? Is what I wanted to ask, but didn't.

Then he implied for the second time that we would be going back to his place after dinner.

Not happening, dude.

My wine threatened to come back up. I had said *no, thanks* already. I had even been polite about it. He went down another notch.

He ignored me. The table next to us kept distracting him. Jason was constantly ogling the pair of giggling college-age girls with low-cut tops. He was probably trying to guess their cup sizes.

I rolled my eyes as he leered at them again. I just had to tough out another half hour to finish dinner and excuse myself.

I picked at my salad, not finding anything with any substance to it. The salad had a fancy name, but to me, it was just goat food, and not much of it at that. My date was quickly making me lose my appetite.

Jason bellowed on. He drove a Maserati.

Lame.

And he had the seats monogrammed.

Lame.

And he added a special sound system.

Lame.

I tuned him out. He mentioned for the third time that he was paying for dinner and we would be going to his place for dessert. He chuckled.

I couldn't believe it. This wasn't funny. It was getting nauseous. I decided that enough was enough. Implying that I could be bought for the price of a dinner was too much.

Screw you, Jason.

I was done here. I considered walking out but decided that there was a chance to salvage tonight if I could meet up with Steven again. I excused myself to go to the ladies' room. I half expected Steven to be waiting for me in the hallway. He wasn't.

Jason had barely noticed me leave as his head swiveled to watch the coeds giggle again.

What an ass.

In the restroom, I took out my phone.

ME: U here tonight?

STEVEN CARTER: Another moron?

ME: pls call I need out

I smiled as I turned on my ringer and returned to the table. I waited for his call to get me away from this disaster date and meet up with Steven instead. Jason was still trying to impress me with the famous people he knew.

Lame.

My phone dinged a text, which didn't faze Jason in the least.

STEVEN CARTER: Be just a minute

I only had to endure a little bit more of Mr. Monogrammed Maserati.

My Maserati blah, blah, blah, Senator, blah, blah, Hollywood, blah, blah, blah.

I started to count the references to himself as he droned on. I was up to sixteen since I had returned to the table.

"Good evening," I heard Steven say as he and his date came up from behind me with red aprons over their street clothes.

My mouth must have dropped to the floor. I had expected a discreet phone call.

Steven bowed. "You two lucky lovebirds have just won tonight's drawing for a free wine tasting. "May I get your names, please?"

Jason was beaming. This was his lucky night. "Jason Biggs."

Quietly, I added, "Miranda Frost."

Steven paused for a few moments then made a note on his pad and raised an eyebrow to me. "Got it. Miranda and Wayson."

My eyes were drawn to Steven's. Those green eyes transfixed me again, and the evening improved one hundred percent.

"Jason," my date corrected him, snapping me out of my daze.

"Yes sir," Steven responded. "I am Steven, and the lovely Jill Masterson will be assisting me tonight." Jill nodded as Steven continued. Now I had a name to put with the pretty blonde's face.

My heart sank as I realized how strikingly beautiful his date was. I had only seen her from a distance before. I didn't recognize her from TV, but she was drop-dead Hollywood gorgeous. There was no way in hell I could compete with her. Jill had one of those faces that hardly needed makeup. Her dress under the apron certainly cost more than one of my paychecks. Her underwear probably cost more than my whole outfit.

Our previous waiter brought out four bottles of wine and glasses on a tray that he placed on a fold-out stand in the aisle. He handed Steven the corkscrew before retreating without a word. Whatever Steven had planned, it had been worked out with the staff somehow, and I was clueless. I would have to wait and see.

A questioning look crossed Jason's face. "Do I know you from somewhere?" he asked Steven.

"I don't think so, sir," Steven responded as he opened the first bottle of wine. "Perhaps the gentleman would like to tell us which of these four reds he prefers." Steven moved Jason's plate to the center of the table as he placed the four wine glasses in front of my smiling date. Being the center of attention suited Jason just fine.

Steven described the first wine as he poured out a large glass. Jason made a show swirling it, sniffing it, and tasting the wine. This was followed by two more glasses that Steven poured and Jason swigged.

Jason had no idea how silly he appeared trying to make a show of being a wine connoisseur.

Jill smiled at me and stepped in my direction, lifting several napkins off the wine tray.

As Steven poured the fourth glass, the lip of the bottle knocked the rim of the glass and the whole thing ended up in Jason's lap.

I squealed and pushed back as Jason gasped.

"Oh, so sorry." Steven fumbled with the glass. Jill quickly placed her napkins on the table, protecting me from the deluge hitting Jason.

"So sorry, Mr. Jasper. Let me help," Steven mumbled as he

moved in with a napkin. The poor guy could not get out of the way as it looked like Steven's foot was behind the leg of his chair.

"You idiot," Jason screamed, drawing more than a few stares from the diners around us as he struggled to get up out of his chair.

"So sorry, Mr. Jester," Steven said, now towering over the struggling Jason.

Jason's face darkened to match the wine stains on his shirt. "It's Jason, you idiot," he yelled at Steven as he surveyed the damage to his suit. "Miranda, we're going to my place."

Fat chance that was happening.

I smiled courteously. "No, thank you."

Jill started to giggle.

Jason's eyes bugged out in disbelief. "Miranda," he pleaded.

Jason winced as Steven grabbed his arm. "I believe the lady said no," Steven told him forcefully. Steven then whispered something in Jason's ear that I couldn't hear.

Jason started mumbling to himself as Steven escorted him to the door.

Jill removed her apron and smiled at me as she offered her hand. "Name's Katie. So nice to meet you. I hope my idiot brother didn't get any on you."

My jaw went slack as I shook her hand. Her name wasn't Jill.

She was Steven's sister? Not his date?

I stood and surveyed my legs and shoes. "No, I think I'm good. Your brother?"

She laughed. "Yeah, somebody had to be his sister, and I drew the short straw."

A chill hit me. Jill Masterson was the name of the girl who got covered in gold paint in *Goldfinger.*

Steven figured out my deception.

Katie moved away from the table. "We would love it if you would join us." She moved to the table directly behind where I had been sitting. "Trust me, he's not always this big of a klutz."

I hadn't seen them arrive.

She took a seat. Their table had three place settings but only two dinners.

Steven returned from escorting my ex-date out the door, and announced to the nearby guests, "I hope you enjoyed this evening's improvisational acting demonstration." He started to clap, and the crowd joined him for a short round of applause, and the previously shocked customers went back to their dinners, now somewhat more at ease, believing that this had all been playacting.

Steven pulled out a chair for me. "Sorry about the theatrics, but I wanted him to leave, not you," he said with a disarming smile. "I took the liberty of ordering the Fettuccine for you when numbnuts wouldn't let you have it."

I was so hypnotized by his lips as he said it that I couldn't manage a coherent response.

This man should have a warning label on his forehead.

They were seated directly behind me and had obviously overheard Jason, not that it was hard with his volume level. Not only had I been saved from another date from hell, but now I was having dinner with Steven the green-eyed hunk and his sister. On top of that, I got the Fettuccine that I had wanted this evening.

They hadn't yet finished their dinners. He brushed his hand across my shoulder, moving behind me to reach his seat. His touch was electric and left a trail of tingles.

The heat rose in my cheeks as I glanced between them. Brother and sister. The resemblance was not close, but I could see it. Good looks certainly ran in the family.

The waiter returned with my entree. "Good job, Mr. C. That guy deserved it."

Katie and I both nodded, and Steven ignited me with his smile and those dimples again.

Katie giggled. "Monogrammed Maserati. What a toad." She had that right.

"What did you say to him?" I asked Steven.

Steven wiped his lips with his napkin. "I just told him that if he

didn't come quietly, he'd be getting blood all over his monogrammed seats."

Katie and I both laughed. I had no doubt that Steven could
have made quick work of little loud-mouthed Jason.

Katie placed a hand gently on mine. "Tiffany, I haven't had this
much fun in a long time, but I have to get going. Hope to see you
again soon." She fixed Steven with a glare. "Now treat her right,
little brother." With a wink to me and a cheek kiss to him, she was
gone. She hadn't finished her dinner.

I waved to her as she left, and suddenly, it was only me and
panty-melting Steven at the table.

"So, you're a *James Bond* fan?" He smirked and his dark green
eyes paralyzed me in place. He stood and offered me his hand with
a sincere smile. "Hello. I'm Steven, and you are…?"

I cringed. I took his hand. "Emma," I responded sheepishly.
Busted.

~

STEVEN

I TOLD THE HOSTESS WHAT I WANTED, AND SHE MANAGED TO SEAT
us out of eyesight, just behind Tiffany after they took a table.

Katie ordered us a bottle of Sauvignon Blanc. She was being a
good sport about this as I listened as discreetly as I could.

I had learned that Tiffany graduated from Santa Clara
University.

The guy had no class. He was sitting across from the prettiest
girl in the room and spent half his time watching two nearby half-
dressed UCLA girls giggle and jiggle. When they ordered, I
couldn't believe it. The dickhead changed her order from the
Alfredo to salad, implying that she needed to watch her calories.

I wanted to get up and deck him, but Katie, sensing my aggravation, leaned over and whispered to me to calm down. When the dickhead started telling the whole room about his Maserati with monogrammed seats, Katie rolled her eyes and I almost burst out laughing. This went on for what seemed like forever.

I couldn't see how Tiffany had the self-control to put up with this for so long. However, she had said last week that it wouldn't be fair. She had to give the guy a chance. I waited for her to text me, but maybe she didn't know I was here. I considered sending her some kind of innocuous message but discarded the thought. I could get up and saunter by the window so she noticed me, or she might take a bathroom break to get away from this dipshit like she did last week's moron.

TIFFANY: U here tonight?

Katie's eyes lit up when my phone announced the incoming text. "That her?" she whispered.

I nodded and turned the screen so Katie could read it. I typed my response.

ME: Another moron?

TIFFANY: Pls call I need out

Katie grabbed at the phone to see the messages.

ME: Be just a minute

I had formulated a plan this afternoon at the office, and just in case, I had called Marco to clear it with him if I wanted to implement it. It helped to be the co-owner's brother. I had also assured him that I would smooth it over with the customers so they didn't freak out.

Showtime.

I got up and motioned for Katie to follow me out to the kitchen. Once there, I recruited Tony, who had been waiting on both of our tables. I filled them both in on my plan.

Katie giggled. This was right up her alley.

Tony was not happy, but he agreed after he checked with Marco. Tony got us two red aprons and a notepad and agreed to follow with the wine.

"Four bottles of your cheapest red," I told him as Katie and I left the kitchen.

My sister was no stranger to practical jokes and was grinning from ear to ear as we walked up.

Tiffany had a slightly puzzled look as I began my little wine tasting speech, but her smile grew as I went along. She threw me a curveball. "Miranda Frost," she said as I asked her name. The moron wasn't fazed, so that must have been the name she had given him.

Tiffany Case last week became Miranda Frost this week. It hit me what she was doing. I knew my *James Bond* as well as the next guy, so I introduced Katie as Jill Masterson and carried on. Katie didn't bat an eye. A real pro practical joker.

I started the tasting charade and made sure to fill the glasses higher than normal for tasting purposes. The guy was acting like the douche he was, trying to impress Tiffany but making an ass of himself instead.

After the third glass, I nodded to Katie, who picked up the extra napkins from the tray and got ready for the finale. I hoped to God that my aim was good and I didn't end up getting any on Tiffany. Katie's napkins were my safeguard.

I positioned my foot behind the leg of Mr. Bigsnot's chair as I poured the fourth glass. I used the end of the bottle to tip the glass into Mr. Bigsnot's lap. He yelped as it drenched him in cheap red wine.

Mr. Bigsnot was pissed. "Miranda, were going to my place," he proclaimed.

As I hoped, Tiffany/Miranda declined and he pleaded
with her.

I grabbed him by his skinny fucking arm. "The lady said no."
Then I whispered to him that I would wipe the floor with him if he
didn't come quietly.

I hauled his whimpering ass out of the dining room and
through the front door.

"You'll regret this. Now I remember who you are," he muttered
before he scampered away.

Sure thing, shrimp.

"And don't come back," I yelled at him.

Back at the table, I pulled out a chair for Tiffany. I explained
that I had ordered her the Fettuccine that the moron had denied her
just before Tony arrived with the plate.

Her smile when the food arrived was payment enough for me.
Katie quickly excused herself with an admonition to me to treat
Tiffany right.

My cock twitched with visions of several right ways I could
treat Tiffany or Miranda or whatever her name was. It was time to
find out the truth. I fixed her gaze with a smile. "*James Bond* fan,
eh?" I rose and offered her my hand. "Hello, I'm Steven, and you
are…?" I waited.

She slumped in her seat, but she took my hand and replied,
"Emma." I couldn't place an Emma in any of the Bond films, so it
figured this might be the real answer. "That's a very beautiful
name. It suits you. You shouldn't hide it," I added.

Emma.

*E*MMA

H*E* PONDERED MY ANSWER AND A SMILE TUGGED AT THE CORNERS

of his mouth. "Emma. That's a very beautiful name. It suits you. You shouldn't hide it."

The heat started in my chest and traveled up to my cheeks. My blush must have been obvious by now. What wasn't showing was the instant heat between my thighs. This man could make reading the dictionary sound sensual. Whereas Jason had leered at me, this man's gaze was pure admiration. I recrossed my legs.

It didn't help.

He leaned in. "Or would you like me to call you Plenty O'Toole?" He made an obvious show of shifting his eyes to my chest. "Or perhaps Pussy Galore?" He was going the have me leaking through my panties if he kept this up. This wasn't merely another guy. This was a man, and one who knew his Bond.

I pasted on my most innocent smile as I loaded some fettuccine onto my fork. "A practical girl takes precautions." Right now, practical was not a good description of what I was feeling. I recrossed my legs again.

He raised his wine glass. "So, Emma, tell me a little about yourself."

Not so fast.

I changed the subject. "Do you rescue girls from bad first dates every week?"

He took a slow, sensual sip from his wine glass before answering. "No, you're the first and only."

Fat chance.

He had no idea what he was doing to me. "Oh, then what makes me so special?" It was a bad idea. Saying the first thing that pops to mind might be good for a *Family Feud* contestant, but it was the wrong thing for a date.

Why did I think this was now a date?

He pinned me with that gaze of his. The piercing green eyes that I had noticed in that first meeting in the hall peered straight into my soul. He pondered his answer for a moment. "I have wanted to meet you since the first time I saw you walk in here." He put his glass down. "Is that so hard to understand?"

The words took a moment to register. He had been watching me. "You don't know anything about me."

His grin expanded as the heat in my face went up a notch. "Let's remedy that, Emma." My name floated dangerously off his lips.

I took another forkful of food and chewed slowly, to calm myself, and glanced down at my plate, not answering his non-question.

"So what is a lady like you doing dining with morons?" he asked.

I finished chewing my mouthful. A lady didn't talk with her mouth full. "And just what makes you think I'm a lady?" I asked, afraid to meet his eyes.

He paused to take a sip of water. "It's not something you can hide. I know one when I meet one."

That was the best compliment I had gotten in a long time. "Nice of you to say."

"So, what do you do when you're not out dining with morons?"

I was concentrating on eating the delicious fettuccine. "I'm an associate curator at the museum."

His eyes warmed. "Paintings or sculpture?" Was he just guessing? Or did he actually know that sculpture was a separate department from paintings?

I forked some more of my dish. "European paintings."

He quickly asked, "How did you get interested in art?" This was a complete change. The deepest question I had gotten from my last several *SuperSingles* dates had been *What's your sign?*

I was slowly getting more at ease with this tall, imposing man. "My great-great-grandmother spent her early years in France and knew some of the painters of her day. She even sat for one. My mother also did a little painting before she got married, and I guess I thought it was in my genes. I started out as an art major in college. I had the interest but not the talent for it, so I switched to art history, with a double-major in psych."

"Interesting combination," he noted.

Interesting was not the normal response I got when people heard my choice of majors. "That was so I'd be qualified to work at Starbucks if I couldn't find a job in the art world." The line that a Psychology degree only prepared one to work at Starbucks was a common joke on campus.

He chuckled at that. "And that was at Santa Clara?"

He'd been listening.

"So, you overheard?" I asked.

He put his glass down. "More than enough to know that he was a jerk." He had that part right. Jason and Steven were as different as night and day. "The dipshit has no idea how to treat a lady."

It was the second time he had called me a lady. "And what makes you so sure I'm a lady?"

"Experience, tempered by judgment. You wasted an entire evening last week with boring Dudley Dipstick because you said it wouldn't be fair to him to cut him off too early. That, my dear, marks you as a lady." He grinned as he peered over his glass, his eyes meeting mine.

I had just been getting control of myself, and then he had to go and compliment me again. I couldn't control my blushing. "And you know how to treat a lady?" I asked coyly.

The lust in his eyes was simmering and unmistakable. His smile widened slowly but surely as his gaze fixed me in place like prey. "Just try me," he said softly. The predator in him was loose.

One word and he would devour me.

I was stricken with an intense desire to respond but helpless to come up with the words.

In an instant, it was over. The predator receded and the gentleman resurfaced. "And how do you manage to find such losers anyway?"

I had blown it.

"Well, my sister, Megan, has been coming over Monday nights to help go through the profiles on *SuperSingles*."

"So, the sister who helped pick these losers for you? Has she managed to find a real keeper for herself?"

I almost spat out some wine with my laugh. "Not exactly."

He wore a knowing grin. "That's what I thought." He sipped his wine. "So, tell me, what are your criteria for picking out a date for the evening?"

"Criteria. Well, let's see. He needs to be honest and have a job."

"No slackers and no criminals then." He grinned. "Perhaps I should apply?"

My heart skipped a beat as I tried to hide my glee at his saying that. This man had a way of making me speechless, which was no easy feat. I recrossed my legs to try to control myself. "And, my number one rule, he can't be a lawyer."

A quizzical look crossed his face. "These criteria working well for you?" He already knew the answer.

I hesitated to admit it. "So far, no second dates."

He finished another bite of his food. "Good choice. For my money, none of those morons met the second date test," he said emphatically.

"And what test is that?" I asked.

He grinned as he picked up his glass. "For a second date, they need to be able to use their eyes to see you as a truly beautiful woman and use their ears to listen to you and learn about you as a truly wonderful person."

I could listen to this man dish out compliments like that all night long.

He sipped some wine. "But enough of them. I want to hear more about you."

I wasn't sure where to start. He already knew I went to Santa Clara. "After school, the only job I could get was as a sales associate at an art gallery. But I kept in touch with my professors from school every few months, and finally, one of them recommended me for this curator job at the museum." I started back on my meal.

"Most people don't have the tenacity to network like that."

It hadn't been easy for me. He was right about that. "Well, it paid off. This is a little museum, but at least I have my foot in the door now."

"And if you could have any job, what would that be?"

I didn't have to think to answer that one. "A senior curator at a major museum, like the National Museum in Washington. Well, actually, there are four museums on my list, including the MET in New York, the de Young in San Francisco, and the Art Institute of Chicago, and I would like to teach kids art in my spare time. That's what I'm going to do one day." That was the truth. I had a goal and I was going to get there, no matter what. I put my fork down. "Enough about me. What about you? What does Steven Carter want to be when he grows up?"

He peered down at his plate, spearing a piece of chicken. "Hard to say, exactly. I don't really like the idea of growing up."

I pointed my fork at him. "You're dodging."

His expression told me I'd hit a nerve. He hesitated before answering. "Right now, I'm just an office temp. But long-term, I want to end up helping people. That's my goal."

He didn't strike me as the office temp type. He was in a suit tonight, and not a cheap one. "An idealist?" I smiled as I picked up my glass again. "And what kind of job do you do to help people?"

"Right now," —he put his fork down— "I'm just a glorified gopher. Yesterday, I spent most of the day running packages back and forth. Today, I spent all afternoon looking over some books." He sipped some wine. "But all I saw on every page was your face, Tiffany… excuse me, Emma."

He was thinking of me and we hadn't even really met yet. That was either very cute, or he was serious stalker material.

A twinkle played in his eyes. "But I didn't know I was two names behind."

I learned that Steven and I both knew a lot of Bond trivia. Both of his parents were dead, and he was the youngest of five in his family, with three older brothers, Bill, Liam, and Patrick, and his sister, Katherine, whom I had met earlier. He had an easygoing way about him, and unlike my last several dates, he seemed to have a genuine interest in me and what I had to say. As things went on, I learned he understood more about Impressionism and Post-Impressionism, which were my focus areas, than any non-art history person I had met. His favorite artist was Renoir, as was mine. We talked about the museum's holdings and the gaps we had in our exhibits. He seemed quite interested in the museum.

Dinner with Steven had been easily the most stimulating time I'd had since, well, forever. Everything about him dripped testosterone, powerful but at the same time gentle, and he was interested in having a true conversation with me. The way he subtly devoured me with his eyes while remaining ever the gentleman was both intimidating and intoxicating. Twice, brief flashes of the predator showed in his eyes, but the gentleman quickly returned each time.

I had finished my plate and was working on my fourth glass of wine, or maybe more. I lost count. "So, you have dinner here every week with your sister?"

He fiddled with the stem of his glass as a gentle smile formed. "Yeah, Katie and I have dinner most every Tuesday, and I've convinced my two local brothers, Bill and Patrick, to alternate meeting me here on Thursdays. Sort of my way of trying to hold us all together as a family since Dad died. Half the time, Bill threatens that he has too much work to make it, but I usually end up shaming him into it when he's in town." He really cared about his family in a very genuine way.

"And why here?" I asked.

He pointed around the room. "My brother Bill put this together. He's one of the owners." That tidbit explained how he'd gotten the staff to go along with his earlier charade. He had spilled wine on the floor, after all.

"I thought you said he worked and traveled."

He finished a bite. "I did, and he does. He and his friend Marco Cardinelli started this place, but since Dad died, Bill had to take on a real job, or at least that's the way Dad would have put it. So now, Marco runs this place, and Bill is just a co-owner."

I ended up filling him in a little on my mom and dad up north and my sister here in LA as we talked on. He told me stories of his childhood with his brothers and sister and summers spent back-packing in Yosemite. He laughed about the time they'd left their food too low and had it devoured by a determined bear. They'd had to hike all day with no food to get back to the main road.

We ordered gelato for dessert. I watched the slow way he sucked on the spoon as he took each bite. I couldn't help but visu-ally undress him for the hundredth time. Everything he did made me hot and wet. I could hear my mother's voice tell me a lady lets the man make the first move. But what if I didn't feel like waiting forever? I had moved my hand to the middle of the table more than once, just short of reaching to touch him, but I hadn't gotten a response.

Before I knew it, the dining room was emptying and only one other couple remained.

"If Jasper Bigsnot drove you, I can offer a ride home."

I laughed at the way he twisted Jason's name. "No, I was smart enough to drive myself."

He rose and offered me his hand.

Finally, a touch. It was electric, sending more signals of lust straight to my core.

Get a grip, Emma.

I let him help me up, and after a few wobbly steps, I regretted the last glass or two of wine.

He put his arm around my waist and pulled me to his side to steady me. After we got out the door, he said, "I'll need your keys." His tone was commanding, not requesting.

"I can drive myself," I protested.

He squeezed my waist. "I always see that a date gets home safely. Sort of a policy of mine."

Wow. He said I was his date.

I located the keys in my purse without any difficulty as we ambled toward the valet. I wasn't really that drunk. It must have been the heels.

He took the keys from me. "Tony, could you please do me a favor and follow me in the lady's car? I'll give you a ride back."

Tony drove my car. Steven helped me into his. After a little coaxing, Siri started giving him directions.

True to his word, Steven walked with me up to the door of my little apartment. As I fumbled with my keys, my eyes found his, waiting for him to make his move.

Hoping.

He smiled innocently.

I ignored my mother's advice about letting the man make the first move and stepped toward him.

That was all the invitation he needed. He pulled me into him. One arm snaked around my waist and the other behind my head as his mouth met mine. He pulled me closer and took control of the kiss. His tongue searched out mine, stroking me, teasing me, claiming me, and lighting my blood on fire as fireworks exploded behind my eyelids. He tasted of wine and pleasure and need. My breasts pressed to his chest as his hand followed my lower back to cradle my ass and pull me against him. His grip was firm, insistent, and powerful.

I melded my body to his. The heat of his body threatened to ignite me. Heat pooled between my thighs as his growing erection pressed against me. He smelled of spice and maleness. I'd been kissed by boys before, but never like this. This was a new experience. A man. A man with a hint of animal.

Things are going too fast.

Then, it didn't matter. I held him tighter. I twined my fingers in his hair as I held on for dear life. My heart was thundering against my ribcage. I relished the heat of him against me, the rod of his arousal pressing against my abdomen, the scrape of his stubble on my cheek. The smell of his hair. The taste of desire on his tongue. Time slowed, and the world dropped away as I was more drunk by the kiss than the wine. It didn't matter that we were in the hall-way… nothing mattered, so long as he held me.

When he broke the kiss, I may have whimpered a bit. Things were fuzzy as passion clouded my brain.

How had I gotten so lucky?

In the space of a few hours, the night that started with another first date from hell had ended with the kiss to define all kisses. I held on tightly, my head pressed into his shoulder, not wanting to let go for fear that I would wake up and it would all have been a dream.

I trembled as his thumb traced the underside of my breast.

He brought his hand to my face.

I pushed into his touch.

He lifted my chin with a finger.

I went weak as I gazed up into those luscious green eyes, awash with passion and desire.

"I think I'll call you Sugar. You taste so sweet." Then, he pushed me away. "Off to bed now, Sugar." His actions suddenly sent the opposite signal of the bulge in his pants. He kissed me on the forehead and turned me toward my door.

Somehow, I had screwed this up.

Why didn't he want to come in? Was I a bad kisser? Maybe I should have squeezed his ass or grabbed for his belt buckle? But it was too late. He backed away down the hallway. "Is it okay if I call you, Sugar?"

"Sure," I mumbled as I turned the key in the lock.

He kept his eyes on me until I got the door open and went inside.

Once behind my door in the empty apartment, the loneliness hit me. I never felt lonely in my little apartment. It was my castle, my refuge from the world outside.

I grabbed a handful of M&Ms from the bowl on the counter. Things were too fuzzy to sort out right now. Move over, Tiffany, Miranda, and Emma. Here comes Sugar.

"Sugar," I repeated out loud to the empty room.

Sugar. I could get used to that.

SNEAK PEEK: THE BILLIONAIRE'S HOPE

Katie

My phone vibrated again in my purse. I sat in the second row of the packed Breakers meeting room at the Mandalay Bay hotel. I was also starting to sweat in my jacket. The air conditioning was set for a T-shirt-and-shorts crowd, not the business suit I had on.

My phone vibrated yet again, and then again. Someone was persistent.

I gave in and opened my purse. My oldest brother, Bill, topped the recent calls list. Actually, there were four missed calls, a voice mail, and a text from him.

My blood froze at the sight of the text.

BILL: Call me ASAP 911

Mr. Cool was not easily excited. It had to be a major issue for him to call it an emergency.

This session of the conference was about the new guidance the Financial Accounting Standards Board had issued for capitalizing software.

I was in the absolute middle of a packed row. It wouldn't be easy to get out. I would have chosen the almost-empty first row, except then I would have had to keep my legs crossed in this skirt, and that would have made typing notes on my laptop harder.

The guys had it so easy, trading suits for jeans. They weren't judged the same way we girls were.

I was deadly serious about beating them all out, and that meant makeup, a proper business suit, and heels——even at a conference in Sin City. I was determined to be kick-ass in this profession, and I intended to make the appropriate impression when I met the presenter after the session. Connections were key in this business. It was something the dolts in the rear didn't seem to get.

I packed my computer into my laptop bag and waited for the man on the stage to turn toward the screen. I didn't want him to notice me walking out.

The presentation was pretty dry stuff. It was putting most everybody to sleep, even worse than the morning session had. But that was the essence of accounting. Knowing all the rules was crucial. *Exciting* was never a word you used in the same sentence with *accounting*. This was like school. Limit my distractions, and I could nail it. I had a high tolerance for boring.

The speaker turned to emphasize something on the screen. I shouldered my Gucci purse and made my way down the row, squeezing past the other attendees as quickly as I could.

This week had been a welcome respite from the office and my boss, Russ Downey. Chewing glass was better than being around Russ. The man yelled at me incessantly, and lately he'd piled increasingly more work on me every day. And that was before you considered his BO.

Russ had stayed in Los Angeles, although he should have been here too. Half the staff called him *Rusty* behind his back, because he wasn't always up on the latest FASB pronouncements. It was sad that several of us new hires knew more than he did, but I'd learned long ago that life wasn't fair.

Anyway, whatever the reason, Russ Downey had it in for me in a big way. I was used to hard work, but the amount he assigned me was way beyond that. I hadn't done anything wrong that I could remember, nothing to make him single me out as the one second-year accountant he was trying to run out of the company, but that seemed to be his goal.

Stubbornness, though, was not something I had in short supply. I was going to leave on my own terms and in my own time. As soon as the firm signed off on my experience hours this fall, I would have everything I needed for my CPA, and I would pull the ripcord. One extra day of Russ was a day too much. The man was such a pig.

The hallway outside the meeting room was teeming with T-shirted nerds attending a computer hacking conference. Black Hat they called it. I moved away from a gaggle of them who didn't seem to have showered as recently as they should have.

Typical computer geeks.

I dialed Bill back.

He picked up on the first ring. *"Katie, where are you?"* he demanded.

"Las Vegas. I'm at a conference this week."

He let out an audible breath. *"Good, I was worried."*

"Worried? Why? What happened?"

"I have some bad news. You might want to sit down."

"No can do." I said, pressing the phone to my ear. The computer geeks were a noisy bunch.

"It's Monica." He hesitated.

I dreaded what might come next. Monica Paisley was a psycho bitch. She had threatened my brother Steven and his wife, Emma, and even torched Emma's car a few weeks ago. Monica was trouble with a capital T.

"It's your house," he said. *"It's on fire."*

My heart stopped, and my stomach lurched. My lunch threatened to come up.

I ran toward the women's room to my left.

I elbowed open the stall door, and the phone hit the marble floor as I went to my knees in front of the porcelain bowl. I almost made it in time. I puked in the toilet, but some splashed on the seat. I couldn't control the upheavals. Remnants of the fish tacos I'd chosen for lunch filled the bowl. After the third and fourth heaves, there was nothing left to expel, but I couldn't stop the convulsions. The urge overcame me again, and I dry-heaved twice more. It felt like I'd torn a stomach muscle.

Once the sickening urges stopped, I spit several times, trying to rid my mouth of the wretched taste of vomit and bile. I picked up my phone and stumbled to a sink. I splashed water into my mouth, spitting again. Some splashed vomit had gotten on my jacket. I wet some paper towels and wiped it off. Some had gotten on my phone too.

Gross.

Bill's call had dropped. I pulled my phone out of the case and wiped it off. I rinsed the cover in the sink, wrapping it in a paper towel to dry and setting it in my bag.

My house. How could she do that?

I had to get home.

Screw everything. This was the last day of the conference anyway. I started for my room, gathered up my courage, and called my brother back.

The elevator door closed. "How bad?" I asked when he came on the line.

"*I'm so sorry, Katie. The fire department is still working it, but there won't be anything left.*"

His words chilled me. Things like this weren't supposed to happen. "I thought she was in jail."

"*She made bail weeks ago. Katie, you need to go stay with Patrick when you get back.*" My younger brother Patrick had a condo in the same building as Bill, but it wasn't anywhere near my work.

"No, that's too far," I complained. My big brother was still bossing me around——the one constant in the universe.

"*Just do it, and don't argue for a change.*" His tone indicated he wasn't going to let this go. "*You'll be safe with him, and the Hanson firm has protection for you at his place. They can keep you safe until we find Paisley.*"

"But why me? I didn't do anything to her."

None of this made any sense. I had never even met her. My sister-in-law's nickname for her had been Cruella. The first time I heard it, it sounded harsh. Today it seemed entirely too kind.

"*Crazy does what crazy wants,*" Bill said with a sigh. "*She's out of control, and there's no telling what she might do next. The Hanson people are even pulling Patrick's girlfriend, Liz, in for protection.*"

I shuddered. The lady was a lunatic. This was terrifying. Dealing with my asshole boss was one type of stress, but this was a whole other level. At least with Russ it was only words and never anything physical.

I stepped out of the elevator and moved down the hall toward my room.

Bill filled me in for a few minutes on the Hanson Security crew's efforts to find Monica and get her back into custody. At the end of the call, he made me promise to go to Patrick's condo when I got back.

I chucked my bag and purse on the bed. My next stop was the bathroom. I brushed my teeth and gargled the entire bottle of complimentary mouthwash to rid myself of that awful barf after-taste. I stripped off my stained suit and grabbed another from the closet. I was glad I always packed extra outfits for a trip like this. It only took me a few minutes to stuff my clothes back into my bag for the trip home. Except I didn't have a home anymore.

I moved my laptop to the desk and powered it back up. The airline website yielded bad news. No seats back to LAX today. I tried Expedia. The same answer: nothing before tomorrow afternoon. My only choice was to rent a car and make the five-hour drive home, unless I wanted to wait. It was almost four... If I left soon, I could make it tonight.

I trundled my bag behind me and shut the door to the empty room. Downstairs, the lady behind the desk gave me even worse news. Because of all the convention-goers, there weren't any rentals available downtown or at the airport, but if I wanted to take a taxi or the shuttle to the airport, I could wait and see if one became available. It seemed like my only choice.

I turned for the door. I brought up the Uber app on my phone. I was typing when I bumped into him, literally. If he hadn't grabbed my arms, I would have ended up flat on my ass.

~

Nick

Hank's morning presentation of my cell phone hack at the Black Hat conference had gone quite well. *Black Hat* was a complete misnomer. This conference was for white hat hackers like me to let targets know how they could be attacked, and put pressure on them to fix their vulnerabilities before the real bad guys got to them.

Hank had presented on stage while I sat in the back and watched. It paid to stay under the radar in my chosen profession. As a member of the Hanson Investigations and Security team, he made a credible presenter. Hank understood the nuances of my technique and answered all the technical questions perfectly. This was the sixth hack I'd gotten out in the open at one of these conferences without anyone realizing I was behind them.

Anonymity, thou art sweet.

I had used the hack for over a year now, and it was time to publish it so the wireless companies could patch it. The feds had a similar thing going the last few years, but it involved driving a truck around with a fake cell tower system in the back. Such a kludge, and only good for a small area. Mine could be launched from my laptop and worked anywhere in the world. Much more elegant. Those feds had no idea how clueless they were.

I had discovered a new alternative vulnerability for my own use, so I wouldn't be giving up any capability when they patched this one.

I had been up to my room and back after the presentation ended, and I now waited in the large lobby to meet up with Hank for a few hours at the tables.

My phone vibrated with a text message.

BRANDI: date Monday night?

ME: bring Candy - six okay?

BRANDI: C U

The twins were expensive, but it was always a pleasure to see Brandi and her sister, Candy. They had great assets and talent to match.

Hank was late.

If he didn't show up soon, I was going to hit the blackjack tables without him. I was looking left, trying to locate Hank, when I heard the clack of her heels coming my way, just before I turned my head to see her.

Too late.

Little miss distracted was looking down at her phone and walked straight into me. She would have ended up on her pretty little ass if I hadn't caught her. Her phone bounced hard on the marble floor. She wasn't very bright. Only an idiot didn't protect her phone with a case these days.

"Careful there, sweetheart," I said. I caught a glimpse of nice cleavage and a black lace bra down her shirt as she leaned over to retrieve the phone. She had a nice figure, probably even nicer if she didn't hide it in a business suit.

"You broke my phone. You…" She looked up and recognition flashed across her face. The anger in her eyes receded. "Nick?"

I hadn't recognized her grown up and dressed like this. But I knew that voice and those eyes anywhere.

"Precious?"

It was Katherine fucking Covington. I hadn't seen her since high school. She had been a nine then, and now she pegged the meter. Her pale blue eyes beguiled me the same way they always had.

A blush rose in her cheeks. "It's been so long," she stammered, a smile growing on her face.

She tucked stray hair behind her ear and shifted her weight. Her hair was up instead of down, and her smile was even brighter than I remembered. The way she filled out her shirt sent a shock to my cock.

She looked down and tapped the cracked screen of her phone. It didn't respond.

"A long time is right, Precious."

I would have preferred her in shorts and a crop top, but she was still stunning.

Tears welled in her eyes. "My phone," she mumbled.

"You should look where you're going next time."

"You ran into me," she blurted defiantly.

Unfortunately, Katie's personality hadn't changed one bit. She'd had an attitude back then, and she hadn't mellowed.

"Well, pardon me for standing still where you wanted to walk, Princess. Now give me that." I wrenched the phone out of her hand.

She huffed. "Give it back, and don't call me that."

She'd always hated the Princess moniker, but today she deserved it. Yelling at me for standing in her way? Give me a break.

"Just a minute. I'm a whiz with these things." That was no joke.

She grabbed for it, but I kept it out of reach. She stomped her foot like the spoiled brat she was.

"Hold on." I ran through the reset sequence, and the phone began to reboot. I glimpsed Hank to my right.

He had heard our exchange. He waved and left me to handle the ungrateful princess on my own.

Katie smiled as the little apple appeared, and she moved closer, oh so close.

I could feel her body heat as she leaned in. When the reboot finished, the display was only partially drawn and the touchscreen still wouldn't respond.

"You're going to need a new screen," I told her. "And, you should get a cover for this."

"I have one," she said with a glint in her eye.

"They work better when you put the phone in them."

"It got dirty."

Typical Princess response. My cover is too dirty to use. Oh my, what will I do now?

I handed her the phone.

"Thanks for trying," she said sweetly, surprising me.

She put it in her purse as a tear escaped down her cheek. She looked lost, hurt, vulnerable, unlike the feisty woman of ten seconds ago.

I lifted her chin and wiped away the tear with a finger. "What's the problem, Precious?"

She bit her bottom lip, seeming unsure how to respond. "I have to get back to LA, and all the flights are booked. I was going to hang out at the airport and see if I could snag a spare rental car."

"Why don't you just rent a limo?"

The Covingtons had money to burn and had never been ashamed of throwing it around. As soon as the words left my mouth, I regretted being as snarky to her as she had been to me.

She huffed, and anger clouded her eyes. "You wouldn't understand. I really have to get back." She grabbed her roller bag and turned to leave.

She didn't deserve to have me ruin her day. I made a snap judgment, the kind that sometimes got me in trouble.

I jumped around in front of her. "Katie, I'm sorry. That was mean. How 'bout I give you a ride back home?"

She hesitated, but the tug of a smile at the edges of her mouth telegraphed her answer. "You sure?"

"Sure. I was leaving tomorrow anyway. This way I avoid the traffic."

"I'll pay you for the gas," she offered.

"Princess, not everything is about money. Your pretty smile is payment enough."

She smiled at the compliment, despite my calling her Princess. She was as tempting now as she had been back in high school, like the apple in the garden of Eden. One bite, and I would regret it for eternity.

I was giving the princess a ride to help her out, and that was all. *It's just a ride, nothing more.*

"If you have a pair of pants in there, pull 'em out," I told her. "It'll get colder as we near LA."

Her brow creased with confusion, but she did as I asked and pulled out a pair of striped yoga pants.

I rolled her bag over to the counter and asked to add it to my bag, which was being delivered to my house tomorrow. I had planned on living out of my backpack tonight. Luggage delivery made these trips so much easier.

She started to object, but my finger to her lips stopped her. The girl had to work on her obsession with rejecting help.

"Just don't call me Princess again," was all she ended up saying.

I nodded. "'K."

The clerk finished adding her bag to my account. My mom's picture dropped out of my wallet as I put my credit card back in.

Katie picked it up and handed it to me.

"You wait here while I get my stuff from upstairs," I told her.

I composed a text to Hank on my way to the elevator.

ME: Heading back 2nite catch up later

I waved to Katie as the elevator door closed.

She waved back.

I was going to enjoy having that body wrapped around me tonight.

Made in the USA
Coppell, TX
26 May 2022

78142239R10203